MW01087218

IOWA
BIKE TOWNS

IOWA
BIKE TOWNS

Eugene H. Schlaman

gatekeeper press™

Columbus, Ohio

Iowa Bike Towns
Published by Gatekeeper Press
2167 Stringtown Rd, Suite 109
Columbus, OH 43123-2989
www.GatekeeperPress.com

Copyright © 2020 by Eugene H. Schlaman
All rights reserved. Neither this book, nor any parts within it may be sold or reproduced in any form or by any electronic or mechanical means, including information storage and retrieval systems without permission in writing from the author. The only exception is by a reviewer, who may quote short excerpts in a review.

The editorial work for this book is entirely the product of the author. Gatekeeper Press did not participate in and is not responsible for any aspect of this element.

ISBN (paperback): 9781662907203

Contents

Introduction

G rowing up in Iowa as a young boy I rode my bike everywhere, but never dreamed of riding across the state. When first learning about the bike ride across Iowa, I said "I need to do this." My first RAGBRAI was in 2005 and I wondered about the history of the towns on the route. In school, we had a class on Iowa history, but that has long since passed from my memory. This prompted me to research the towns on the bike route to discover each town's history and unique facts about each community. I have continued to ride each year and accumulated many stories about the towns on the route. Each night before the next day's ride, I would gather my fellow bikers for my "nightly reading," telling them about the towns on the next day's route. They enjoyed these stories and each night they would look forward to hearing about the towns on the following day's route. They even asked others to join. After gathering several years of stories, my biker friends encouraged me to write this book. Since in 1973, some 800 towns have been on the route. Each year thousands of bikers have enjoyed many of the towns previously visited and a few new towns. This book should interest bikers who have biked or will bike Iowa, those traveling through Iowa and Iowans who enjoy the history and trivia of their state.

My research revealed some of the following themes in Iowa's history:

Towns got their names in unique ways. One town got its name from a flip of a coin, two from the first letter of the names of ladies getting off a train at a new depot and others from the name of a settler's previous community. Some investors required the town bear their name for their investment.

Coal was mined in Iowa. Coal mining grew from 1870 to 1920 before mining started to decline. Coal mining ended in 1994. Most was surface mining and shallow underground mining in central and southern Iowa.

Members of the Church of Jesus Christ of Latter-day Saints (LDS) traveled through Iowa on what is known as the Mormon Trail. The trail started at Montrose Landing, Iowa across from Nauvoo, Illinois and went through Council Bluffs, Iowa. From 1846 to 1869 more than 70,000 Mormons travelled across Iowa on their way to Salt Lake City, Utah.

Iowa played an important part in the Underground Railroad. It was a free state and had a lot of activity because it shared a border with Missouri, a slave state. Quakers, who opposed slavery, assisted slaves as they escaped on their way to Canada. Slaves were often housed in people's homes or somewhere on their property. Assisting an escaped slave was considered an act of theft according to U. S. Law because slaves were considered property. Helping a slave escape would subject a person to a fine and imprisonment. John Brown, the famous abolitionist, spent several months in Iowa planning for his raid on the Federal Armory in Harpers Ferry, West Virginia.

The railroad contributed to the growth of Iowa communities. With the coming of the railroad, goods could easily be imported and exported, travel became easier and faster, and mail arrived on a regular basis. With the old steam locomotives (Iron Horses), a depot was required approximately every 30 miles so the steam engines could fill-up with water to make steam to operate. This created a network of depots where communities would spring up. Many Iowa towns were named by or for employees of the railroad companies. John Insley Blair, a railroad official, named several towns after himself, family members, and even his dog. The first railroad bridge to cross the Mississippi river was in Davenport and the Transcontinental Railroad started in Council Bluffs. With the demise of the steam locomotive, consolidation of the railroads and the increased network of paved roads, many miles of railroad tracks were abandoned. Many of these abandoned tracks have now been transformed into Iowa's great network of Rails- to-Trails.

In this book, you will find how towns got their names as well as stories and facts about the communities. You will discover the man who grew the longest beard, a town which was the setting for a Broadway musical, the birthplace of actors and actresses and a famous late night TV host along with other trivia. It is my hope that should you chose to pass through these towns this book will give you some history and trivia that will enrich your journey. This book has not included all the interesting stories associated with the approximately 800 communities that have been on the route.

I cannot guarantee all of the information is totally accurate because the sources may not have had accurate knowledge.

To the reader: If there are additional items of interest or facts about these towns that you would like to share, feel free to submit them to IowabikeTowns@gmail.com.

Bio

I was born in Anamosa, Iowa. Then at the young age of two we moved to Hampton, Iowa. I graduated from Hampton Community High School in 1963 and in the fall of that year joined the Navy to become a missile technician on nuclear powered submarines. After the Navy, I attended Clemson University and graduated with a degree in financial management then received a Master's of Business Administration from Appalachian State University. My first job out of college was in the tax department of a Fortune 500 company and then in 1989 I took a position in public accounting. In 2007, I retired from public accounting. Researching this book proved to be more enjoyable than tax research.

Acknowledgments

I would like to thank my Sister-In-Law, Helen Everhart, who helped with the editing of the book and my biking friends for encouraging me to write this book. The acknowledgments would not be complete without acknowledging the patience and support provided my wife Freda.

Iowa Bike Towns
(1973-2019)

A

Ackley (Franklin and Hardin)
(1983), (1995), (2004), (2015)
Ackley was formed in 1857 and incorporated in 1869. It was named for William Ackley, who purchased the land for the railroad route.
<u>Item of interest</u>
Since 1902, Sauerkraut Days has been an annual event that takes place in June. This is a three-day event with carnival rides, live entertainment, free wieners and sauerkraut, a grand parade, and many other events.

Ackworth (Warren)
(2009)
Ackworth originally started by a group of North Carolina Quakers and was first known as the South River Meeting. In the spring of 1868, the Ackworth Academy was established and it was decided to change the name of the town to Ackworth, after the oldest Friends School in England called Ackworth. The town was laid out in 1874 and incorporated in 1881.

Adair (Adair and Guthrie)
(1991), (2001), (2019)
The town officially became Adair in 1872 and was named for General John Adair, a general in the War of 1812, who became the 8th governor of Kentucky. The town is located in an area known as the Summit Cut

in reference to the ridge that forms the watershed divide between the Missouri and Mississippi Rivers.

Item of interest

Jesse James and his notorious gang of outlaws staged the world's first robbery of a moving train on the evening of July 21, 1873, a mile and a half west of Adair.

Early in July the gang learned that $75,000 in gold from the Cheyenne region was to come through Adair on the recently built main line of the Chicago, Rock Island, & Pacific Railroad. Jesse sent his brother, Frank James, and Cole Younger to Omaha to learn when the gold shipment was to be shipped while Jesse, Jim and Tom Younger, Clell Miller and Bill Chadwell remained camped. Finally, Frank and Cole got their tip that the gold shipment was on its way east and reported this to Jesse, who had made plans for the train robbery. On the afternoon of the robbery, the bandits went to the section house and obtained some pies and other food from Mrs. Robert Grant, wife of the section foreman.

In the meantime, the bandits broke into the handcar house, stole a spike-bar and hammer with which they used to pry off a fish-plate connecting two rails and pulled out the spikes. This was on a curve of the railroad track west of Adair, near the Turkey Creek bridge on old U.S. Highway No. 6. A rope was tied on the west end of the disconnected north rail. The rope was then passed under the south rail and led to a hole they had cut in the bank where they would hide. When the train came along, the rail was jerked out of place and the engine plunged into the ditch and toppled over on its side. The engineer was killed, the fireman died of his injuries, and several passengers were injured.

Two members of the gang, believed to have been Jesse and Frank James, climbed into the express car and forced the guard to open the safe. In the safe they found only $2,000 in currency, the gold shipment had been delayed. They collected about $3,000, including the currency and loot taken from the passengers.

Levi Clay, a railroad employee, walked to Casey where the alarm was sent by telegraph to Des Moines and Omaha. Soon the news spread throughout the nation. A train loaded with armed men left Council Bluffs for Adair and dropped small detachments of men along the route where saddled horses were waiting. They spread over the countryside searching for the robbers. The trail of the outlaws was traced into Missouri where the outlaws had split up and were sheltered by friends. Later the governor of Missouri offered a $10,000 reward for the capture of Jesse James, dead or alive

The reward proved too tempting for Bob Ford, a new member of the James gang, and on April 3, 1882, he shot and killed Jesse in the James home in St. Joseph, Missouri.

Adaza (Greene)
(1988)
Adaze is an unincorporated community founded in 1881. Originally known as Cottonwood, but was renamed in 1882 by Captain Albert Head, which resulted from his statement while visiting the town, "ain't she a daisy," which was shortened to Adaza.

ADEL (Dallas) (County Seat)
(1984), (2000), (2006)
Adel was incorporated in 1847. Originally called Penoach, but in 1849 a surveyor renamed it Adel after a very pretty child.
<u>Item of interest</u>
The Adel bank was robbed on March 6, 1895. Two men entered town in a buggy then went to the bank and shot a teller. Though wounded, the teller managed to close the vault and turn the tumblers, preventing the thieves from taking off with a substantial amount of money. George W. Clarke had a law office on the second floor and was descending the stairs when a robber fired his gun. The weapon misfired, sparing Clarke's life. Clarke lived to become a future Governor of Iowa. It is not known if the robbers were ever found.

Adelphi (Polk)
(1988), (1992), (2013)
The name Adelphi comes from the Greek word adelphi, meaning "brothers." Formed in 1856 it remains an unincorporated community.

Akron (Plymouth)
(1982)

This town used to be named Portlandville. In 1872, Mr. Sargent and Mr. Crill plated the town. They originally intended to call the town Portland, but since there was another post office in Iowa by that name, the Post Office Department added "ville" to its name. In an 1882 petition for incorporation, the name was changed to Akron, after Akron, Ohio, a name selected by Mr. Sargent since he felt that the old name was too long.

Albert City (Buena Vista)
(1977), (1979), (2007)
Albert City was established in 1890 and incorporated in 1900. It was initially named Manthorp after a town in Sweden. The post office department was concerned that the town's name would be confused with the nearby community of Marathon, so Manthorp was renamed to Albert City for Albertina Anderson, the founder's wife.
Items of interest
Around 3 p.m. on the afternoon of November 16, 1901, three men, one a person of mixed race, entered the depot restaurant. The small town had only one central telephone for the entire community and the robbers assumed that no one knew that the night before they had just robbed a bank in the neighboring city of Greenville. The thieves came to Albert City simply in search of a meal, but miscalculated how fast news of a crime could travel on the prairie.

Word had reached Albert City's Marshal, Charley Lodine, that the robbers were in town so he rounded up some fellow citizens to go to the depot and arrest the three men. After entering the depot fully armed, the Albert City residents expected the robbers to surrender quietly. Instead their appearance touched off the biggest shootout that the area had ever seen, claiming the lives of three men.

The robbers weren't afraid to start shooting when confronted. They knew how to use their weapons. The three suspects each drew two guns from their hips and unloaded gunfire on the posse. They then took cover behind a black pot-bellied stove in the corner of the restaurant. The posse fired their guns in the area where the robbers hid; but, the thieves slipped out the back door and continued to spray bullets at the citizens of Albert City, which resulted in two of residents becoming casualties.

Marshal Lodine was the first to be hit, a bullet ripped through his left hip at the upper part of the thigh in the outer part of the leg, which lodged near the groin area. A man named Sundblad was the next to be shot. A bullet penetrated his shoulder and pierced the upper lobe of the left lung, numbing his left arm almost immediately. Despite being hit, Sundblad continued to pursue the robbers to the grain elevator next to the depot, but then received a second gunshot wound in the hip and collapsed near the elevator. After seeing one of their partners struck by gunfire while attempting to steal a horse and buggy to use in the getaway, the two surviving robbers fled southeast of town. They came upon Charley Peterson, who had stopped his team of horses after hearing the gunfire and seeing the smoke near the railroad. The pair quickly hijacked Peterson's horses and attempted to ride southward, but after one of the horses refused to go any further, they met the traveling buggy of Mrs. John Anderson. They threw her off and used the buggy to continue their escape. Using the Anderson buggy was one of the most interesting parts of the entire event, as the robber of mixed race was calm enough to write a letter of apology to Mrs. Anderson. He stuffed the note and $11 of the stolen money under the back-seat cushion of the buggy.

After abandoning the Anderson buggy, the men then changed teams of horses two more times, hoping to throw their pursuers off track before nightfall, when an escape would have been much easier. Their plan was spoiled when one of the robbers was thrown from his horse as the posse closed in on them. They surrendered and were marched into town just as the sun began to fade from the horizon.

The men were identified as Albert Phillips and Lewis Brooks, but those were fictitious names because they did not want to bring shame upon their families by revealing their true identities. The third robber died the next morning, refusing to the end to reveal his name. His tombstone reads only "Bank Robber," and still has never been identified. Sundblad passed away from the puncture to his lung and Lodine survived for several days after the attack, but also died from his injuries.

It was amazing that only three people died in the confrontation, 64 thirty-eight caliber bullet shells were picked up in the depot alone after the battle.

From 1936 to 1942, Thieman tractors were manufactured in Albert City. They offered two in types of tractors: $185 kit or a complete tractor with a Ford Model A engine for about $500. With the kit, farmers had to procure his own engine, driveshaft and rear end from a Ford Model A, 1928 Chevrolet or Dodge Four, and then build a tractor. The object was to cobble together pieces of used equipment to make an inexpensive tractor.

The Albert City Threshermen & Collectors Show has been an annual summer event since 1971.

ALBIA (Monroe) (County Seat)
(1984), (2000)
Albia was incorporated in 1856 and first known as Princeton, but changed its name to Albia for Albia, New York, the former home of some of the early settlers.
Item of interest
The Albia area was known for its coal mines. On Feb. 14, 1893, there was a coal mine explosion about 2.5 miles west of Albia. One miner was killed outright and seven died later of their injuries. The explosion happened after a gunpowder charge, used to bring down the coal, ignited the coal dust causing an explosion in the mine. This was one of only two major mine disasters in Iowa between 1888 and 1913.

Albion (Marshall)
(2008)
Founded in 1852, the town was called La Fayette until 1858, when the name was changed to Albion because there was another town that was named La Fayette. It was renamed after Albion, Michigan, the former home of some of the early settlers. Albion is another name for the island of Great Britain and is sometimes used poetically to refer to the island.

Alburnett (Linn)
(1978), (1990)
In 1887, Albert Burnett donated land to the Illinois Central Railroad to build a depot. Because he had given the land for the depot, the name "Burnett" was chosen for the town. Mail delivery problems soon developed between Burnett and the community of Bennett in Cedar County. Consequently, Al Burnett changed the name to Alburnett. The town was incorporated in 1912.

Alden (Hardin)
(1995), (2015)
Alden was laid out in 1855 and was named for its founder, Henry Alden, a native of Massachusetts.
Items of Interest
Alden is believed to have the smallest endowed Carnegie Library built in the United States, build in 1913 at a cost of $9,000.

Famous people from Alden include Gordon Jones, an actor known for his parts in The Rifleman, The Green Hornet, Abbot & Costello movies, John Wayne movies, the Son of Flubber, and the Ozzie & Harriet show. Jones has a star on the Vine St. Hollywood's Walk of Fame.

Alexander (Franklin)
(1980), (1990), (2007)
Alexander was platted in 1885 and incorporated in 1902. According to tradition, it was named for a man connected with the building of the railroad.

ALGONA (Kossuth) (County Seat)
(1977), (1990), (1999), (2005), (2010), (2017)
Algona was founded in 1854 and named after the Algonquian (North American native language) word for "Algonquin waters." The following is a line from the Algonquin water song: "We sing this song like a lullaby.

The song means the water is the life's blood of our mother the earth. Water is the life's blood of our own bodies."

Items of interest

In 1894, Algona, along with other Iowa communities became part of the project known as the "Orphan Trains." As New York City saw booming immigration and also saw a rise in the number of orphans in its orphanages. Unable to provide adequate care for the orphans, the people who ran the orphanages saw fit to ship nearly 100,000 orphans westward to start a new life with families across America. The recent best-selling historical novels such as The Orphan Train by Christina Baker Kline has brought new interest to this chapter of history. Algona itself welcomed nearly 100 orphans into the town, many of whom remained lifelong residents.

Algona was the site of a German prisoner of camp during World War II. From 1943 to 1946, Camp Algona housed nearly 10,000 prisoners, many of whom were put to work on farms owned by Americans who were fighting overseas. The war prisoners were credited with saving crops. A museum now commemorates the camp's history and features a nativity scene built by the POWs.

In 2003, Algona drew national attention with the purchase of the world's largest Cheeto. A local radio DJ hoped that the Cheeto would bring tourism to the town.

Alice (Linn)
(1978), (1985)
Alice was name for Alice Cushman Kirk.

Alleman (Polk)
(2011)
Alleman was named for the early settler John L. Alleman. The city did not incorporate until May 18, 1973, making it the most recent city to incorporate in Polk County.

ALLISON (Butler) (County Seat)
(1980), (1990)
In 1881, Allison was named for Iowa's U. S. Senator William Boyd Allison. Allison was incorporated in 1881.

Alpha (Fayette)
(1999)
Alpha was founded in 1871 and named for the first letter of the Greek alphabet, because it was the first community on Crane Creek.

Alta Vista (Chickasaw)
(1987), (1996)
Alta Vista was established and incorporated in 1894 and first named Elk Creek, but later changed to Alta Vista, meaning "high view" in Spanish.

Alton (Sioux)
(1975), (1993), (1996), (2002), (2005), (2012), (2017)
Alton was originally called East Orange Station. The town was renamed Alton in 1882 for an early settler name Alton. It was incorporated in 1883.
Items of interest
St. Mary's Catholic Church is the oldest, neo-gothic church west of the Mississippi River and features the largest square footage of stained glass in the nation.

Alton has the oldest continuously operated golf course in Iowa. Course founder W.S. Slagle, was first introduced to golf in 1888 during a trip to the East Coast who then proceeded to convert a pasture into the course.

When the liquor store burned in February of 1937, good Samaritans helped carry the hooch off the premises in wash baskets to get it safely across the street to Elmer Goebel's building. The story goes that some of the booze actually got there, understandably, some did not.

Altoona (Polk)
(1973) (2011)
Incorporated as a city on March 11, 1876. Its named came from the Latin word for "high," altus, after a surveyor discovered that Altoona was the highest point on the Des Moines Valley Railroad between Des Moines and Keokuk.

Item of interest

In August of 1877, central Iowa experienced record amounts of rainfall. Farm fields were flooded, rivers and creeks were overflowing, and livestock retreated to safety on higher ground.

During the night of August 29, 1877, Little Four Mile Creek became a swollen, raging torrent. It was reported that the Creek was fifty feet wide at some points. The force of the water caused the stone arches under a railroad bridge to be washed away. Early that morning, a passenger train heading for Des Moines sped around a curve but the engineer could not see that only part of the bridge was standing. He opened the throttle and the train plunged into the water.

The Iowa State Register reported that the locomotive had jumped the stream and landed hard against the western bank of the creek. A coal car and a Barnum Bailey circus poster car were pulled in behind the engine. A mail car, an express car, and three passenger cars also plunged into the creek. A sleeper car was saved because there was no room for it in the creek bed. Twenty people died and 35 were injured. The disaster was called the worst train wreck in Iowa history.

Amana Colonies (Iowa)
(1976), (1991) (2011)
The new colonies were originally to be named "Bleibetreu," German for "remain faithful;" however, residents found it difficult to properly pronouncing the word in English, so they settled on Amana, a Biblical name with a similar meaning.

The Amana Colonies are seven villages: Amana (or Main Amana), East Amana, High Amana, Middle Amana, South Amana, West Amana and Homestead. They are a group of settlements begun by radical German Pietists (a movement within Lutheranism that combines emphasis on biblical doctrine with the reformed emphasis on individual piety and living a vigorous Christian life). They first settled in New York State near Buffalo, but in 1855 in order to live out their beliefs in more isolated surroundings, they moved west to the rich soil of east-central Iowa.

A striking feature of the Amana Colonies is that for eighty years, until 1932, they maintained an almost completely self-sufficient local economy, importing very little from the wider, industrializing U.S. economy. At the same time the level of physical comfort, housing, possessions, education, and social and cultural amenities were comparable to that enjoyed by average middle class Americans. The Amanians were able to achieve this independence and lifestyle by adhering to the specialized handcrafts and farming occupations they brought with them from Germany. Master craftsmen passed on their skills from one generation to the next. They shared their knowledge, techniques, artisan iron and copper smith skills, wood wrights, weavers, shoemakers, cheese makers, etc. They used hand, horse, wind, and waterpower, and lived a sustainable community life.

Most residents of the Amana Colony are considered tri-lingual. They speak American English, High German, and a dialect known as Amana German. This dialect is High German in origin, but has strong influences of American English. They lived a communal life until the mid 1930s. The Amanas are sometimes mistaken as Amish.

Amber (Jones)
(1991), (2002)

The town was originally called Blue Cut, due to a wide strip of the nearby blue clay. On July 1, 1878, the name was changed to Amber for the name of a character in a novel a resident had read.

Item of interest

Amber is home of the Hula Hoop Tree. In 2015, a storm blew through the community and two hula hoops appeared on a roadside tree where the storm had passed. Now people come there to toss their own hoops up onto the tree making a unique display that draws tourists.

Ames (Story)
(1973), (1976), (1983), (2008), (2018)

Ames was founded in 1864 as a station stop on the Cedar Rapids and Missouri Railroad. It was named for the 19th century U. S Congressman

Oakes Ames of Massachusetts, who was influential in the building of the transcontinental railroad.

Items of interest

Ames has been rated as the 5th "Smartest City in America," "Healthiest City in the Country" and one of the "Happiest Small Places in America."

Ames is the home of Iowa State University of Science and Technology (ISU), a public research institution with leading Agriculture, Design, Engineering, and Veterinary Medicine colleges. ISU is the nation's first designated land-grant university and the birthplace of the world's first electronic digital computer.

Ames was home to George Washington Carver for five years. Sometime in the early 1860s he was born into slavery at Diamond Grove, now known as Diamond, Missouri. The exact date of his birth is uncertain and was not known by Carver himself; however, it was sometime before January of 1865, when slavery was abolished in Missouri. His master, Moses Carver, was a German American immigrant who had purchased George's parents on October 9, 1855, for $700. At an early age, George showed an interest in education, but was not allowed to attend the all-white school. Mrs. Carver taught him to read.

When he was older, Carver applied to several colleges before being accepted to Highland University in Highland, Kansas. When he arrived, they rejected him because of his race. In early 1888, Carver obtained a $300 loan for education and in 1890 started studying art and piano at Simpson College in Indianola, Iowa. His art teacher recognized Carver's talent for painting flowers and plants and encouraged him to study botany at Iowa State Agricultural College in Ames. When he began in 1891, he was the first black student. Carver's bachelor's thesis was "Plants as Modified by Man," dated 1894.

Iowa State professors convinced Carver to continue at the college for his master's degree. Carver did research at the Iowa Experiment Station during the next two years. His work at the experiment station gained him national recognition and respect as a botanist. He was the first black faculty member at Iowa State.

In 1896, Booker T. Washington, the first principal and president of Tuskegee Institute (now Tuskegee University), invited Carver to head its Agriculture Department. Carver taught there for 47 years, developing the department into a strong research center. He taught methods of crop rotation, introduced several alternative cash crops for farmers that would also improve the soil of areas that had been heavily depleted by growing cotton, initiated research into crop products, and taught generations of black students farming techniques for self-sufficiency. Iowa State University did the world a great favor when it accepted its first black student and teacher.

ANAMOSA (Jones) (County Seat)
(1978), (1982), (1991), (1994), (2002), (2004), (2012)
Anamosa was founded as the settlement of Buffalo Forks in 1838 and incorporated as Lexington in 1856. At that time, Lexington was a very popular name for towns, so when Lexington chose to become incorporated in 1877, the name was changed to Anamosa to avoid mail delivery confusion. There are many different stories of how the name of Anamosa was chosen, but all center around a local Native American girl named Anamosa, which means "white fawn" or "you walk with me."

The story goes that a Native American family was passing through town in 1842. The family stayed at the Ford House. The little girl, named Anamosa, endeared herself to the townspeople and when the family departed from town, local citizens decided to name their town for her.

Items of interest
The Wapsipinicon River, called "Wapsi," runs through Anamosa. Legend of the river's name is that a Native American maiden and her lover threw themselves off a bluff overlooking the Wapsipinicon River. Legend has it that one was named Wapsi, the other Pinicon.

Anamosa was named the Pumpkin Capital of Iowa by the Iowa State Legislature in 1993, and now hosts a pumpkin fest, a pumpkin festival and a pumpkin weigh-off each October.

Anamosa is home to the Anamosa State Penitentiary, formerly known as the Iowa Men's Reformatory, a medium/maximum security prison that was the largest in Iowa, housing over 1,200 male inmates. It was established in 1872 and constructed from locally quarried Anamosa Limestone in the style of a castle, which inspired its nickname as "The White Palace of the West." The prison grounds also house the Anamosa State Penitentiary Museum, which contains artifacts and exhibits on prison life from throughout its history.

In the massive annals of Anamosa prison history, few stories are stranger or more compelling than that of John Wesley Elkins. If nothing else, his case demonstrates that youthful violence is not solely a modern-day problem.

Elkins was only 11 years old when he murdered his father and stepmother in the remote farmhouse they shared in rural Clayton County. A motive was never definitively established; however, young Elkins was known to be angry over being required by his parents to care for his infant stepsister more frequently than he wanted. The brutality of the crime, its senselessness, and the tender age of the alleged murderer, caused a stir across the state and beyond.

In 1890, weighing just 73 pounds and standing 4'8" tall, Elkins was committed to the maximum-security Anamosa prison to serve a life sentence. He spent the next 12 years working in the prison library and chapel, educating himself and becoming proficient with the written and spoken word. After a long and bitter public debate about his case, in 1902 the Governor of Iowa issued parole papers for Elkins. He eventually settled in St. Paul, Minnesota, where he lived until 1920, working for a major railroad. In 1922, he married a Hawaiian woman in Honolulu. He became a farmer in San Bernardino County, California, where he resided until his death in 1961. There is no evidence that he ever committed another crime.

Also in prison was Mrs. Anna Taylor who was sentenced for the crime of murder. John S. Taylor became enamored of her and she returned his passion. They had clandestine meetings but became impatient by the restraint imposed upon them by Taylor's wife. They resolved to get rid of his wife and planned to kill her by poison. Anna bought the poison and John administered it. The wife died suddenly and the day the wife was buried, John married Anna. Suspicion pointed to their crime and they were soon arrested. Both were convicted and sent to the penitentiary for life. She protested her innocence to the last and the thoughts of being buried in the convicts' cemetery continually filled her mind. Every cent of money she made by making fancy-work and selling it was saved for the purpose of buy a lot in Riverside Cemetery and to pay the expenses of a civilian's funeral. At the time of her death, she had gathered enough money for that purpose. Warden Martin directed that her wishes should be carefully carried out. The body was placed in a nice coffin and a traveled through the town to the Riverside cemetery.

Anamosa is home to the National Motorcycle Museum, which features many vintage motorcycles, including the only original "Captain America bike" from the movie Easy Rider.

Anamosa was the birthplace of the artist Grant Wood. He is best known for his paintings which depicted the rural American Midwest, particularly the paintings of "American Gothic" and "Stone City." When Wood died, his estate went to his sister, Nan Wood Graham, the woman portrayed in American Gothic.

Andrew (Jackson)
(1989), (1991), (1998), (2000), (2002)
Because the town was located in Jackson County, Andrew was named for the seventh United States President, Andrew Jackson. It was incorporated in 1863.

Angus (Boone)
(1994)
Angus was originally named "Coaltown," and was established as a coal mining community in the 1870s. The name was changed to Angus in 1881, named after a railroad official. In 1885 Angus was the largest coal mining town in Iowa.

Anita (Cass)
(1991), (2000), (2001), (2019)

Anita was platted in 1869 and incorporated in 1875. This is how the town came to be called Anita: One day in 1869, a number of railroad officials were having dinner at Mr. Beason's house, when the subject of the new station and its potential name was being discussed. The railroad men proposed calling it Beason, but there were objections. Mrs. Beason suggested the town be called Anita, in honor of her niece. The topic was dropped, but soon afterward Mr. Beason was informed by the railroad that Mrs. Beason's suggestion had been adopted and the towns name would be Anita. The name is Spanish, and is pronounced as though spelled with a long "e" thus: An-e-ta. Translated it would mean, "little Anna."

Ankeny (Polk)
(1973), (1974), (1984), (2000)
Ankeny was founded in 1875 by John and Sarah Ankeny and was incorporated on February 28, 1903.

Anthon (Woodbury)
(1988), (2006)
The town was founded in 1888 and named for J. C. Anthon, a railroad engineer.

Aplington (Butler)
(2007), (2015)
Aplington was founded in the 1850's on land donated by Thomas Mask, R. R. Parriot, Theodore Wilson, and Zenas Aplington. In honor of his generous donation of land, the town was named for Mr. Aplington.

Arbor Hill (Adair)
(2000)
The town is an unincorporated community and name Arbor Hill in 1895.

Arcadia (Carroll)
(2006),
Arcadia was laid out in 1871 and incorporated in 1881. It was named for the region of Arcadia, in Greece.

The town was originally called Tip-Top. It is located on the Mississippi-Missouri Divide. The name Tip-Top was significant because it divides the waters which flow toward the Mississippi River Valley from those that flow to the Missouri River Valley. The dividing line runs though Arcadia and one may stand there to see the parting of the waters.

Archer (O'Brien)
(1993), (1996), (2005)
Archer was founded in 1888 and named for John Archer, who owned the town site.

Ardon Creek Vineyard (Louisa)
(2016)
Ardon Creek Vineyard and Winery was founded on a 164-year-old family farm which has a rich Irish heritage. They offer wines to suit any palate from sweet, semi-sweet, semi-dry and dry in whites, rose, and red varieties.

Aredale (Butler)
(1980), (1990), (1999), (2007)
The name Aredale is derived from a variation of the Pennsylvania town of Airville, from which several Aredale residents were from. When it was submitted to Washington, D.C., the spelling was changed and the town became Aredale. The plat was recorded on June 28, 1900.

Argyle (Lee)
(1981), (1992)
Argyle is unincorporated and is named after Argyleshire, Scotland.

Argo (Scott)
(2008)
In Greek mythology, Argo was the ship on which Jason and the Argonauts sailed from Iolcos to Colchis to retrieve the Golden Fleece. A post office was established in 1897, but was discontinued in 1902.

Arlington (Fayette)

This village was settled in 1854 and incorporated in 1875. It was originally called Brush Creek for the brush willows that lined the creek. In 1895, the town council recommended the town change its name to Arlington, which was approved by a vote by the towns people. Another suggestion for the town was Allentown or Allenton for Theo Allen, who was the town's first railroad depot agent.

Item of interest

Glacial gold has been found in Brush Creek in Arlington. Big gold nuggets do exist in Iowa, but they are exceptionally rare. The glaciers that transported gold down from Canada pulverized the gold and in most cases, all that is left is extra fine gold dust.

Arnolds Park (Dickinson)

(2014)

Arnolds Park was named after Wesley Arnold who purchased the property in 1864. Arnolds Park is in the center of the Iowa Great Lakes.

Items of interest

Arnolds Park is known as the city of five lakes. The lakes are West and East Lake Okoboji, Lake Minnewashta, and Upper and Lower Gar Lakes.

Built in 1927, the amusement park is home to the legendary roller coaster which is the 13th oldest wooden roller coaster in the world.

Arnolds Park is also home to the Iowa Rock'n Roll Hall of Fame.

Arthur (Ida)

(1987), (1988), (2001)

Arthur was platted in 1885 and incorporated in 1887. It was named for Chester A. Arthur, 21st President of the United States. Arthur became President after the death of President James A. Garfield in September of 1881. Garfield was shot by an assassin on July 2, 1881, but didn't die from his wounds until September 19, 1881.

Asbury (Dubuque)
(1983), (1993)
Asbury was first settled in the 1830s by Methodists who named it for British-born Bishop Francis Asbury, one of the first two bishops of the Methodist Episcopal Church in the United States. The city was incorporated in 1933, following the passage of the Twenty-First Amendment to the United States Constitution, which ended prohibition. The city incorporated so they could gain the legal standing necessary to sell alcohol, as liquor licenses were still forbidden in rural unincorporated areas.

Ashton (Osceola)
(1999), (2007)
Ashton was laid out in 1872 and incorporated in 1885. It was first called St. Gilman but changed its name in 1882 to Ashton from a grove of white ash trees near the town site.

Aspinwall (Crawford)
(2018)
Aspinwall was incorporated in 1914. One of the legends of how Aspinwall got its name is that while standing where Main Street is today, the early settlers could look north and view a mile-long stretch of Aspen trees which extended westward. This view reflected a "wall" of aspen trees thereby giving the pioneers the idea to call their new town "Aspinwall." Aspen trees closely resemble Cottonwood trees, but the Aspen is not native to the area. It should be noted that Aspen was spelled Aspin.

Atalissa (Muscatine)
(1976), (2001), (2006), (2015), (2018)
Atalissa was platted in 1859 and named by its founder, William Lundy, for a mining town in California, which was named for the Indian queen Atalissa.
Items of interest
Atalissa was the home of a few dozen intellectually challenged men who, for several decades, worked in a nearby turkey processing plant. They lived together in an old schoolhouse and were taken each workday to the

plant and paid $65 a month after expenses. They were relocated by state agencies in 2009, after being found to be living in unacceptable conditions. A 2013 verdict awarded the men a total of $240 million in damages, but was reduced to $50,000 a man. A Texas labor broker received as much as $40,000 a month in wages earned by the group of mentally disabled men. The men's plight has had a profound effect on social services in Iowa.

Atkins (Benton)
(1994), (2004)
Atkins was first settled in 1881, under the name of Hague. Early German settlers were not happy with the city's name. Some called the town "Poker Flat" because in the winter a local storekeeper warmed the beer he sold with a red-hot poker. This technique gave the drink an odd "flat" taste. In 1882, the town was officially named Atkins, for one of the officials of the railroad.

ATLANTIC (Cass) (County Seat)
(1974), (1980), (1989), (1991), (2001), (2011) , (2019)
Historians cannot agree on how Atlantic got its name. Local legend has it that the founding fathers estimated the town was about halfway between the Pacific Ocean and the Atlantic Ocean, so it led them to flip a coin and Atlantic won. Atlantic was incorporated in 1869.
<u>Items of interest</u>
Atlantic was named the Coca-Cola Capitol of Iowa in 2001. The Atlantic Bottling Company trails only Atlanta, where the soft-drink company is based, in the production of Coke products.

Another story told about Atlantic is how the placement of Main Street was decided. Someone asked Whitney (the founder) where it should be placed. He marked the center at the current 6th and Chestnut Streets, then plowed two furrows 100 feet apart all the way up to the railroad. This became Main Street.

Atlantic is the birth place of Ethel Theresa Wead Mick, the founder of the Masonic girls' organization, The International Order of Job's Daughters (now known as Job's Daughters International) where she served as its first Supreme Guardian.

The group takes its name from the biblical Book of Job, in particular to a reference in the 42nd Chapter that reads, "And in all the land were no women found so fair, as the Daughters of Job."

Job's Daughters was founded in 1920 to provide an opportunity for young women to work together, learn about themselves, and help others. Job's Daughters is open to girls ages 10 to 20 who have a Masonic relationship (through either a relative or sponsorship.) They do not follow any specific religion, but do require their members have a belief in God.

Attica (Marion)
(2003)

Attica is named for a historical region of Greece, which includes Athens, the current capital of Greece. It was platted in 1847, under the name of "Barkersville." On December 28, 1852, Governor Hempstead approved an act of the Iowa Legislature entitled "An act to change the name of Barkersville in Marion County to Attica." It is said this action was taken in response to a petition by some of the citizens of the town, who considered Mr. Barker's conduct (in particular his attachment for another man's wife) a public disgrace.

AUDUBON (Audubon) (County Seat)
(1986), (2006)

The city is named for John James Audubon, the world-famous ornithologist artist, and painter. The town of Audubon was laid out on September 23, 1878.

Auburn (Sac)
(1975), (1980), (2012)

Auburn was platted in 1888. It was named after the city of Auburn, New York.

Aurelia (Cherokee)
(2012)

Aurelia was founded in 1873 and named for the youngest daughter of the owner of the railroad, John Isley Blair.

Item of interest

Aurelia is also known as the town that denied a disabled man his service dog because the dog was a mixed breed containing part pit bull. A judge ruled in favor of a couple seeking an injunction against the Aurelia law that bans pit bulls.

Aurora (Buchanan)
(1990), (2002)

Aurora was founded in 1886 and incorporated in 1899. The town was laid out on land donated by Bishop Warren and his wife Alice. It was named after Warren's birthplace of East Aurora, New York

Austinville (Butler)
(2015)

Austinville is a small-unincorporated town that had its beginnings in the early 1880s. It was originally called Evergreen. When it was discovered that another town in Iowa had the same name, it was changed to Austinville, for Henry and William Austin, who came to Washington Township in 1868.

Avoca (Pottawattamie)
(1976), (2019)

Avoca was established in 1869 when the Rock Island Railroad came through from Des Moines to Council Bluffs. The name came from a poem by Thomas Moore called "The Meeting of the Waters." This image came from an old Irish tale, "Vale of Avoca," meaning "where the bright waters meet."

Item of interest

Avoca is known for its unique turret (small towers) architecture as well as being home to Farmall-Land-USA. This is a 26,500-square foot museum housing a collection of more than 150 International Harvester (IH) full-size tractors, pedal tractors, toy tractors, artist's prints, and other IH memorabilia. The impressive collection represents a lifetime of collecting by Jerry Mez.

Ayrshire (Palo Alto)
(1990), (1993), (1999), (2002), (2017)

Ayrshire was incorporated on September 20, 1895 and named for a breed of cattle popular in the area.

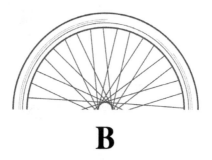

B

Badger (Webster)
(1987)

Badger was organized in 1865 and laid out and plotted by Charles Knudson. Knudson is known as the "Founder of Badger." Badger has been recognized as a town since 1882, but it was not incorporated until February 8, 1900. There are several stories on how Badger got its name:

- One story is that it came from soldiers at the nearby fort.
- Another is that a group of mounted infantry soldiers came across a real mean animal who took on the men's dogs and whipped them. They shot the animal and back at the fort it was identified as a badger.

Baldwin (Jackson)
(1978),

Baldwin was incorporated in 1881. It was originally called Fremont. The present name comes from Edward Baldwin, the original owner of the town site.

Bancroft (Kossuth)
(1982), (1996), (2014)

Bancroft was platted in 1881 and named for George Bancroft, an American historian.

Item of interest

Bancroft's claim to fame was George and John Holloway's world famous diving horses. After watching their horses dive into the river, the Holloways constructed a 75- foot chute at the east end of Main Street. The horses would dive into the water at the end of the chute. In 1900, a special show was held in Bancroft on Easter Sunday. The act was later shown throughout the nation and also exhibited in Ireland and for England's Queen Victoria.

Bangor (Marshall)
(1979), (1998), (2004)
Bangor was founded by Abijah Hodgins in August of 1854 as a Quaker settlement. Quakers came to Bangor from North Carolina to get away from the slave trade. The town played a role in the Underground Railroad. Bangor was named after the township where it is located.

Bankston (Dubuque)
(1983), (2010)
Bankston was founded by and named for Colonel Bankston. It was incorporated in 1933.

Barnum (Webster)
(1995), (2004)
Barnum was platted in 1869 by the railroad. The source of the towns name cannot be confirmed but there are several theories:
- The town was named after P. T. Barnum and his circus.
- The town's blacksmith was named Barnum.
- It was named for William Henry Barnum, a United States Senator from Connecticut who was a nationally important Democrat.
- The most likely was J. H. Barnum, a big land speculator from New York who owned a construction company which may have been into railroad construction.

Bartlett (Fremont)
(1984), (1989), (1992)
Bartlett was named after Annie Bartlett Phelps, wife of a railroad engineer. Bartlett was founded as a railroad town. Rail service was established between Bartlett and Council Bluffs in January 1867.

Battle Creek (Ida)
(1977), (1988), (2006)
Battle Creek had its start in 1877 with the building of the railroad through that territory. The town was incorporated in 1880. The town was first called Bluff Dale, then changed to Willow Dale. It was determined that there was another Willow Dale so the town was named Battle Creek, after the nearby Battle Creek stream. The Battle Creek stream got its name

from the 1849 fight that took place between government surveyors and the Sioux Indians.

Bauer (Marion)
(1991)
Bauer was named for one of the early settlers.

Baxter (Jasper)
(2001), (2011), (2018)
Baxter was platted in 1883. In 1870, the town was named Independence Center; however, that name was not accepted because there was already an Independence. The next name selected was Sidney, but that town name was already in use. The third name submitted was Baxter and that became the town name in 1872. The town was named for Sidney Baxter Higgins.

Bayard (Guthrie)
(1989)
Bayard was platted in 1882. It was named for Thomas Francis Bayard who was from Delaware. He served as a Delaware Senator and Secretary of State under President Cleveland.

Beacon (Mahaska)
(2003), (2013)
Beacon was platted in 1864 as a coal mining town under the name of Enterprise. When the Keokuk and Des Moines Railroad was completed, it was called Oskaloosa Station. The town was incorporated in 1874 and then took the name Beacon.

Beaman (Grundy)
(1986), (1995)
Beaman was incorporated in 1884. The town was first called Wadiloupe, but in 1875 was renamed Beaman after the original owner of the town site.

BEDFORD (Taylor) (County Seat)
(1992), (2003)

Bedford was first named Grove, but the current name is thought to have come from Thomas J. Bedford, who was the first westbound Pony Express rider to deliver the mail on its final leg from Benicia, California to Oakland, on April 23, 1861. It was incorporated in 1866.

Beebeetown (Harrison)
(1991), (1994), (1997), (2008)

Beebeetown is an unincorporated community. The town was named for its first postmaster, Frederick K. Beebee.

Belle Plaine (Benton)
(1986), (1995), (2008)

The history of Belle Plaine started in the early 1840's with the end of the Black Hawk war and treaties with the Native Indians. It was founded in 1862 when it was certain the railroad would be extended to that point. "Belle Plaine" is derived from the French meaning "beautiful plain."

Item of interest

On July 28, 1984 Robert Liddle, a blacksmith, was working at his forge repairing an iron wagon wheel. The wheel needed to be red hot for him to shape it. Sparks flew as he was hammering. The nearby livery was insuring they had enough feed in the stable for horses that would be staying for the week-end. Hay was being delivered and a stray spark from the blacksmith's forge flew into the dry hay as it was being lifted up. The fire spread as a result of the hot July winds. It was three hours before the fire was over, five city blocks of downtown Belle Plaine was destroyed. This included, 27 building which was home to 80 businesses. The first buildings destroyed were the city hall and the fire department. Some of the firefighting equipment was also destroyed. Calls went out to Cedar Rapids, Blairstown and Tama who, with the help of the railroad, responded to help extinguish the fire. Before the smoke had cleared, the town was busy replacing goods and building materials. Immediately after the fire the town motto became "Keep coming our way. We'll take care of you OK."

Bellevue (Jackson)
(1989), (1991), (1999), (2002), (2007)

Bellevue was incorporated in 1851. The city attributes its name to the French words "belle" and "vue", meaning beautiful view as well as to an early settler, John D. Bell.

Item of interest

Bellevue had a history of division that led up to what became known as the Bellevue War. This was really a shoot-out between a posse led by Sheriff W. A Warren and his friend Thomas Cox against W. W. Brown and his friends.

It started in 1837 when a large group of settlers from Michigan settled in the town who were not trusted by the original settlers. Among the settlers was W. W. Brown, a man of wealth who purchased the hotel. The original settlers came to appreciate his open handedness with credit and willingness to pay high wages for wood they hauled across the Mississippi River to his hotel in the winter. The other group of settlers didn't trust Brown and thought he had gained his wealth dishonestly. Politics caused further division. Brown decided to run for Sheriff and was opposed by W. A. Warren who won. Brown; however, was named Justice of the Peace by Thomas Cox, who won the election to be a representative of the Iowa Territorial General Assembly. Further division came when Brown was accused of being an accessory in a horse theft incident. Cox was angry with Brown about this and even more so when a few years later, Brown beat him to be a candidate for a seat in the Territorial House. Cox won the election as an independent, but towns people were divided in their loyalties. There was a shooting incident followed by Sheriff Warrens formation of a posse to arrest Brown because of his association with criminal activities. When they went to Brown's hotel to arrest him, it appears that Brown accidently fired his weapon in the process of surrendering it. A gun fight broke out which resulted in three deaths on each side. The posse set the hotel on fire and captured Brown's friends as they tried to escape. After receiving a whipping, Brown's friends were told to leave the county. Incidents continued to happen between Cox's followers and Brown's "gang." Finally, after attempts to negotiate peace failed, Sheriff Warren and Cox wrote a warrant for Brown's arrest. Cox took his posse and advanced on Brown who stood in the hotel door. In the transfer of Brown's rifle, it fired ripping through Cox's coat. In the ensuing exchange of fire, Brown was killed along with three members of the posse and two members of the Brown's gang.

While there was some public outrage, Cox was re-elected to the State House and named Speaker. He later served in the territory council (Senate) before his death in 1844. As for Warren, he remained Sheriff until 1845.

Belmond (Wright)
(1980), (1993)
A post office was established in Belmond in 1856. Mr. Drmond wanted to name the town from where he came from, but the community was not in favor of that, so they took his name, dropped the "Dr" and replaced it with "Bel" resulting in Belmond.
Item of interest
On October 14, 1966, an F5 tornado ripped apart the community, destroying or damaging about 600 homes and 75 businesses. Six people were killed and large swaths of the town was left in ruins.

Bennett (Cedar)
(2008)
Bennett was incorporated in 1896. It was named for a railroad contractor.

Bentley (Poattawattamie)
(1974), (1991), (1997)
The town of Bentley began in the late 1800s.

Benton (Ringgold)
(1992), (2003)
Benton was organized in 1887. It is thought to be named for Thomas Benton, an early settler.
Item of interest
When the Fertig family came to Iowa ahead of an Indian massacre at Pine Bend, Minnesota, they stopped at a settlement north of Benton. Their animals were tired and the people were friendly, so they decided to stay. With the help of the people, they soon had a house and barn built. At times when wild animals destroyed their gardens, they had to forage for their food such as: nuts, berries, and fish. With the wild game, they could live off the land.

Salt was a necessity for the Fertigs and their livestock. The only way they knew how to get salt was to go to a deer lick. The deer found salt by licking the ground. It was late summer and the trip to the deer lick was long and hard. They wanted to be home before the Fall rains. They used two wagons, taking extra horses, as the horses were easily lame and the creeks were full of quicksand.

William Henry Fertig was a young boy who rode ahead of the wagons on a spotted Indian pony named Chief. The trail they followed had been made by Indians and buffalo and often times had to be cleared of fallen trees and limbs. His job was to check all the streams to find where the animals could safely cross the streams, which were often filled with quicksand.

He had two guard dogs. The mother dog named "Balto" stayed with the wagons. After the wagons were loaded with salt, they started home. The wagons were heavy and the old trail was bad. They had to cross the streams without getting the salt wet. While his father watched the horses graze, the men would sit on a log and read from the Bible.

Time passed fast and they needed to get across the swampy ground before the rains came. They had gone a short distance when "Balto" warned of danger. They stopped and heard a low rumbling sound. They got off the trail just in time. A small herd of buffalo passed them coming from Canada on their way to Kansas to spend the winter.

At the end of the herd were two cows and two calves. The men butchered the two calves for their winter meat. They loaded the meat onto the wagons and sent ahead for fresh horses and men. The men rode beside the wagons with ropes to help pull the heavy load. The meat and salt were divided and all were happy.

These Buffalo were the last to be seen using the trail to Canada in the Spring and returning to Kansas in the Fall.

Bentonsport (Van Buren)
(1981), (1997), (2003), (2013)

The village was platted in 1836 and named "Benton's Port" for Thomas Hart Benton and later changed to Bentonsport.

<u>Items of interest</u>

The Bentonsport bridge opened in 1883 and is "the oldest wagon bridge" of its type remaining on the Des Moines River. There are several extremely rare and significant pin-connected truss bridges on the lower section of the Des Moines River. The Bentonsport Bridge stands out as an example of a large, relatively complete, pin-connected truss bridge. The bridge is a long, five-span truss bridge with each span containing eight panels.

The first paper mill in Iowa was located in Bentonsport. The town also had a grist, saw, linseed oil, and woolen mills.

The village is home to The Indian Artifact Museum which is filled with over 4,000 arrowheads and artifacts collected by Tony Sanders in Southeast Iowa, Missouri, and Illinois.

The Mason House Inn Bed & Breakfast is a hotel built in 1846 by some Mormon craftsmen for those coming to the area on steamboats. It was also a station on the Underground Railroad as were many of the buildings in this area of the state. The Mason House has a real railroad caboose from the Roscoe, Snyder & Pacific Railway line that came from Texas and is one of the options for rooms. Today the village has approximately 40 residents, many of them artists and bed & breakfast keepers.

Bernard (Dubuque)
(1999), (2007)
Bernard started with the building of the railroad. It was platted in 1896 and incorporated in 1897. In 1849, a party of monks, including Father Bernard, landed in New Orleans and made their way up the Mississippi River to Iowa. The town was named for Father Bernard.

Bethesda (Page)
(2016)
In 1870, Swedish settlers came to the area and in 1877 built the Bethesda Lutheran Church. The town took its name from the church. The Bethesda name came from the Bible story (John 5:2) of when Jesus healed the man who was at the healing pool. This is where Jesus said, "Rise up and

pick up your bed and walk. The biblical meaning of Bethesda is "House of Mercy."

Bethlehem (Wayne)
(1981), (1997), (2009), (2016), (2019)
Bethlehem was platted in 1853.

Bidwell (Wapello)
(1984)

Birmingham (Van Buren)
(2013)
Birmingham was incorporated in 1856. The story of the town's name, as told by descendants of the Norris family, is that Birmingham received its name as the result of an incident at a spelling match. A child was asked to spell the name Birmingham (a city in England) and he spelled it "Burmingham." The child was so embarrassed by the incident that Dr. Norris, who ran the spelling bee, later remembering it when he and John Harrison platted the town. He suggested the town be named Birmingham.
Item of interests
In 1854, the town's fire alarm was a great steel triangle on the roof of a hotel. A hammer was used to strike the triangle which could be heard for miles.

Blairsburg (Hamilton)
(1995), (2009), (2015)
In 1869, John I. Blair, a chief engineer of a railroad, came to the area to gain some incentives of land from investors for having the railroad come to town. When they refused, he platted his own town and named it for himself.

Blairstown (Benton)
(1986), (2008)
Blairstown was platted in 1862 and incorporated in 1868. It was named for John Insley Blair, a railroad official.
Item of interest

Jim Cox was known as a shiftless ne'er do well living at Blairstown. The citizens of that village had a wholesome respect for his sharp shooting. He lived with a sister at the east edge of town and lived too well on the neighbors' chickens to suit the neighbors. He believed chickens that trespassed on or near another's property belonged to those who could get them. He believed that if a chicken came close enough for him to shoot it in the head, it would be fair game. Many young chickens died that way.

The citizens protested, but to no avail. They finally issued a warrant for his arrest and Marshall Will Gearhart went out armed with a warrant and his gun to bring him in. Cox evidently was expecting the Marshal and took a quick shot at the Marshal befor3e he had time to act. Cox then barricaded himself in the house and dared them to get him. They tried to smoke him out and finally threw some cotton soaked with kerosene on the house and set it on fire. Cox then went to the south door of the house, shot in the air a few times, then went out the back door and down the railroad track to Watkins.

Word was sent ahead to be looking for him and someone filled him full of bird shot in his posterior extremity. However, he kept on going. No one dared face him in the open. He finally succumbed to the pain from the bird shot and went to a doctor in Marengo to have the bird shot removed. He was arrested there and returned to Benton county, where he was sentenced to fifteen years in the penitentiary. The Marshal recovered from his wounds, which was the reason for the light sentence.

Blakesburg (Wapello)
(2000), (2003), (2016)
The town was laid out in 1852 and named for one of its founder, Theophilus Blake.
Item of interest
Three miles northeast of Blakesburg is the Airpower Museum which features approximately 25 mostly pre-World War II aircraft as well as the Library of Flight, early flight simulators, propellers, engines, and original art. A fly-in of vintage aircraft is held each year on Labor Day Weekend where up to 25 pre-registered crews fly antique/classic aircraft from all over the United States to rendezvous with hundreds of other antique and classic aircraft at the airfield.

Blockton (Taylor)
(1992)
Blockton was founded by Mormons in 1861 and was originally known as Mormontown. After the Mormons left the area, the Chicago Great Western Railway came through the town and renamed it Blockton, in honor of W. T. Block, a railroad official.

BLOOMFIELD (Davis) (County Seat)
(1981), (1997), (2003), (2019)
In 1843, the site of Bloomfield was surveyed and incorporated in 1852. Three names were proposed for the town, Jefferson, Davis, and Bloomfield. The names were put into a hat and the name Bloomfield was drawn.

Item of interests
On August 27, 1924, Henry "Dare-Devil" Roland, "The Human Fly," attempted to climb the northwest corner of the courthouse. He fell to the ground from about 25 feet, breaking his hip. He was hospitalized in Bloomfield for six weeks, before returning East with his wife and daughter. On June 28, 1932, Roland made a return trip to Bloomfield to remove the blot from his record of successful climbs. This time, in just eleven minutes, he was sitting perched alongside the statue of Blind Justice on top of the courthouse. Roland died October 7, 1937, as a result of a trapeze fall at Ottway, Tennessee.

Bloomfield has the distinction of being the furthest north location reached by any Rebel from the Confederate lines. Twelve Confederates dressed in stolen Union uniforms snuck into Iowa on October 12, 1864. They spread havoc along 15 miles into the state where the raiders stopped to rob, kidnap, and kill civilians. The rebels then hightailed it back into Confederate-held Missouri.

Walter A. Sheaffer, who developed the first commercially successful lever-filling fountain pen and founded the W. A. Sheaffer Pen Company, was born in Bloomfield. (See Fort Madison)

Blue Grass (Muscatine and Scott)
(2018)
Blue Grass was a spot on a Native American trail between the Mississippi River and Cedar River. This was a choice camping spot for the Native Americans. When the Native Americans and ponies went through the grass, they noted that the newer grass sprouted up with a bluish tint. (The grass was similar to Kentucky bluegrass.) Blue Grass was incorporated in 1903.

Bode (Humboldt)
(1993)
Bode had its start in the year 1881 with the building of the Burlington Cedar Rapids and Northern Railway and was named by its founder T. A. Rossing.

Bolan (Worth)
(1987), (1996)
Bolan began in 1886 when the Chicago Great Western Railroad started building through that territory. It was named by the road master at the time, Matt Bolan.

Bonaparte (Van Buren)
(1981), (1997), (2003), (2013)
Founded in 1837, Bonaparte was originally named Meeks Mills. The name was changed in 1841 to Bonaparte in honor of Napoleon.

Item of interests
The riverfront district was added to the National Register of Historic Places in 1989. The old grist mill is now a restaurant is called Bonaparte's Retreat.

Bonaparte has been named the smallest Main Street Community in the United States and has the honor of having been named a winner of the "Great American Main Street Award."

On May 24, 2007, in a sensational trial, Shawn Bentler was found guilty of killing his parents and three of his younger teenage sisters in order to acquire his family's inheritance. His father, Michael Bentler, was the owner of a lumber and elevator company. Shawn's guilty verdict of mass murder was read to a court room filled with over 100 family members.

Bondurant (Polk)
(1974), (1984), (2000), (2006) (2011)
Bondurant was named for Alexander C. Bondurant, who was the area's first settler in 1857.

Boondocks Station (Hamilton)
(2015)
Boondocks Station is a truck stop near the town of Williams that closed in 2018.

BOONE (Boone) (County Seat)
(1973), (1975), (1976), (1988), (1998), (2008), (2011), (2018)
Boone was established in 1865 by John Insley Blair. It was first named Montana, but in 1881 was renamed Boone in honor of Captain Nathan Boone, son of Daniel Boone.

<u>Item of interests</u>
On the afternoon of July 6, 1881, heavy thunderstorms caused a flash flood of Honey Creek, washing out timbers that supported the railroad trestle. A pusher locomotive with a crew of four was sent to check on the track condition, but plunged into Honey Creek when the bridge over the Des Moines River collapsed.

Katherine Carroll "Kate" Shelley heard the crash and knew that an eastbound passenger train was due in Moingona about midnight. It would stop shortly before heading east over the Des Moines River and then to Honey Creek. She found the surviving crew members and shouted that she would get help. To get help she had to cross the Des Moines River bridge. She started with a lantern but it went out, so she crawled on the bridge span on her hands and knees with only lightning for illumination. Once across, she had to cover about two miles on the ground to the Moingona depot to sound the alarm. The passenger train, with about 200 aboard, was stopped at Scranton. Katie then led a party to rescue the crew members. Edgar Wood, who was perched in a tree, grasped a rope thrown to him and came ashore hand-over-hand. Adam Agar couldn't be reached until the floodwaters began to recede. Pat Donahue's corpse was eventually found in a cornfield a quarter mile downstream from the bridge and A. P. Olmsted was never found.

Because of her efforts, Katherine Carroll "Kate" Shelly became the first woman in the United States to have a bridge named for her and one of a few women to have a train named for her: The Kate Shelly 400.

In 1941, Boone commissioned the largest ever statue of Theodore Roosevelt. This statue was to be eight times larger than life-size and was scheduled to be completed in 1943. However, before casting, its 4,000 pounds of bronze was appropriated for uses in WWII. It was thought that Roosevelt would have approved of the decision by putting the service of the country first. In 1946, the Roman Bronze Corporation produced the casting in the original mold and on January 6, 1948, it was placed in McHose Park. It rests on three large granite blocks and the 6' 3" statue depicts Roosevelt rising out of a mountainous landscape with his hand outstretched as if addressing a crowd. Below the statue are ten reliefs telling of Roosevelt's outdoor accomplishments.

Boone is the birthplace of Mamie Geneva Doud, wife of President Dwight Eisenhower.

This historic railroad town offers trips on the Boone and Scenic Valley Railroad, where it crosses the Kate Shelley Memorial High Bridge, the longest and highest double-track railroad bridge in the country.

Bouton (Dallas)
(1983), (1986), (1994), (2001)
James L. and Sarah E. Bouton purchased the land in 1875. In 1885, they sold some of the land to the railroad who suggested the town be named Bouton.

Boxholm (Boone)
(1975), (1979), (1989), (1998)
Boxholm was mainly settled by Swedish immigrants and platted in 1900. The town was named for Boxholm, Sweden, the native home of its first postmaster, John B. Anderson.

Boyden (Sioux)
(2014)
Boyden was founded in 1878 and incorporated in 1889.

Boyer (Crawford)
(1981), (2006)
Boyer was laid out in 1889 and took its name from the Boyer River. The Boyer River was named for a settler who hunted and trapped in the watershed before the time of Lewis and Clark.

Bradford (Chickasaw)
(1982), (1983), (2002)
Bradford is not to be confused with Bradford, an unincorporated community in Franklin County. Chickasaw County was first inhabited by the Chickasaw Indians whose chief was named Bradford. The county was named for the tribe and the town was named for the chief. Bradford is an unincorporated community first settled in the early 1850's.
<u>Item of interest</u>
In 1857, Dr. William S. Pitts' stage coach stopped in Bradford on its way to Fredericksburg. The stop allowed Pitts to walk around the area and noted the beauty of the wooded valley where he envisioned a brown church building. He kept the vision in his mind and after returning to his home in Wisconsin, he wrote "The Church in the Wildwood." He was surprised when he later returned to the area to find a church being erected where he had imagined it five years earlier. The building was even being painted brown, because that was the least expensive color of paint to be found.

> There's a church in the valley by the wildwood
> No lovelier spot in the dale
> No place is so dear to my childhood
> As the little brown church in the vale

(Oh, come, come, come, come)

Come to the church by the wildwood
Oh, come to the church in the vale
No spot is so dear to my childhood
As the little brown church in the vale

Bradgate (Humboldt)
(2007)
The first settlement in this location was named Willow Glen; however, when the town was platted, the name was changed to Bradgate. There are several theories of how the town got its name but the most widely accepted is that Bradgate was named after Bradgate Park in England.
<u>Item of interest</u>
In 1854, the last battle between two Iowa American Indian tribes took place at nearby Avery's Hill. The two tribes were the Sioux and Winnebagos. Some eighteen Sioux warriors under the leadership of Coustawa (Big Tree) surprised the tribe of the Winnebagos, but they were driven back after the death of Coustawa. One of the Sioux warriors was reported to be Inkpaduta, who later led a band of Sioux in the famed Spirit Lake Massacre. (See Spirit Lake)

Brandon (Buchanan)
(1974), (1983), (1985)
The village of Brandon was platted and laid out in 1854 and incorporated in the 1905. It was name for Thomas Brandon, who was an early settler.
<u>Item of interest</u>
Brandon is home to Iowa's largest frying pan which was constructed in 2004. The frying pan promotes the Brandon Community Club's annual Cowboy Breakfast. The pan weighs over 1,000 pounds.
It took over forty volunteer man hours to construct the frying pan. It was made out of scrap steel donated by local farmers. They chose to build a large frying pan because a cowboy's breakfast is cooked over open flames using mostly cast iron frying pans. Although the frying pan is not used on the third Sunday in September when the town celebrates their annual Cowboy Breakfast Festival.

The pan:
- Weight: 1,200 pounds
- Total length: 14 feet 3 inches
- Rim diameter: 9 feet 3 inches
- Base diameter: 8 feet
- Handle length: 5 feet

The frying pan is calculated to hold 88 times as much as a 10-inch frying pan.

It can cook:
- 528 eggs (44 dozen)
- 352 pork chops (1/2 pound chops)
- 88 pounds of bacon
- 440 hamburgers (1/2 pound Burgers)

Breda (Carroll)
(1988), (1994)

Breda had its start in 1877 with the building of the Maple Branch of the Chicago and North Western railroad through that territory. It was named for the Dutch city of Breda by a settler native to that place.

Bremer (Bremer)
(2014)

The first Post office in Bremer was established in 1888. Bremer is an unincorporated community. The county and town were named for Fredrika Bremer (1801-1885), a Swedish feminist writer and reformer. She is regarded as the Swedish Jane Austen. Her 1850s novel Hertha, prompted a social movement that granted all Swedish women legal majority at the age of 25 and established Sweden's first female post-secondary school.

Item of interest

At one time, The Jahnke Dance Hall was a popular place which featured big-named bands.

Bremer Station (Bremer)
(1980), (1999), (2002)
(See Bremer)

Brighton (Washington)
(1992), 2009)

Brighton was laid out in 1840. The town was named for Brighton, England.

Item of interest

Brighton was the scene of a famous shoot-out where Dr. Hough killed Dr. Sales on Main Street in August of 1868. Dr. Hough escaped.

Bristow (Butler)
(1980), (1990), (1999)

Bristow was incorporated in 1881 and was first called West Point after West Point township. In 1876, the towns name was changed to Bristow because there was already a town named West Point.

Item of interest

Ed Yost was born in Bristow and considered the Father of the modern day hot-air-balloon. His historic 25-minute 3-mile flight on Oct. 22, 1960, in Bruning, Nebraska, was on a contraption that resembled a lawn chair dangled from a nylon balloon, which was propelled by a propane-burner system that gave rise to the modern hot air balloon.

Britt (Hancock)
(1985), (1987), (2010), (2017)

Britt was incorporated in 1881. It was named for a brakeman or engineer on the Chicago, Milwaukee and St. Paul Railroad.

Items of interest

Since 1900, on the second weekend of August, Britt holds the National Hobo Convention. The highlight of this festival is the election of the King and Queen of the Hobos. The hobos come to town and set up a hobo jungle, sell their crafts and provide free entertainment for visitors. Britt is also home to the National Hobo Museum, where many authentic hobo artifacts are on display.

Hobos were migratory workers who helped satisfy America's labor needs after the Civil War. They were "homeless" by choice; they worked to travel and traveled to work. Their chief mode of transportation has always been freight trains.

Hobos, tramps, and bums are all terms used for persons who are homeless and without a steady job. While most folks use these words interchangeable, there is a slight difference between the three. A hobo is someone who travels from place to place looking for work, a tramp is someone who travels but avoids work whenever possible, and a bum doesn't care to work or travel.

Britt is also home to the largest Draft Horse Hitch Show in North America which is held every Labor Day Weekend.

Bronson (Woodbury)
(1988), (2006)
Bronson was laid out in 1901 and named for Ira D. Bronson, an early settler.

Brooklyn (Poweshiek)
(1976), (1979), (1991), (2006), (2011)
The founders changed the name of their town from Greenfield to Brooklyn in 1859. As current residents tell it, the town renamed itself when the downtown was moved a half-mile south to be better situated next to the new railroad line. To come up with a name, the mayor went to the highest point to look out over the landscape. After observing that the town sat between two small rivers, he reportedly said, "There's a brook over there and a brook over there, and all this land in the middle. We should be called Brookland." The name was shortened to the better-sounding Brooklyn.
Item of interest
Brooklyn boasts a large display of flags from each of the fifty states, the four branches of the military, along with several other flags. Brooklyn is known as the "Community of Flags."

Brookville (Jefferson)
(1984)
Brookville started in anticipation of the railroad coming through the community; however, the railroad did not come through the community

and without the railroad, the community dried up and it is currently listed as a ghost town.

<u>Item of interest</u>

One of the early settlers was Isaac Newton Williams who opened a tannery. He hired a man to help run the business while he went off to fight in the Civil War. When he returned, there was an argument between them about the war which resulted in the man stabbing Williams.

Brunsville (Plymouth)
(1998)

Brunsville was platted in 1909 and incorporated in 1911. It was named for Mrs. Bruns, who originally owned the land.

Buck Creek (Clayton)
(1998)

Buck Creek is surrounded by over 100 acres of forested land along the banks of Buck Creek Trout Stream. It flows into Lake Rathbun.

Buckeye (Hardin)
(2015)

Buckeye had its start about 1901 with the building of the railroad through that territory. It was incorporated in 1903. Many of the early settlers were from Ohio and it is thought that this is how the town was named Buckeye. Ohio is known as the Buckeye State because of the many buckeye trees that covered the Ohio's hills and plains. The name "buckeye" came from Native Americans who called the nut "hetuck" which means "buck eye" because the marking on the nut resembles the eye of a deer. The buckeye state slogan started in 1840 during William Henry Harrison's presidential campaign. His supporters claimed he was "the log cabin candidate" and his campaign emblem was a log cabin made of buckeye timbers with a string of buckeyes decorating the walls.

Burchinal (Cerro Gordo)
(1977), (1985)

Burchinal is an unincorporated village.

BURLINGTON (Des Moines) (County Seat)
(1979), (1984), (1990), (2000), (2009), (2019)

This area was first a neutral territory for the Sac and Fox Indians, who called it "Shoquoquon" (Shok-ko-kon), meaning Flint Hills. This was the first name of the town. In the spring of 1834 John Gray purchased the first lot with his wife Eliza Jane and chose the name Burlington in honor or his hometown in Vermont.

Items of interest

Iowa's nickname, "The Hawkeye State" came about when the Burlington newspaper changed its name from the Iowa Patriot to the "Iowa Hawk-Eye and Patriot."

From 1838 to 1840, Burlington served as the first capital of the Iowa Territory. In 1803, President Thomas Jefferson organized two parties to explorer the Louisiana Purchase. Lewis and Clark followed the Missouri River and while Zebulon Pike followed the Mississippi River. In 1805, Pike landed at the bluffs below Burlington and raised the United States Flag for the first time on what would become Iowa soil.

"Ripley's Believe It or Not" calls Burlington's Snake Alley the "Crookedest Street in the World." Perhaps this is Burlington's most famous landmark which consists of five half-curves and two quarter-curves. The alley is composed of limestone and blue clay bricks. The constantly changing slant from one curve to the next required some complicated construction to keep the high grade to the outside. Snake Alley curves over a distance of 275 feet, rising 58.3 feet, a 21% grade, from Washington Street to Columbia Street.

Kurtis Eugene Warner was born in Burlington. After graduation from high school, he attended the University of Northern Iowa and was the third string quarterback until his senior year, when he became the starting quarterback. That year he was named the Gateway Conference's offensive player of the year.

In 1994, he was signed by the Green Bay Packers as an undrafted free agent. He played for three NFL teams: the St. Louis Rams, the New York Giants and the Arizona Cardinals. Warner went on to be considered the best undrafted NFL player of all time. He was inducted into the Pro Football Hall of Fame in 2017 and is the only person inducted into both the Pro Football Hall of Fame and the Arena Football Hall of Fame.

Burt (Kossuth)
(2014)
Burt was platted in 1881 when the railroad was extended. It was named for Horace G. Burt, a railroad official.

Bussey (Marion)
(1984), (2000), (2003), (2013)
Bussy was named for Jesse Bussey who originally bought the land for the town in 1867.

<u>Item of interest</u>
The mural in downtown Bussey has a story behind it. In 1994, Todd Spaur's car flipped off a highway. He lay trapped and hidden in the underbrush for more than 16 hours. He could not call for help or crawl away because he'd broken his back, his neck and most of the bones in his face. "I just wanted to die," he said. The doctors told him that he would never walk again. "I could only wiggle one toe," he recalled. Doctors told him that he was looking at a life in a wheelchair. "If I can't get some relief," Spaur thought, "I'm going to kill myself." His neighbors in Bussey offered to look after Spaur while he set out to prove the doctors wrong. "It was hard," he said. "But friends and family believed in me, and that meant a lot. I looked at myself in the mirror and asked the nurse for a comb."

Sixteen years after his car accident, Spaur was finally able to stand up straight. A slow smile spread across his face. "My doctor's name was Smucker. He had to be good." Spaur can now walk with a cane and he decided to do something special for all those people who helped when he needed them most. Spaur has nine steel plates and a fractured fifth vertebra, but he said "thank you" by working for ten months on a mural which depicts a Fourth of July parade with images of family and friends.

To do his work he dangled from a cherry picker on the side of an old building two stories above downtown.

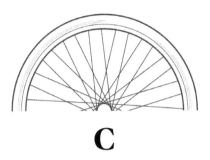

C

Cambria (Wayne)
(1981), (2016)
Cambria is an unincorporated community that has existed since 1848. Cambria was founded by Arbuckle Nelson, a farmer who laid out the village. The name Cambria is a Welch name for Wales.

Cambridge (Story)
(1994), (2001)
Cambridge was incorporated in 1881. It was founded and named by Josiah Chandler.

Camp Dodge (Johnston)
(1974)
Camp Dodge was named for Brigadier General Grenville M. Dodge, who organized Iowa's first National Guard unit in 1856. It is the headquarters of the Iowa National Guard. Camp Dodge is located in the town of Johnston.
Item of interest
Camp Dodge is Iowa's largest military base and trained thousands of soldiers for World War I.

Canby (Adair)
(2000)
Canby is an unincorporated community. A post office was established in 1873 and remained in operation until 1908. Little remains of the original community.

Canton (Jackson and Jones)
(1991), (1998), (2002)

Canton is an unincorporated community. Because many of the early settlers were from Ohio, Canton could have been named for Canton, Ohio.

Carnavon (Sac)
(1975)
The unincorporated community of Carnavon was named for Caernarfon, in Wales, the former hometown of its first settler.

Carnes (Sioux)
(1993)
A post office was established at Carnes in 1890 and remained in operation until 1914. The community was named for Edward Carnes, a railroad road master.

Carnforth (Poweshiek)
(1976), (1991), (2006), (2011)
A post office was established in 1884 and after two months was named Carnforth. A railroad official selected the name Carnforth from a book he was reading at the time.

Carpenter (Mitchell)
(1996), (2005)
In 1854, Neks Severson and members of the Lee Family came to the area as its first settlers. Carpenter was named when the Chicago, Milwaukee & St Paul Railroad was coming through the area. It was incorporated in 1897.

CARROLL (Carroll) (County Seat)
(1980), (1988), (1994) (2011)
Carroll was laid out in 1867 and took its name from Carroll County, which was named in honor of Charles Carroll, the only Roman Catholic to sign the Declaration of Independence.
Item of interest
Before the county was settled, there was a line that separated the Pottawatomie and Mequakie Indians from the Sioux Indians. One day a group of Sioux warriors chased a buffalo over the separation line and

a battle began. At Swan Lake three hundred Pottawatomie Indians were hidden in ambush on the southeast side of the lake when seven hundred Sioux came from the west. Rifles were used until the ammunition gave out. Then they used bow and arrows and when the arrows were gone, they went to hand to hand combat with tomahawks.

Legend has it that only three Pottawatomie and one Sioux Indian survived. It was noted by early trappers and hunters that the ground where the battle took place was white with bleached bones, rusted rifles and weapons.

Carson (Pottawattamie)
(1997), (2011)

Carson was formed in 1881 when a depot was establishment on the Burlington and Rock Island Railroad and was named for a railroad officer.

Item of interest

Carson's Rodeo has been described as the "Best Small Rodeo in the Country." The annual rodeo takes place on the first weekend of August.

Cartersville (Cerro Gordo)
(2010), (2017)

The community of Cartersville was named after the 1891 novel Col. Carter of Cartersville by Francis Hopkinson Smith.

Item of interest

On the RAGBRAI route in 2010, the Cerro Gordo County Sheriff's Department and the Iowa State Patrol shut down what they called a wild party at a private pond in Cartersville, after swimmers allegedly started taking off their clothes. The partiers were swinging on a rope that went out over a pond. Sheriff Kevin Pals said in the afternoon that many of the thousands at the pond were not wearing shorts or were females without tops. He later said there were "several" people who were partially undressed. It was estimated that 1,500 to 1,700 people went through the pond before it was shut down.

Cascade (Dubuque and Jones)
(1974), (1989), (1999), (2007)

Cascade was incorporated in 1880. The town takes its name from Cascade Township which was derived from the cascade, or water power, with which early settlers used to power their mills. The town's most notable historic event was the flood of 1925.

Casey (Adair and Guthrie)
(1981), (1991), (2001), (2019)
Casey was platted in 1869 and named for a railroad man. In 1868 when the railroad bypassed the town of Dalmanutha, the town of Casey was created. The people of Dalmanutha picked up their houses and belongings and moved to the new town of Casey,
Item of interest
In 2015, the City Clerk, Dorothy Dillinger, was indicted for embezzling city funds and burning down the city hall. She stole up to $300,000 of city funds and spent it on purchases at Victoria's Secret, Wal-Mart and other places. She pleaded guilty in federal court and received a prison sentence of five years. Construction of a new city hall and community center was started in 2018.

Castalia (Winneshiek)
(2017)
Castalia was incorporated in 1901. The origin of the town's name is uncertain, but it may have come from Greek mythology where Castalia was the daughter of Achelous. Some sources say that water was a gift to Castalia from the river Cephisus. A Latin poet wrote that to escape amorous advances from Apollo, Castalia transformed herself into a fountain at Delphi.
Castalia was incorporated in 1902. In early times Castalia was referred to as Rattletrap.
Item of interest
Near Castelia since 1851, the Green family owns and operates Green's Sugar Bush, where each year about 2,250 sugar maple trees are tapped on the farm to make maple syrup.

Castana (Monona)
(1977), (1995), (2004)

Castana was platted in 1886 by the railroad. The name Castana was selected by an early settler who believed it was a Latin word meaning "chestnuts." The word in Latin is spelled "castanea."

Item of interest

The Western Iowa Experimental Farm, a part of Iowa State University, is located just outside Castana, where, research is carried out on beef and swine and the effects of fertilizer on soybeans and corn.

Cedar (Mahaska)

(2003), (2013)

Cedar is an unincorporated community. The Post Office was established in 1873. It took its name from being in Cedar township.

CEDAR FALLS (Black Hawk)

(1985), (1989), (1998), (2007), (2015)

William Sturgis founded Cedar Falls in 1845. It was originally named Sturgis Falls, for the first family who settled the site. The city was renamed Cedar Falls because of its proximity to the falls on the Cedar River. The Cedar River takes its name from the large number of red cedar trees growing along its banks.

Item of interest

In 1863, what is now known as the University of Northern Iowa (UNI) began as a Civil War Soldier's Orphan Home. It has had several name changes which include Old Central, Iowa State Normal School, Iowa State Teacher's College, State College of Iowa and currently the University of Northern Iowa.

CEDAR RAPIDS (Linn) (County Seat)

(1990), (1994), (2012)

When the town was first established, it was named Columbus and in 1841 renamed Cedar Rapids for the rapids in the Cedar River. The river was named for the large number of red cedar trees that grew along its banks. Cedar Rapids is nicknamed the "City of Five Seasons," the "fifth season" is time to enjoy the other four.

Items of interest
An island, now named Municipal Island, in the channel of the Cedar River was, until 1851, the headquarters of the Shepherd gang, who were notorious horse thieves.

During the flood of 2008, the Cedar River reached a record high of 31.12 feet on June 13, which surpassed the 500-year flood plain. The previous record was 20 feet. 1,126 city blocks were flooded and 561 city blocks were severely damaged. In total, 10 square miles were effected. This was 14% of the city's total area.

Cedar Rapids has the largest newspaper archive in North America with a repository of more than 150 million pages assembled over 250 years.

Cedar Rapids is one of the largest corn processing cities in the world.

Cedar Rapids has always had the highest percentage of exported products, per capita, in the United States.

Czechoslovakians, known as Bohemians, began arriving in 1852 to work in local meat packing plants, and soon a "Little Bohemia" was established in the southwest sector of the city, which is now known as "Czech Village." Josef Sosel, the first Czech lawyer in the United States, was smuggled out of his native country in a barrel after he was accused of revolutionary activities. Sosel settled in Cedar Rapids, where he played a prominent role in the Czech community.

Cedar Rapids has played an important role in Muslim culture in the United States. The National Muslim Cemetery is said to be the first exclusively Muslim cemetery in North America. Graves in the cemetery face Mecca. The Mother Mosque of America, dedicated on June 16, 1934, is the longest standing mosque in North America.

Coe College claims to have the shortest name of any
American institution of higher education, but the school
has actually carried five titles through its history: The
School for the Prophets, Parsons Seminary, Coe Collegiate
Institute, and Cedar Rapids Collegiate Institute.

Center Junction (Jones)
(1974), (1985)
Center Junction was laid out in 1871 and named with the hope it
would become a junction near the geographical center of Jones County.
The town, for many years was a junction of the Chicago & North Western
Railroad and the Chicago, Minneapolis, St. Paul & Pacific Railroad.
Item of interest
Center Junction was once an incorporated community but because
of financial difficulties, in a special election in 2015, it voted to sell off its
assets, disband, and turn the administration of the community over to the
county.

Center Point (Linn)
(1974), (1978), (1983), (1985)
Naming this new village proved to be controversial. Some wanted it
to be call McGonigle's Point after the first settlers, but the majority wanted
it named Central Point, because of its central location between Cedar
Rapids, Quasqueton, and Independence. A compromise name of "Centre
Point" was selected. The spelling of the name was later changed to Center
Point due to popular usage.
Items of interest
There are several stories about "Horse Thief Cave" located west of
Center Point. Horse thieves were thought to have hidden stolen horses in
this cave that had its access on the banks of the Cedar River. This prevented
trackers from finding the horses. The story that has been passed down
is that one morning in 1880, a mob of locals captured an alleged horse
thief named Brody. Brody claimed he found the horses but his "gang" was
known for stealing horses, counterfeiting, and selling whiskey to Native

Americans. The mob of locals proceeded to Vine and Summit streets where Brode was hanged on a large pine tree. This story of the hanging cannot be confirmed, but several gangs of horse thieves have been documented in Linn County from the 1840's to the 1850's. One of the prominent gangs was the Brody gang.

In 1872, William Langsdale was indicted for killing Joseph Barnes at Langsdale's Store. The records indicated that Barnes was drunk when he started a fight with another customer. Mr. Langsdale pulled a pistol from behind the counter and shot Mr. Barnes. Barnes was taken to a doctor's office where he died. Langsdale was tried in March 1873. The jury returned a verdict of not guilty.

CENTERVILLE (Appanoose) (County Seat)
(1981), (2016), (2019)
Centerville was founded in 1846 by Jonathon Stratton, who named it "Chaldea." The name was later changed to Senterville, for William Tandy Senter, a prominent Tennessee politician. When incorporation papers were filed in 1855, someone mistook the name for a misspelling and "corrected" it to Centerville.
Items of interest
Centerville claims to have the world's largest town square.

During the Civil War, the Centerville area sent 1500 men to fight and three hundred died in battle. The last to die was a 15-year-old boy.

Coal mining began in 1868 resulting in immigrants from over 40 countries coming to Centerville to work. The mines were closed in the 1930s. Today the city remains the home of many Swedish, Italian, Croatian, and Albanian American descendants of immigrants who worked in the mines.

Beginning in 1987, on the last Saturday of July, Centerville
has held the Croatian Fest to celebrate the area's Croatian
Heritage.

The city is home to the Appanoose County Historical & Coal Mining
Museum.

In the 1950s and 1960s a civic movement resulted in the
building of nearby Rathbun Dam and the formation of
Rathbun Lake. Rathbun Lake is known as "Iowa's Ocean."
It was dedicated on July 31, 1971 by President Richard M.
Nixon.

Centerville has been named one of the top five outdoor
towns in America by Outdoor Life Magazine.

Central City (Linn)
(1974), (1982), (1985), (2002)
Central City was founded in 1850 and its name refers to its close
proximity to railroads.

Centralia (Dubuque)
(1974), (1993)
The town was started in 1850 and first named Dacotah, but later
change its name to Centralia. The town is located in Center township.

CHARITON (Lucas) (County Set)
(1997), (2009), (2019)
The town was platted in 1850. After much discussion, some wanting
to call the town Polk; however, it was named Chariton for Chariton Point,
a landmark along the native and pioneer trail on the Chariton River. The
river is believed to have been named for Joseph Chorette, who drowned
while swimming in the river as he accompanied the French Jean Baptiste
Trudeau 1795 expedition up the Missouri.

CHARLES CITY (Floyd) (County Seat)
(1977), (1982), (1996), (2002), (2010), (2017)
Charles City was incorporated in 1869. The town was originally
named Charlestown for the son of the first-known white settler to the
area. It later became St. Charles and eventually Charles City, to avoid
duplication of another towns name in Iowa.

Items of interest

Charles City played a role in the development of the American
tractor. Charles Walter Hart, the son of a man who had three local farms,
met Charles H. Parr in college. After graduating from the University of
Wisconsin in 1897, they developed a two-cylinder gasoline engine and set
up their business in Charles City. It was here in 1901 that Hart and Parr
created the term "tractor" which was derived from Latin roots from the
combination of the words traction and power. In 1903, they built fifteen
"tractors," the first successful production-model tractor line in the United
States. In 1929, Hart-Parr was one of the four companies that merged
to form Oliver Farm Equipment and finally the White Farm-New Idea
Equipment Company.

The Hart-Parr company also made some of the first washing
machines. Selling for $155.00 in the 1920s, the buyer had the option of
ordering either an electric or gasoline engine.

On January 9, 1907, Charles City was the scene of the last
lynching in Iowa. A mob of several hundred men, some
masked with handkerchiefs, used a rail iron to knock down
the doors of the Floyd County Jail. The Sheriff and several
deputies only offered little resistance. The mob seized the
prisoner, James Cullen. This man was a wealthy white, sixty-
two-year- old contractor who had murdered his wife and
stepson the previous day. As the mob hauled Cullen to the
Cedar River bridge, Frank Roper, a Salvation Army officer,
interceded to say a prayer for Cullen over the protests of
some of the less patient members of the mob. Cullen then
offered his own prayer stating that he had acted in self-
defense. Some in the mob wanted to fill Cullen's body with
bullets, but one of the leaders said that a simple hanging

would suffice. Afterward the mob quickly departed, leaving Cullen's lifeless body as a reminder of the events of the previous 48 hours. Approximately five hundred residents of Charles City, including women and children, witnessed the hanging.

Carrie Lane Chapman, a national women's rights leader grew up on a farm south of Charles City. She was well known as a prominent leader of the woman's suffrage movement and her efforts helped pass the 19th Amendment granting women the right to vote in 1920. She was also the founder of the "League of Women Voters."

Charles City is home to the Alvin Miller House, a home designed by Frank Lloyd Wright. The house is located at 1107 Court Street.

Charlotte (Clinton)
(2004), (2012)
Charlotte was platted in 1871 and named for the first postmaster's wife, Charlotte Gilmore. The town pronounces its name as SHAR-LOT.

Item of interest
At one time Charlotte had a cannon from the Civil War. Someone wanted to see the cannon in action, so he filled it with rocks instead of a cannon ball, added some powder and lit the fuse. The cannon went off and the rocks hit the depot creating a hole in the roof. Later the cannon was scrapped to help with the World War II war efforts.

Charter Oak (Crawford)
(1987), (2018)
Charter Oak was incorporated in 1891. The town was named by the American Emigrant Company as a result of an event that happened during a rain storm while the territory was being surveyed. When the heavy rains came, the surveyor protected his maps and papers by bundling them up and putting then into a hollow spot in a large oak tree. The tree became the Charter Oak and later became the town's name.

Chelsea (Tama)
(1986), (1995), (2008)
Chelsea was incorporated in 1878. There are two stories about where the town got its name. One is that S. G. Breese, one of the original owners of land near the site, named it for Chelsea, Massachusetts, from where he had come from. The other story is that John I. Blair named it for Chelsea, England.

CHEROKEE (Cherokee) (County Seat)
(1975), (1982), (1998), (2002) (2012)
Cherokee was laid in 1870 and named for the Cherokee Indian tribe.
<u>Items of interest</u>
In April of 1857, there was a rumor that 400 Sioux were coming down the river on the war path. This rumor caused the settlement to be abandoned. For the next 3 years, the setters would leave and return due to Indian scares.

In 1861, the State government created the Iowa Border Brigade to protect the frontier. In 1862, a fort was constructed near the present site of Cherokee. In 1862, the last Indian battle was fought in Iowa. Sam and Andrew Purcell, scouts for the Border Brigade, shot and killed a Sioux warrior and wounded another during a horse-stealing raid.

The Cherokee Mental Health Institute is a state-run psychiatric facility. In 1901, to relieve overcrowding in the state's other three facilities, a fourth hospital was opened under the name of "Cherokee Lunatic Asylum." The purpose was to take care of alcoholics, those with old age diseases, the mentally-ill, and the criminally-insane. The hospital was set up to serve 700 patients. In August of 1902, special trains brought to 306 patients to Cherokee from Independence and 252 from Clarinda. The early years were dark and brutal for the patients. The hospital name has changed several times over the years, going from Iowa Lunatic Asylum to Cherokee State Hospital and to its current name of Cherokee Mental Health Institute.

> Mardi Gras Fat Tuesday is celebrated every year by women racing through downtown wearing a dress, apron, and kerchief and carrying a frying pan, complete with a pancake. The women must flip the pancake at the beginning and end of the 415-yard course.

Pilot Rock, located two miles south of Cherokee, is an enormous boulder of red Sioux quartzite that measures 160 feet in circumference and 20 feet in height. It was revered by the Native American population that once lived in the region.

Chillicothe (Wapello)
(2003)
Chillicothe was incorporated in 1881. The word "Chillicothe" came from the ancient Shawnee word meaning "Principal Place." The main chief of the Shawnee could only come from the Chillicothe clan. When a village was called Chillicothe, it meant it was home to the principal chief. It was the capital city of the Shawnee until the death of that chief when the capitol would move to the home village of the next main chief. Then that village would then become Chillicothe.

Item of interest
Chillicothe is the burial place of Curtis King, the oldest man to serve in the Civil War. In 1863, the Lt. Governor of Iowa asked the War Department for permission to form a regiment of men over the enlistment age of 35 to relieve the younger men from non-combat duties, resulting in the 37th Iowa Volunteer Regiment (known as the "Gray Beards.") Mr. King enlisted at the age of 80 years. He served for several months before being discharged due to ill health.

Churdan (Greene)
(1975), (1979), (1988), (1994), (2011)
Churdan (pronounced - Sure-Dan) was incorporated in 1884 and named for Joseph Churdan, a pioneer settler.

Clare (Webster)
(1973), (1987), (2015)
Clare was settled around 1882 by immigrants from County Clare, Ireland, which resulted in the town's being named Clare. In the early days, the town was referred to as "The Irish Settlement," because a number of residents were from Ireland.

CLARINDA (Page) (County Seat)
(1989), (2003)
Clarinda was incorporated on December 8, 1866 and named for Clarinda Buck, who according to legend, carried water to the surveyors while Page County was first being surveyed.
Items of interest
In 1943, an internment war camp was built in Clarinda for 3,000 prisoners of war. The camp had sixty barracks and a 150-bed hospital. The camp held prisoners from Germany, Italy, and Japan.

Glenn Miller, the famous band director, was born in Clarinda. While he was traveling to entertain U.S. troops in France during World War II, his aircraft disappeared in bad weather over the English Channel. His body nor the plane was ever found.

In 1884, The Clarinda Treatment Complex was built as the Clarinda State Hospital. It was the third asylum in the state for the treatment of alcoholics, those with old age diseases, the mentally-ill and the criminally-insane. (see Cherokee)

CLARION (Wright) (County Seat)
(1980), (1983), (1993), (2007)
Clarion was originally named Grant, but changed its name to Clarion after Clarion, Pennsylvania. It was incorporated in 1881.
Item of interest
Clarion is the birthplace of the four-leaf clover emblem used by 4-H Clubs of America. It was conceived in 1907 by the local school superintendent, O.H. Benson.

Clarksville (Butler)
(1980), (1985), (1990), (1999), (2010), (2014)
In 1852, traveling from Indiana, the Clark-Poisal wagon train, with 32 family members, arrived in what would be called Clarksville. They decided to stop and build one large log cabin for everyone to stay for the winter. Thomas Clark then traveled to the land office in Dubuque to claim the strip of land. The town was then named for him.

Clayton Center (Clayton)
(1996), (2005)
An unincorporated community.

Clear Lake (Cerro Gordo)
(1977), (1985), (1999), (2010), (2014), (2017)
Clear Lake was founded in 1852 and incorporated in 1856. The city is named for the large spring-fed lake formed by glacial action some 14,000 years ago. It covers approximately 3,600 acres and measures seven miles long and two and one-half miles wide.
Items of interest

> The region around the lake was the summer home to the Dakota and Winnebago Indians. In 1832, Nathan Boone, the son of Daniel Boone, noted the lake on his survey of the area.

Clear Lake is home to the Surf Ballroom, an American cultural icon and an important landmark which opened on April 17, 1934. The Surf got its name from the original owners who wanted to create a ballroom to resemble an ocean beach club. The murals on the back walls were hand-painted to depict pounding surf, swaying palm trees, sailboats and lighthouses. The furnishings were bamboo and rattan and the ambience was that of a south sea island. The stage is surrounded by palm trees and the clouds overhead makes it seem as if you were dancing outside under the stars.

In the 1930's and 1940's, the Surf was a must stop for big bands to make a nationally recognized reputation. Some of the bands that played at the Surf included Count Basie, Duke Ellington, and The Dorsey's band. In the early years, the main entertainment was ballroom dancing. In the 1950's, when rock and roll became a hot item, it drew names such as The Everly Brothers, Roy Orbison, Ricky Nelson, Little Richard, Jan and Dean, and Conway Twitty.

On February 2, 1959, the Surf held its Winter Dance Party which featured Buddy Holly, Ritchie Valens, The Big Bopper, and Dion. It was this show that made the most lasting mark on the Surf Ballroom.

In the early hours of February 3, 1959, after performing at the Surf, a Beechcraft Bonanza airplane carrying Buddy Holly, Ritchie Valens, and the Big Bopper took off from the nearby Mason City airport for their next show in Moorhead, Minnesota. The plane crashed soon after takeoff, killing all aboard. This event was later eulogized by folk singer Don McLean's famous song, "American Pie," in which the death of these '50s icons serves as a metaphor for greater changes within American society. This happening is often referred to as "The Day the Music Died."

Clemons (Marshall)
(1986), (1998), (2012)
The settlement of Clemons began in 1851 when the Robert Elder family arrived and name it Elder's Grove. The land was granted to Elder by the government for his father's services in the Mexican War.

In 1853, Robert Elder's brother-in-law, William M. Clemons, came to the area for the purpose of surveying the land and making it his future home. The only land that suited him was his brother-in-law's. Robert Elder agreed sell him his land. The town was then known as Clemons' Grove then finally Clemons after William Clemons.

Cleves (Hardin)
(1978), (1983), (1995), (2004), (2015)
The village of Cleves, was platted in 1880 by a railroad company. It was named after Cleves (Kleve) Germany.

CLINTON (Clinton) (County Seat)
(1978), (1985), (1994), (2004), (2012)
Clinton was incorporated on January 26, 1857 and named for DeWitt Clinton, the sixth governor of New York.

Items of interest

Between the 1850s and 1900, Clinton and neighboring Lyons became a center for the lumber industry and were regarded as the "Lumber Capital of the World." Huge log rafts were floated down the Mississippi River from Wisconsin and Minnesota to Clinton where they were cut into lumber and then shipped out on the river or railroad.

Clinton is home to The Sawmill Museum. The museum houses original pieces from the Struve Mill which operated from 1860's to the 1980's. The exhibit shows how lumber was processed from live trees to finished products and used for commercial and residential purposes.

In the 1880s and 1890s Clinton boasted 13 resident millionaires, more millionaires per capita than any other town or city in the nation at the time. The era of opulence came to an end by 1900, as the northern forests were depleted and the sawmills closed. The city still boasts a number of magnificent Victorian mansions.

Clinton is home to The L'Arche Clinton community which provides homes where people with and without intellectual disabilities live and work together as peers. The home creates an inclusive community of faith and friendship, and transform society through relationships that cross social boundaries.

The first L'Arche home was opened in 1964 in the village of Trosly, France in response to the call to bring people with intellectual disabilities out of the degrading conditions of institutions. No longer were people with disabilities seen as something shameful that needed to be quarantined, but as full human beings inherently deserving of respect. That first L'Arche home, in its simple beginning, became the model for today's federation of over 150 L'Arche communities in 38 countries worldwide.

In 1968, Sister Marjorie Wisor of the Sisters of St. Francis in Clinton, was studying French in Paris, and made a visit to the L'Arche community in Trosly. According to Sister Marjorie, her visit left a great impression as she felt layers of her being stripped away as those with disabilities met her person-to-person. There were no barriers.

In 1972, Sister Marjorie and Father Mottet of Davenport Catholic Social Services discussed the effects of the Scott County Home closing and consideration was given to using it to opening a L'Arche home. When that did not work out, The First Presbyterian Church of Clinton donated a house and on June 6, 1974, Gerry Potter became the first community member welcomed by L'Arche Clinton.

Bennett Warren and his family owned a farm and also kept a house of entertainment for travelers. During the days of horse-thieving and counterfeit money, the house had become notorious and was a stopping place for those engaged in these unlawful practices. It was also believed he was aiding and abetting these criminals by hiding them and their stolen horses. No sufficient evidence could be obtained to convict him of actively participating in these crimes. He had been indicted once for stealing a trapper pelt traps, but was acquitted at the trial. It became almost impossible to secure a conviction because of the difficulty in selecting a jury.

In June of 1857, vigilantes, numbering about two hundred, left their meeting place at Big Rock. They had with them two prisoners and upon reaching Warren's house, took him with them to a small nearby grove of trees where a tragedy was to take place. There were no riotous proceedings, nor semblance of a mob. Everything was done with a kind of rude decorum and gravity befitting the occasion. No one was masked, or in any manner concealed their identity. Upon their arrival at the grove, the leader, whose authority was recognized by all, called the meeting to order and a jury of twelve was selected by nomination and then they took their places. Witnesses were sworn in and testified. The jury then deliberated and returned their verdict that Bennett Warren was guilty of harboring horse-thieves, knowing them to be such; of keeping and concealing stolen horses, knowing them to be such; and of habitually passing counterfeit money, knowing it to be such." The jury passed no sentence, but upon rendering the verdict, the leader called for an answer to the following question: "Shall he be punished?" In taking this vote, those who wished to vote in the affirmative were to step to one side of the road which passed through the grove, and those voting in the negative, to the other side of the road. The vote was unanimous, or nearly so, for punishing the man. The next question put was, "Shall the punishment be whipping or hanging" and the vote was taken in the same manner as the previous one. At the first, the majority was largely in favor of whipping, but then they had an argument to discuss the pros and cons of this punishment. Those who favored hanging said, "What satisfaction will there be in whipping an old, gray-headed man?" "What good will come of it?" "We are here to make an example that will protect our property and deter others for these crimes." As the arguments progressed, one by one, or in groups of twos and threes, the people passed over the road until a clear majority stood for the death sentence. The leader called for a rope, which was soon forth-coming. It was placed around Warren's neck. He was informed that his time was short and given the opportunity to say anything he desired. If his executioners expected any confession or appeal for mercy, they were disappointed, for the man was brave, and died without remorse. His only reply was, "I am an old man and you can't cheat me out of many years." A number of men grasped the rope which had been thrown over the projecting limb of a convenient tree. Amid silence the signal was given and Bennett Warren was hanged. He was taken down, carried to his house, where the men who had executed him prepared him for burial and quietly dispersed. No proceedings were taken against any engaged in this transaction.

This was the second husband that Mrs. Warren lost to hanging. Her first husband was hanged for the murder of a peddler.

Clutier (Tama)
(1986), (2004), (2012)
Clutier was founded in 1900 by Wm. E. Brice, the principal capitalist and promoter of the railroad project known as the Iowa, Minnesota, and Northern Railroad. Mr. Brice named the town for his sister, Maude, and brother-in-law, Bertram L. Clutier.

Coalville (Webster)
(1973), (1995)
Coalville started around 1860. The early settlers were coal miners, therefore; the town took its name from the coal mines in the area.

Coburg (Montgomery)
(1992)
The community was first settled around 1911. The town was named for Coburg, Kentucky.

Coin (Page)
(2003)
Coin was incorporated 1881. It has been reported that the name Coin was selected when a workman came to the saloon and found a five-cent piece and remarked, it would be a good name for the town, hence, the new town was called Coin.

Colfax (Jasper)
(1973), (1975), (1984), (2000), (2006), (2011)
Colfax was founded in 1866, and named for Schuyler Colfax who was Vice-President under Ulysses. S. Grant.
Items of interest
Near Colfax in 1875, while drilling for coal, a well containing high mineral content was discovered. With this new discovery, and over the next four decades, thousands of people visited the town for the healing powers of its fourteen mineral springs. The springs resulted in the building of nine hotels which offered guests mineral baths and spa treatments. Four bottling companies opened to produce bottled mineral water. The city's mineral springs industry declined and died out as a result of the Great Depression.

The Weirick Drug Store was built in the late 1800's and still has an old fashion soda fountain where a soda jerk still serves malts, cherry cokes and milkshakes.

Colfax has a train museum where train buffs depict the development of the railroad across the United States frontier. Both steam, and diesel eras are represented. There is over 2,600 square feet of display areas and around 25 model trains can be operated. Some 60 operating Lionel accessories in their original state are also displayed.

Colfax is the birthplace of James Norman Hall, author of
<u>Mutiny on the Bounty</u>.

College Springs (Page)
(2003)
The city started in the 1850s. It took College in its name because
Amity College was in the town and Spring because of a nearby spring with
very clear water. The college closed in 1917.

Colo (Story)
(1974), (1976), (1994), (2008), (2018)
Colo was incorporated in 1876 and John I. Blair, a railroad official,
named the community for his dog.
<u>Item of interest</u>
Colo is known as the "Crossroads of the Nation" because here the
Jefferson Highway (North and South) and the Lincoln Highway (East to
West) intersect.

Columbus Junction (Louisa)
(2016)
Columbus Junction began as Clifton around 1858 when the Chicago,
Rock Island and Pacific Railroad passed through the area. Then in 1870 the
Burlington, Cedar Rapids and Minnesota Railroad crossed the Rock Island
at Clifton and the name was changed to Columbus Junction, because of
the junction of the two railroads. It took the name Columbus from nearby
Columbus City.
<u>Item of interest</u>
Columbus Junction is home to the historic Swinging Bridge. It was
constructed in 1886 and called the Lovers Leap Bridge because of a legend
that a heartbroken Indian maiden jumped to her death in the ravine below.
The historic Swinging Bridge is located one block south of Highway
92 near downtown. The 262-foot long steel cable and wood suspension
bridge was built in 1922 as an elevated walkway connecting Third and
Fourth Streets.

Colwell (Floyd)
(1996)
Colwell was named for James Colwell who built the first three houses and owned the land. The Charles City Western Railway originally planned to extend their line to Cresco, but their plans didn't materialize and Colwell became the end of the line.

Communia (Clayton)
(1987)
The area was established as a German Colony in 1847. Communia was the most successful of Iowa's secular communal societies. Communal groups generally share common characteristics and are formed for either religious or economic reasons. Historically, religious communal groups tended to last longer and were more successful. Communica was formed in 1847 but disagreements led to dissolution of the colony in 1858, after much of the land and property was sold off by various families.

During the 19th century, thousands of Americans formed communal societies. The people within the communes worked for the common good, but no one received wages or owned property.

Confidence (Wayne)
(1981), (1997), (2009), (2016), (2019)
Confidence is an unincorporated community originally platted in 1858. Its population and economic activity peaked in the 1920s as a result of coal mining activity in the area. The town changed drastically as a result of the Great Depression and by the end of the 20th century was virtually a ghost town.

Conrad (Grundy)
(1986), (1995)
A post office has been in operation since 1880 and the city is named for John Conrad, an early settler.
<u>Item of interest</u>
Conrad holds the honor of being known as the "Black Dirt Capital of the World." This title resulted from what the early settlers discovered. Twelve thousand years of prairie grass had seeded, sprouted and withered

on these poorly drained plains, laying down a thick layer of black organic matter that extended two feet deep. When combined with the thick covering of minerals deposited from centuries of dust storms, the soil of Conrad had become a magical mixture of humus (a layer of organic matter), sand, silt and clay. The settlers soon found that if they planted corn, oats, wheat or hay, all grew remarkable well.

Coon Rapids (Carroll and Guthrie)
(1976), (1980) (1981), (2008), (2018)
Coon Rapids was established in 1863 and took its name from the Middle Raccoon River.
<u>Item of interest</u>
Coon Rapids was the home of Roswell "Bob" Garst, a farmer and seed company executive who developed hybrid corn seed in 1930 that resulted in greater crop yields than open-pollinated corn. In 1959, he is known for hosting Nikita Khrushchev on his farm in Coon Rapids. He sold hybrid seed to the Soviet Union beginning in 1955 and played a role in improving US-Soviet communication.

Cooper (Greene)
(1980)
Cooper was founded in 1881 with the arrival of the railroad. It was named for a Des Moines railroad executive F.M. Hubbell's father-in-law, Isaac Cooper.

Coppock (Henry, Jefferson and Washington)
(1992)
A post office opened here in 1882 and was named Coppock. It was closed in 1955. The town was named after William Coppock.

CORALVILLE (Johnson)
(1995), (2001), (2006), (2011), (2015)
Coralville was incorporated in 1857. The city's name came from fossils that are found in the limestone along the Iowa River.
<u>Items of interest</u>

In 1856 at Coralville, some 1300 Mormon immigrants stopped and made camp in their migration to Salt Lake City. They built handcarts out of native woods during their encampment so that an adult could haul a 600–700-pound load and cover about 15 miles per day on foot as they traveled west.

> The Coralville Dam was authorized in 1938 by Congress and begun in 1949 with completed in 1958 by the United States Corp of Engineers. It has been successful in preventing serious flooding except in the exceptionally wet years of 1993 and 2008.

Coralville is home to the firefighter's memorial and visitor's center. Iowa is the first state to have this type of establishment. This demonstrates Iowa's national leadership in fire service training and safety education.

Cornelia (Wright)
(2007)
Cornelia was originally called "Little Wall Lake," because of the wall of rocks around part of the lake. The lake was formed by leftovers of the glaciers. In 1868, a group of state geologists arrived in the area to survey and chart the lakes and rivers. They found Miss Cornelia Eastman, "a very popular and talented young lady of the city" so attractive, that they renamed the lake and town in her honor.

CORNING (Adams) (County Seat)
(1984), (1992), (1997), (2009), (2016)
Corning was platted in 1855 and named for Corning, New York, where an early settler came from.
Items of interest
The first European settlers were a group of French Icarians who came to establish a community based on utopian principles, which in turn was based on the democratic principles of the American and French Revolution.

> Corning is perhaps best known as the birthplace of John Carson, who was host of The Tonight Show.

Corwith (Hancock)
(1985), (1987), (1990)
The city of Corwith started in 1880 as a result of the construction of the Minneapolis & St. Louis Railroad. It was named for J. E. Corwith who was one of the land owners of the town.

Cosgrove (Johnson)
(2006)
Cosgrove is an unincorporated community. The town was named for Bishop Henry Cosgrove, the bishop of the Davenport Roman Catholic Diocese.

Cottonville (Jackson)
(1999)
Cottonville was named for Samuel D. Cotton who, with his family, arrived in the area in 1839. Mr. Cotton was the first postmaster. The post office was established in 1850 and discontinued in 1900. Cottonville is an unincorporated community.

COUNCIL BLUFFS (Pottawattamie) (County Seat)
(1974), 1986), (1994), (2000), (2009), (2013), (2019)
Between 1846 and 1852, Council Bluffs, then known as Kanesville, served as the headquarters for a substantial Church of Jesus Christ of Latter Day Saints (LDS) presence. In 1853 Kanesville was renamed Council Bluffs for a bluff where a meeting took place on August 2, 1804, between Lewis and Clark and Oboe and Missouria tribesmen.
<u>Items of interest</u>

Council bluffs is known as a "Gateway to the American West."

Council Bluffs is a historic point on the Mormon Trail and the northernmost anchor town for other emigrant trails. Council Bluffs saw many settlers and explorers pass through its limits. At one time, as many as thirty-one small encampments were in and about Kanesville. At its height, it consisted of 350 log cabins, two log tabernacles, a post office, and numerous shops, stores, and other business establishments. Wheat, corn, and many vegetables thrived then, as they do today, in the rich riverbed soil near the bluffs. The town's most pressing problem was to provide adequate food, shelter, employment, and wagon outfits for large numbers of poor emigrants passing through. This was made easier by the California Gold Rush of 1849-1851. This resulted in a boom for Kanesville and other outfitting towns. The gold rush greatly expedited LDS migration while transforming Kanesville from a Mormon town into a secular town. By the summer of 1852, more than 12,000 Latter-day Saints, 6,100 from Great Britain alone, had traveled west via Kanesville.

Arnold Potter (January 11, 1804 – April 2, 1872) was a self-declared Messiah and a leader of a sect in the LDS Movement. Potter referred to himself as Potter Christ. By 1861, Potter and some of his followers left California with the intention of settling near Independence Missouri, the traditional location of Zion for the Latter-Day Saints. They settled at Saint Mary's in northwest Mills County, Iowa. When Saint Mary's was destroyed by flooding in 1865, they moved to Council Bluffs. Potter spent his days wandering the streets in Council Bluffs wearing a long white robe and became a local oddity. Potter's followers in Council Bluffs were described as "few but devout." The men wore black robes and the women followed normal grooming practices of the day. Potter and his followers held enthusiastic prayer meetings which would often result in Potter declaring new revelations from God. In 1872, Potter announced at a meeting of his church that the time had come for his ascent into heaven. Followed by his disciples, Potter rode a donkey to the edge of the bluffs, whereupon he leapt off the edge intending to "ascend," he instead fell to his death. His body was collected and buried by his followers.

Perhaps one of Council Bluffs' most famous residents was Gen. Grenville M. Dodge, who has been called "the greatest railroad builder of all time." A Civil War veteran, Dodge's involvement in political, financial and military affairs made him an associate of many of the most influential

Americans of his time and counsel to presidents, including Abraham Lincoln and Ulysses S. Grant.

During the 1865 campaign in the Laramie Mountains in Wyoming, while escaping from a war-party, Dodge realized he had found a passage for the Union Pacific Railroad, west of the Platte River. In May 1866, he resigned from the military, and, with the endorsement of Generals Grant and Sherman, became the Union Pacific's chief engineer for the Transcontinental Railroad from Council Bluffs to Sacramento.

Dodge's job was to plan the route and devise solutions to any obstacles encountered. He had been hired by Herbert M. Hoxie, a former Lincoln appointee and winner of the contract to build the first 250 miles of the Union Pacific Railroad. Hoxie assigned the contract to investor Thomas C. Durant, who later was prosecuted for attempts to manipulate the route to suit his land-holdings. Seeing that Durant was making a fortune, Dodge bought shares in Durant's company. He made a substantial profit, but when the scandal of Durant's dealings emerged, Dodge moved himself to Texas to avoid testifying at the inquiry.

The 1869, Dodge built a Victorian home at 605 Third Street at a cost of $35,000, a lavish sum for that day. The home still stands. The fourteen-room, three-story mansion is located on a high terrace overlooking the Missouri Valley. It displays such architectural features as parquet floors, cherry, walnut and butternut woodwork, and a number of "modern" conveniences quite unusual for the period.

A 56-foot golden concrete spike is located at South 21st Street and Ninth Avenue. It was constructed to mark the 1939 premiere of the film "Union Pacific."

Lee de Forest was born in 1873 in Council Bluffs. He was an American inventor, self-described "Father of Radio," and pioneer in the development of sound-on-film recording used in motion pictures. He had over 180 patents. His most famous invention was the three-element Audion (triode) vacuum tube, the first practical amplification device. Although De Forest had only a limited understanding of how it worked, it was the foundation of the field of electronics, making possible radio broadcasting, long distance telephone lines, and talking motion pictures, among countless other applications.

The unique Squirrel Cage Jail served as the Pottawattamie County Jail from 1885 until 1969. The design and size of the Squirrel Cage Jail was a one-of-a-kind structure. It was one of 18 revolving "squirrel cage," "human rotary," or "lazy Susan" jails built, but Council Bluffs has the only three-story jail ever built. Built at a cost of about $30,000, the jail had three floors of revolving pie-shaped cells inside a cage. The front part of the building had offices for the jailer, kitchen, trustee cells, and quarters for women. The object was to produce a jail in which prisoners could be controlled without the necessity of personal contact between them and the jailer." It was to provide "maximum security with minimum jailer attention." As one deputy put it, "If a jailer could count he could control the jail."

Covington (Linn)
(2012)
Covington was formed when the Chicago, Milwaukee and St. Paul Railroad came through the area. It is an unincorporated community.

Craig (Plymouth)
(1998)
Craig was incorporated in 1911. It was named for Wright L. Craig, a Northwestern railroad attorney.

CRESCO (Howard) (County Seat)
(1993), (1996), (2005), (2017)
Cresco was platted in 1866, when the railroad was expanding into the area. It was first known as Schook's Grove. Cresco is a Latin phrase meaning "I grow."

Items of interest
Cresco was the boyhood home of Dr. Norman Borlaug, a recipient of the Nobel Peace Prize, the Medal of Freedom, and in the Fall of 2007, received the Congressional Gold Medal from the President of the United States. Only 4 other people in the entire world have received all three

honors. Dr. Borlaug developed improved strains of food grains and trained thousands of scientists and small land owners in their use. His scientific and humanitarian contributions have led the way in the fight against malnutrition and starvation. He is also known as the "Father of the Green Revolution."

Cresco is also home to Ellen Church, the first airline stewardess. She is credited with starting the flight attendant industry by convincing Boeing Airlines that having nurses on board would help the airline industry convince the public that it was safe to fly.

CRESTON (Union) (County Seat)
(1981), (1984), (1997), (2016)
Creston was originally settled in 1868 as a survey camp for the workers with the Burlington and Missouri Railroad. The campsite was on the crest of the railroad line between the Missouri and Mississippi Rivers; hence, the name Creston.

Crocker (Polk)
(1984), (2000)
Crocker was platted in 1880 and took its name from Crocker Township, which was named for General Marcellus M. Crocker, a General in the Union Army during the Civil War.

Crystal Lake (Hancock)
(1977), (1982), (1987), (1999), (2002), (2005), (2014)
Crystal Lake was platted in 1898 and incorporated in 1899. It was named for Crystal Lake and Crystal Lake township.

Cumming (Warren)
(1997), (2019)
Cumming was established following the arrival of the Chicago, St. Paul, and Kansas City Railroad and incorporated in 1924.
<u>Items of interest</u>

St. Patrick's Catholic Church is a parish church that Pope John Paul II visited on his first pastoral visit to the United States in 1979.

Cumming is home to the Iowa Distilling Company, whose straight bourbon is said to be "like a warm hello from an old friend." With the sophisticated aroma of baking spice and pipe tobacco, Iowa corn has never tasted so fancy. It has a rich, complex flavor with a hint of butterscotch and caramel. It is distilled and hand-bottled in Cumming.

Curlew (Palo Alto)
(1990), (1999), (2017)

Curlew had its start in 1882 with the building of the Des Moines and Fort Dodge Railroad through that territory. It was named by the railroad president, an avid hunter, for the Curlew birds found in the area.

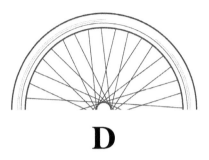

D

Dahlonega (Wapello)
(1984)
Dahlonega was organized in 1844 and named by James Woody who came from Dahlonega, Georgia.

<u>Item of interest</u>
An episode known as the Dahlonega War came about as a result of a dispute over a land claim. An early settler, James Woody, having made a claim, sold it to Martin Koontz for $200. Having second thoughts about the price, he reoccupied the land, built a cabin on it and attempted to legally reclaim it. Koontz issued an eviction notice but Woody refused to leave. A claim committee issued a second eviction warrant resulting in Woody's refusal and arming himself. About sixty of Koontz's friends armed themselves and went to the cabin and demolished it with Woody inside. Woody's friends rallied around him and engaged Koontz's friends in a battle where one of Woody's party was killed. Civil authorities were outraged. Deputy Sheriff Woodward, from Fairfield, was sent to make arrests and restore order, but found himself arrested by the offenders and was held overnight. The next morning, he was brought out and placed on his horse then escorted to the public square. Here the Koontz forces announced that his services were no longer needed and he was free to go, but should he return without being summoned, he should have his last will and testament in order. The officer departed hastily. Because of legislation changes in jurisdiction, the case it was never tried. The Dahlonega War ended with Woody losing his claim on the Koontz land.

DAKOTA CITY (Humboldt) (County Seat)
(1978), (1985), (2007)
The city was laid out in 1855 and named for the Dakota people. A post office was established as Dakotah in 1856, but in 1924, was renamed Dakota City.

Dalby (Allamakee)
(1977)
In 1869, a post office was opened in Dalby and remained in operation until it was discontinued in 1885.

Dallas Center (Dallas)
(1984), (2000), (2013)
Dallas Center was incorporated in 1880. It started with the building of the railroad through the territory and was named for President James K. Polk's Vice President, George M. Dallas.

Dana (Greene)
(1976), (1988), (2008) (2011), (2018)
Dana was incorporated in 1907 and named for Samuel Dana, a pioneer settler.

Danbury (Woodbury)
(1977), (1995)
A post office called Danbury has been in operation since 1877. The city's name is a combination of the name of its founder, Daniel Thomas, and Woodbury, the county in which it is located.

DAVENPORT (Scott) (County Seat)
(1973), (1982), (2011), (2015), (2018)
Davenport was founded on May 14, 1836 by Antoine Le Claire and was named for his friend George Davenport, a former English sailor who served in the U.S. Army during the War of 1812. He served as a supplier to Fort Armstrong and worked as a fur trader with the American Fur Company. Davenport was appointed as quartermaster with the rank of colonel during the Black Hawk War.

Items of interest

The land where Davenport is located was originally owned by the Sauk, Meskwaki (Fox), and Ho-Chunk (Winnebago) people. In 1803 France sold it to the United States under the Louisiana Purchase. In 1832, a group of Sauk, Meskwaki, and Kickapoo people were defeated by the United States in the Black Hawk War. The United States government then finalized the Black Hawk Purchase, sometimes called the Forty-Mile Strip or Scott's Purchase, by which the United States acquired lands in what is now eastern Iowa. The purchase was made for $640,000 on September 21, 1832 and contained an area of some 6 million acres, at a price equivalent to 11 cents per acre. The Black Hawk Purchase was named for defeated Chief Black Hawk, who was being held prisoner at the time. The purchase was agreed to by Sauk Chief Keokuk, who had remained neutral in the war. The treaty was made on the site of present day Davenport. Army General Winfield Scott and Governor of Illinois, John Reynolds, acted on behalf of the United States, with the future Davenport founder, half-native, Antoine LeClaire serving as translator.

Lieutenant Zebulon Pike was the first United States representative to officially visit the Upper Mississippi River area. On August 27, 1805, Pike camped at the present-day site of Davenport.

In 1856, The Rock Island Railroad Company built the first railroad bridge across the Mississippi River. It connected Davenport with Rock Island, Illinois and improved the flow of goods between Chicago and Iowa. Steamboat companies saw nationwide railroads as a threat to their business and on May 6, 1856, just weeks after the bridge was completed, a steamboat captain deliberately crashed the Effie Afton into the bridge. The owner of the Effie Afton, John Hurd, filed a lawsuit against the Rock Island Railroad Company. The case went to the United States Supreme Court which upheld the right to bridge navigable streams; therefore, the bridge was allowed to remain. Abraham Lincoln was the lead defense lawyer for the railroad company.

In 1865, the Iowa Soldiers' Orphans' Home opened in Davenport to take in children left orphaned by the Civil War.

African Americans settled in Davenport as early as the 1830s. Dred Scott, whose legal fight for freedom was ruled on 1857 by the United States Supreme Court, lived with his family in Davenport as he followed his master to various military postings in the Midwest. Scott and his wife based their appeal for freedom on the fact that they had been held for extended periods of time in free states and territories, including Scott's stay with his master in Davenport from 1834 to 1836.

The Court had ruled that African Americans had no claim to freedom or citizenship. Since they were not citizens, they did not possess the legal standing to bring suit in a federal court. Slaves were considered private property and Congress did not have the power to regulate slavery in the territories and could not revoke a slave owner's rights based on where he lived. This decision nullified the essence of the Missouri Compromise, which divided territories into jurisdictions, either free or slave. Speaking for the majority, Justice Taney ruled that because Scott was simply considered the private property of his owners, he was subject to the Fifth Amendment to the United States Constitution, prohibiting the taking of property from its owner "without due process."

Davis City (Decatur)
(1981)
Davis City was laid out in 1855 and named for William Davis, who operated a sawmill there.

Dayton (Webster)
(2012)
A post office called Dayton has been in operation since 1877. The city was named for Dayton, Ohio.
<u>Items of interest</u>
An event known as "The Dayton Riot" happened in January of 1894 at a New Year's dance in Burnquist's Hall. At a signal from an attendee, some hoodlums from nearby Boone entered the hall and cleared out the hall of dancers. Women ran screaming and men fought using chairs as weapons. After destroying the hall, the hoodlums went to supper in a nearby restaurant. The aroused citizens accompanied Marshal Larson to arrest the hoodlums. The marshal was shot in the hip with his own pistol by Paris Winters. A citizen, Frank Dowd, heroically came to Larsen's aid, but the marshal died. The whole gang of rioters were sent to Fort Dodge for trial.

Decatur City (Decatur)
(1992), (2003), (2016)
Decatur City was incorporated in 1875 and named in honor of Stephen Decatur, a naval hero of the War of 1812. Decatur City was the first county seat of Decatur County, but in 1853 the seat was transferred to Leon.

DECORAH (Winneshiek) (County Seat)
(1977), (1993), (1999), (2017)
Decorah was the site of a Ho-Chunk Indian village beginning around 1840 and named for Ho-Chunk leader Waukon Decorah who was a United States ally during the Black Hawk War of 1832.
Items of interest
Decorah is home to Luther College, a private liberal arts college established as a Lutheran seminary in 1861 by Norwegian immigrants. The school today is affiliated with the Evangelical Lutheran Church in America.

Decorah is also home to Vesterhelm, the national Norwegian-American museum and heritage center. With over 33,000 artifacts, 12 historic buildings, a Folk-Art School, a library, and archives showcases the most extensive collection of Norwegian-American artifacts in the world.

Dedham (Carroll)
(1980), (2011, (2018)
Dedham got its start in 1881 with the building of the Chicago, Milwaukee and St. Paul Railroad through the territory. It was named for Dedham, Massachusetts.
Items of interest
Local lore contends that the town's name came from a train wreck that killed a shipment of hogs in the 1800s (thus, "dead ham").

A local specialty is Dedham Bologna, a German bologna that is predominantly beef with some pork and spices

enclosed in natural casings that are tied by hand. The mild
rings are hickory smoked for three and a half hours and are
fully cooked ready to serve.

Deep River (Poweskiek)
(1973), (1975), (1979), (2001), (2018)
Deep River was established in 1884. The town was named Sap-Pom-
Ah (meaning Deep River) by the Fox and Sac Indians that lived along its
bank before the arrival of the white man. Deep River was not named for
the depth of the water, but for the depth of the ravine through which it
flows. At some places the banks are 20 feet above the normal water level.

Deerfield (Chickasaw)
(1996)
The area was first settled by whites in 1854 and named for Deerfield,
Massachusetts

Delaware (Delaware)
(1989), (1993), (1999), (2010)
Delaware was platted in 1860 and name for the state of Delaware.

Delmar (Clinton)
(2012)
Delmar was platted in 1871, and first called Brookfield. On the
Midland train's inaugural run, the train paused to name the new station.
In keeping with the alphabetical order of stations coming from Clinton
(Almont, Bryant and Charlotte) the conductor wanted this stop to begin
with the letter D. There were six ladies on the train with the first names of:
Della, Emma, Laura, Marie, Anna, and Rose. Using the first letter of each
lady's name, they came up with the pronounceable name of Delmar.
    Item of interest
Delmar is home to the Orphan Train Research Center. Over a 150,000
orphan and street children immigrated from the New York slums to
Midwestern farms from 1854 to 1929. Poor and homeless children roamed
the streets of New York City in the mid-1800s. They sold newspapers,
matches, and flowers to earn money in the days before school attendance

was required. Called "street arabs," they sometimes begged for food and turned to stealing. Homeless children lived in boxes or under stairwells with only rags for clothing. Disease spread quickly through overcrowded areas where new immigrants to the United States lived. Many children died. Those who survived sometimes lost both parents to illness. The dirty, congested streets of New York City were miles and worlds away from the open prairies of middle America. The children were sent to "western" states to live in new homes with total strangers. These programs were intended to provide homes and families for children, while fulfilling the demand for workers on farms.

In 1850, when New York City's population was 500,000, an estimated 20,000 homeless children lived in the streets or were warehoused in more than two dozen grossly overcrowded orphanages. The first "orphan train" went to Michigan, in 1854. The trains would run for 75 years with the last one pulling into Missouri in 1929.

Deloit (Crawford)
(1987), (2001)
Deloit was platted in 1899 and named for Beloit, Wisconsin, but altered the spelling to avoid repetition.

Delta (Keokuk)
(1992)
Delta was incorporated in 1877. In 1874 two trains came through the county and where they crossed formed a triangle. It was noted that the triangle actually formed the symbol for the Greek letter delta, so it was decided that the town should be called Delta.

Denhart (Hancock)
(1987)
Denhart is an unincorporated village. The town was originally named Bangall but renamed Denhart for Henry Denhart who owned the property.

DENISON (Crawford) (County Seat)
(1987), (2001), (2018)
Denison was incorporated in 1875 and named for a Baptist minister, J.W. Denison, who owned 200,000 acres in Harrison and Crawford

Counties. He offered to build a courthouse, hotel and store if the site was named the county seat. His offer was accepted and the place was called Denison.

Items of interest

Denison was the boyhood home of Clarence D. Chamberlin, the pilot of the first trans-Atlantic passenger flight on June 4, 1927.

Denison is the birth place of Donna Reed (born Donna Belle Mullenger; 1921 – 1986) an American film and television actress and producer. Her career spanned more than 40 years, with performances in more than 40 films. She is well known for her role as Mary Hatch Bailey alongside James Stewart the film "It's a Wonderful Life." In 1953, she received the Academy Award for Best Supporting Actress for her performance as Lorene Burke in the war drama "From Here to Eternity." She may also be remembered for her role as Miss Ellie Ewing in the TV show "Dallas" and as the host for "The Donna Reed Show."

Denmark (Lee)

(1975), (2003), (2019)

Denmark is an unincorporated community that was first settled in 1836. The founders were mostly devout New Englanders that were brought up under Pilgrim influence. Many settlers were professors of religion. It was first called "Yankee Heaven" because of the number of settlers from New England. It was next called "Haystack" because the settlers stored their hay in haystacks. It was then renamed Denmark, but the origin of that name is unknown.

Denova (Henry)

(1992)

The town was first called Bengall but in 1890 changed its name to Denova.

Denver (Bremer)
(2007)
Denver was incorporated in 1863 and was originally called Jefferson City. The name was changed to Denver when a federal post office was established in 1863. It is believed that name Denver was selected because many of the people were heading to Denver, Colorado for the gold rush.

DES MOINES (Polk) (County Seat)
(1973), (1988), (1992), (1997), (2013)
The City of Des Moines can trace its origins to 1843, when Captain James Allen supervised the construction of a fort on the site where the Des Moines and Raccoon Rivers merge. Allen wanted to use the name Fort Raccoon; however, the United States War Department told him to name it Fort Des Moines. The city was incorporated in 1851 as Fort Des Moines, but shortened to Des Moines in 1857. The river from which the city got its name was likely adapted from the early French name, Rivière des Moines, meaning River of the Monks

Items of interest
Des Moines was originally a frontier fort; but, unlike most of the frontier forts in the west, this fort was not established to protect the whites from the Indians. Fort Des Moines was established to protect the Sac and Fox Indians and to secure for them the peaceful possession of their hunting grounds. Also, it aimed to protect them from land agents, the encroachment of whites, and attacks by the bloody Sioux.

In 1921, The Iowa General Assembly in Des Moines became the first state to passed a state cigarette tax. The tax rate was 2 cents per pack.

DeWitt (Clinton)
(1994)
De Witt was platted in 1841 under the name Vandenburg, but was later named DeWitt for DeWhitt Clinton, an early American politician who served as a United States Senator and the 7th Governor of New York.

Dexter (Dallas)
(1991), (2019)

Dexter was founded in 1868 and incorporated in 1870. The town's slogan is "original one horse town" because the town was named for "Dexter King of the Turf," a famous trotting horse.

Items of interest

Dexfield park opened in 1915 and was likely the most famous amusement park in the state. It was located between Dexter and Redfield on the south side of the Raccoon River. Every Sunday people came from miles around and over 4,000 people could be there at one time. The park had a large cement swimming pool fed by the nearby Marshall springs. The spring water was said to have healing qualities for arthritis sufferers. West of the pool was a large open-air dance hall where they held dances on Sundays and during the week, accompanied by many good orchestras. The park closed in the 1930s.

Though abandoned, Dexfield Park was the scene of excitement in 1933 when Bonnie and Clyde and the Barrow Gang were discovered hiding out there. Buck Barrow had a bullet in his skull and Blanche had pieces of glass in her eye as a result of a gun battle with lawmen in Platte City, Missouri. While they were hiding out, Clyde went into Dexter a few times for food and medical supplies. On Sunday, July 23, a local farmer, Henry Nye, discovered the campsite by chance and reported it to Marshal John Love, who in turn called the Dallas County Sheriff, Clinton Knee. About fifty lawmen, including some from the Des Moines Police Department, surrounded the Barrow camp. After an extended gun battle between the lawmen and the outlaws, Clyde, Bonnie and gang member W. D. Jones escaped by an unguarded route over the South Raccoon River. Blanche stayed behind with Buck, who was too seriously wounded to travel. The escapees made their way to nearby Vallie Feller's farm where they stole a car. In Polk City, they abandoned the Feller car and stole another. People reported seeing the escapees in LuVerne, Sutherland, Denison and Des Moines, but the sightings were never substantiated. Buck Barrow died in the Perry hospital five days after the incident. Blanche was returned to Missouri and sentenced to ten years in prison. Bonnie and Clyde; however, were back in Iowa in 1934. They robbed banks in Rembrandt and Knierim and were suspected of robberies in Stuart and Lamoni. After several months on the run, they were killed in a roadblock ambush in Gibsland, Louisiana. W. D. Jones left the gang just before going to Louisiana and went to Houston, Texas. He was arrested tried and sentenced and after 6 year, was paroled. He died in 1974 when a friend shot him.

On September 18, 1948, Dexter was the site of a national plowing match where President Harry Truman delivered a speech attacking the 80th Congress for their record regarding the American farmer. This speech is considered one of the most important of his 1948 Whistle Stop campaign that turned the tide of the election and returned him to the White House.

The first death in town was a little boy named Miller, who was thrown from the platform of a rail road car, as he was getting off. One of his limbs was crushed almost off and several wheels passing over him. He lived a few days in great pain, and then died. Some eye-witnesses say it was one of the saddest sights ever witnessed.

Diagonal (Ringgold)
(1981), (2016)
The town was incorporated in 1888 and named for the fact that two railroads intersected diagonally near the town site.

Dickens (Clay)
(1979), (1990), (1999), (2007), (2017)

Dickens was founded in 1886. The town is believed to be named for the Dickinson brothers who were early settlers in the area.

Dickeyville (Adams)
(1984), (1992)
The settlement of Dickeyville was named in 1849 for Charles Dickey, an early settler and surveyor. The village was incorporated in 1947.
Items of interest
The Dickeyville Grotto was built by Father Mathius Wernerus, the pastor of Dickeyville's Holy Ghost Parish, from 1920 to 1930. The site includes the Grotto of the Blessed Virgin, Christ the King Shrine, Grotto of the Sacred Heart, the Eucharistic Altar, the Holy Ghost Tree, the Patriotism Shrine and the Crucifixion Group. Although most of the site's components are religious in nature, the Patriotism Shrine includes depictions of Columbus, Washington and Lincoln. According to Anne Pryor, a cultural anthropologist, this shrine was erected to demonstrate the patriotism of Catholics. Protestant Americans of that time believed that Catholics' allegiance to the Pope conflicted with their allegiance to the United States.

Dike (Grundy)
(1989), (1998), (2010)
Dike incorporated in 1901 and named for the railroad construction engineer Chester Thomas Dike.

Donnellson (Lee)
(1981), (1992), (2019)
Donnellson was incorporated in 1892, and named for Esten A. Donnell, a surveyor in the region.
Item of interest
Donnellson is the site of the Lee County Fair, "Iowa's Oldest Fair."

Doon (Lyon)
(1985)
The city was incorporated in 1892. Doon is located on a plateau on the eastern bank of the Rock River and named for the River Doon in

Scotland, which was made famous as the subject of Robert Burns' poem, "The Banks O' Doon."

> Ye banks and braes O'Bonnie Doon,
> How can ye bloom sae fresh and fair:
> How can yet chant ye little birds?
> And I sae weary, fu' O' care!

Dougherty (Cerro Gordo)
(1985), (1993), (1999)
Dougherty was organized in 1870 and named Prairie, but in 1871 the name was changed to Daugherty in honor of a pioneer settler, Daniel Dougherty.

Douglas (Fayette)
(2005)
Douglas was first settled in 1850 and named for Thomas Douglas, an early settler.

Dows (Franklin and Wright)
(1978), (1983), (2004)
Dows had its start in 1880 with the building of the railroad through that territory and was named for Dows, a railroad contractor.

Drakesville (Davis)
(1981), (1997), (2003)
Drakesville was founded in 1847 and named for its founder, John A. Drake.

Dublin (Washington)
(2000)
Dublin was first known as Swire's corner then Dutch Creek Center before the being named for Dublin, Ireland. This was because the many of the settlers were from Ireland. Dublin in currently listed as a ghost town.
<u>Item of interest</u>
Dublin cheese was once famous all over the United States.

DUBUQUE (Dubuque) (County Seat)
(1974), (1983), (1993), (2010)
Dubuque was officially chartered in 1833, and named for Julien
Dubuque, who settled in the area.
Items of interest
Dubuque is located in an area that was part of the Louisiana Territory
which was purchased from Spain during the Jefferson administration.
Historically the land belonged to France. After the British defeated France
in the Seven Year's War (French and Indian War) the known American
continent was divided. Britain claimed all land east of the Mississippi
River plus Canada. France got the land west of the Mississippi River. Later
Napoleon sold a large tract to Spain for money needed to fight his European
wars. In 1803, Spain sold what is known as the Louisiana Purchase to the
United States. Most of what is now Iowa, was in that purchase.

The first permanent settler in what is now Dubuque was
pioneer Julien Dubuque, who arrived in 1785. In 1788,
he received permission from the Spanish government
and the local Meskwaki Indians to mine the area's rich
lead deposits. Dubuque died in 1810, but The Meskwaki
continued to mine the lead with full support of the United
States government until 1830, when the Meskwaki were
illegally pushed out of the region by American prospectors.

In the early 1990s the city experienced racial strife that attracted
national attention. The problems began when a cross was burned next to
the garage of an African-American family which caused the barn to burn.
In the ruins, parts of the cross were found with the inscription "KKK Lives."
Another cross was burned a few weeks later. This was found to be the work
of a group of young men who were well known racists. Those responsible,
many of whom had criminal records, eventually were convicted and sent
to prison.

About this same time, the city embarked on a plan to
encourage more minorities to move into the area. Some
critics tried to stir up fear by telling people that the city

was planning to take a bus to a large city and grab the first 100 African-Americans they found. In reality, the city was planning to recruit African-American professionals to the city.

The city's program, and the cross burning polarized the community. People took up strongly held views. Dubuque police had to be summoned to Dubuque's Senior High School at one point because racial tension almost boiled over into a large fight at the school. Jim Brady, who was mayor at the time, had gone to the schools in Dubuque to talk about his experiences with racism over the years. When the Guardian Angels arrived in Dubuque, it was felt that their presence would only complicate the matter. Brady told them that if they caused problems he would have them arrested. The cross burnings and the city's plans had the effect of bringing negative media attention to the city. An ABC's news segment on race relations was felt by many to be biased against the city and the people who lived in it.

The problems also attracted the unwelcome attention of hate groups. One hate group held a parade through the city, which was attended by only a few hundred people. The Ku Klux Klan held a rally in downtown Dubuque. To counter the Klan rally, the city held a free diversity public gathering at Dubuque's Eagle Point Park.

In 2007, racial tension heated up once again with the stabbing of a white male at a party in downtown Dubuque by a group of African-Americans.

In 1882, Dubuque reported that frogs had fallen from the sky. A Tornado or waterspout was believed to have swept up the frogs from their natural habitats and dropped them on the city streets.

Dumont (Butler)
(2007)
A post office in Dumont has been in operation since 1882. The city was named for John M. Dumont, a miner in Colorado. It was incorporated in 1896.

Duncombe (Webster)
(2015)
Duncombe is named for The Hon. J. F. Duncombe. It was incorporated in 1893.

Dundee (Delaware)
(1999), (2007)
Dundeee was incorporated in 1917. Some say Hiram Wood named the town after Dundee, Scotland; however, after some research, it was learned that Wood's ancestors originated was in England, not Scotland. Hiram Wood's mother was of Scotch Irish descent. One source says the town was first called Wood until it was renamed Dundee by the railroad company. In 1987, the Dundee postmaster was informed this railroad village was named by Fritz Mchugh, an engineer on the crew that laid the rails through this part of the county and that its name did come from the town in Scotland.

Item of interest

Early one morning in 1922, four robbers dynamited a safe at the Dundee Savings Bank and escaped with $1,200 in cash and $4,500 in bonds. Plans for the robbery had been carefully laid. The men drove into Dundee about 2 a.m., after cutting all telegraph and telephone wires. The Chicago Great Western passenger train number 2 was due at that hour and it is believed that the robbers waited until the arrival of the train so the train's noise would cover them while they robbed the bank. Six charges of high explosives were fired in the safe, completely wrecking it. The bank vault was untouched. Two people heard the explosions, but the telephone lines were "dead," so they were unable to sound a warning until after the robbers had completed their work.

Earl Watt, a Dundee merchant, gave the alarm about half an hour later. The sheriff, accompanied by several deputies, immediately started in pursuit of the robbers, who were driving a new Buick Six touring car bearing a Minnesota license. The pursuing party was unable to find the robbers and it is believed that they had crossed into Minnesota. The bank's loss was covered by insurance.

Dunkerton (Black Hawk)
(1982), (1989), (1998), (2007)
In 1853, two brothers, James and John Dunkerton, walked from Dubuque to stake out a claim of land near Lester. This claim became the town known as Lesterton, and later Dunkerton.

Dunlap (Harrison and Crawford)
(1983)
Dunlap was platted in 1867 and incorporated in 1871. It was named for George L. Dunlap, a railroad official.

Durant (Cedar, Muscatine, and Scott)
(1973), (1982), (2011), (2015)
Durant was platted in 1854 and first named for Benjamin Brayton, its founder, but the name was later changed to Durant for Thomas C. Durant, one of the pioneers of the Transcontinental Railroad and an individual who contributed the bulk of funds needed to build the town's first public school.

Dyersville (Delaware)
(1983), (1989), (1993), (2007), (2010)
Dyersville was laid out in 1851 and named for an early landowner, James Dyer.
Items of interest
Dyersville is the home of The Basilica of St. Francis Xavier, a parish church in the Archdiocese of Dubuque. In 1888, many farmers and merchants mortgaged their properties to build a new Catholic church large enough to accommodate one thousand people. The church was named in honor of the missionary Saint Francis Xavier. In 1956, Pope Pius XII elevated the church to a Minor Basilica.

The basilica features Ruskinian Gothic Revival architecture. The two steeples are 212 feet tall with 14 feet crosses that cap the spires. This helps make the church visible from miles away across the rolling lightly forested farmland. The church is a rectangular structure that measures 174.5 by 70 feet and is 76 feet high. The interior includes columns and vaulted ceilings.

The church has 64 large cathedral glass windows. There are two notable windows in the church. The first is the rose widow above the entrances to the church which replaced a conventional church window on which the framework had deteriorated. An Indian motif was selected for the second in recognition of many local Indian tribes that inhabited this area 150 years earlier. There are about 5,000 people total in the parish.

> In 1945, Fred Ertl, Sr. began making scale models of farm tractors using molds he created and fired in his basement furnace. This hobby led to a family business and eventually to the Ertl Company, which produces toy tractors and farm implements. The popularity of these toys over the years has supported two large toy shows which are held every June and November.

Dyersville is known as the "Farm Toy Capital of the World" and is home to the National Farm Toy Museum. The Museum houses memorabilia and farm toys of today and yesterday.

> Just outside Dyersville is the Field of Dreams. In 1982 screenwriter Phil Robinson became interested in the novel <u>Shoeless Joe</u>, the story of Joe Jackson, a major-league player in the early 1900's. He recognized the potential for this heartwarming story and looked for a setting for a film. In the early months of 1988, Robinson came upon the Lansing farm near Dyersville and said, "That's it! That's my farm!" The movie was called "The Field of Dreams," Starring Kevin Costner and James Earl Jones. Today the site is well maintained and visited by many baseball enthusiasts One famous line from the movie is "Build it and they will come."

Dysart (Tama)
(1978)
Dysart started in 1872 with the building of the Burlington, Cedar Rapids and Northern Railroad through the territory and the town takes its name for Joseph Dysart, a farmer and founder of the town.

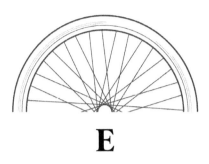

E

Eagle Center (Black Hawk)
(1978), (1983)
The Eagle Centre post office was established in 1879 but changed the spelling to Eagle Center. Eagle Center is an unincorporated community.

Eagle Grove (Wright)
(1978), (2004), (2007)
Eagle Grove was incorporated in 1881. It was named by early settlers for the eagle nests seen in a large grove of oak trees.

Earlham (Madison)
(1991), (2019)
Earlham was incorporated in 1870 and named after Earlham College, a Quaker college in Richmond, Indiana.
Items of interest
Earlham's greatest claim to fame is that in the early 1900's, Marion Michael Morrison, a.k.a. John Wayne, lived in Earlham. His father, Clyde, owned a pharmacy until his poor health forced the family to move to California.

Earling (Shelby)
(1983)
Earling was platted in 1882 by the Milwaukee Land Company and was first known as Marthan. However, there was already a town called Marathon whose name was too similar to Marthan. The name of the town was soon changed to Earling, in honor of Albert J. Earling, the division superintendent of the Chicago, Milwaukee and St. Paul Railroad.
Items of interest
Earling was well known for being the site of a 1928 exorcism. Over a period of 23 days the Roman Catholic friar, Theophilus Riesinger, worked

to exorcise demons from Emma Schmidt at the local Franciscan convent. During the exorcism, Schmidt reportedly flew across the room, landed high above the door, and clung tightly to the wall. Despite attempts by church officials to keep the exorcism secret, townspeople soon began hearing strange noises coming from the convent as well as horrid odors. Finally, after 23 days, the demons in Schmidt's body gave up when Father Riesinger commanded, "Depart, ye friends of hell! Be gone, Satan." After the exorcism, Schmidt reportedly led a fairly normal life.

Earlville (Delaware)
(1983), (1989), (1993), (1999), (2007), (2010)
Earlville started in 1857 with the building of the railroad through the territory. It was named for its first settler, George M. Earl.

East Amana (Iowa)
(1991)
(See Amana)

East Peru (Madison)
(2009)
East Peru was incorporated in 1897 with the building of the railroad through that territory. It was named for Peru, Indiana.

Edgewood (Clayton and Delaware)
(2014)
Edgewood was incorporated in 1892. It was first known as the Yankee Settlement. In 1842, the first settlers were from New York. When the Davenport and St. Paul Railroad came through the town, the Railroad changed the town's name to Edgewood because west of town was mostly prairie and east of town was wooded.

Elberon (Tama)
(1994), (2004)
The post office of Elberon has been in operation since 1882. A temporary name for the town was Halifax; however, patriotic fervor was high at the time because of the assassination of President, James Abram

Garfield, who died September 19, 1881, at Elberon, New Jersey. Elberon was named in honor of that eastern suburb.

ELDORA (Hardin) (County Seat)
(1986), (1998), (2004), (2015)
Eldora was incorporated in 1895 and named by a local mother in honor of her infant daughter who had died. Eldora is derived from the Spanish name for "the gilded."
<u>Items of interest</u>
In 1868, Iowa Governor Samuel Merrill signed a bill creating a reform school for delinquent boys, known as the Boys Training School in Eldora. The school is now called the State Training School which provides supervision and rehabilitation programs that meets the needs of male delinquents in a manner consistent with public safety. These services and programs have individualized treatment, which control the offender for his own benefit and the protection of society.

The city was the location for the filming of the 1996 movie <u>Twister</u>.

Eldridge (Scott)
(2008)
Eldridge was incorporated in 1871 and named for Jacob M. Eldridge, who arrived in central Scott County in 1846.

Elgin (Fayette)
(1987), (1993), (1999), (2005)
The town was laid out in 1851-1852 and named Elgin, which was the native town in Illinois of surveyor M. V. Burdick.

ELKADER (Clayton) (County Seat)
(1980), (1987), (1996)
Elkader was incorporated in **1891** and named for the Algerian leader known as Emir Abdelkader. He led his people in resisting the French in their conquest of Algeria. Elkader is the only United States town named after an Arab Jihadis, a 19th century Algerian Muslim.

Elkhart (Polk)
(2006), (2011)
Elkhart was incorporated in 1904 and named by early settlers who came from Elkhart Indiana.

Elk Horn (Shelby)
(1974), (1980), (1986), (2000), (2008), (2011, (2013)
Elk Horn was incorporated in 1910. The name came from the Elk Horn Creek which received its name from settlers who saw the bones of an elk near the stream.

<u>Items of interest</u>
The Danish villages of Elk Horn and nearby Kimballton are the two largest rural Danish settlements in the United States.

Elk Horn has a historic windmill that in 1848 was brought to America from Norre Snede, Demark and rebuilt by over 300 volunteers to honor the area's rich Danish Heritage. The windmill was restored to working condition in 1976. It needs a 20-mph wind to operate. It is the only working Danish windmill in America.

Another acknowledgment of its Danish heritage it the sculpture of "The Little Mermaid," a character in the fairy tale by Hans Christian Anderson about a young mermaid, who is willing to give up her life in the sea as a mermaid to gain a human soul.

Elkport (Clayton)
(1980), (1987), (2014)
Elkport was laid in 1855 and named for the Elk Horn Creek, which received its name from settlers who saw the bones of an elk near the stream.

<u>Item of interest</u>
The town was severely damaged by floods in May of 2004. After the floods, all the town residents chose the federal buyout of their homes. By September 2006, the Federal Government had nearly all of the buildings in Elkport demolished.

Elk Run Heights (Black Hawk)
(1974)
Elk Run Heights was established in 1951. It started when a small group of people wanted to escape the problems of big city life. The town got its name from the Elk Run River that runs through the town.

Ellendale (Plymouth)
(1993)
An Ellendale post office was established in 1874.

Ellston (Ringgold)
(1981)
Ellston was formerly known as Wirt. The name was changed to Ellston in 1895 because it was located on the same railroad line as Van Wert, which made mail delivery confusing. The town was renamed for a Mr. Ellston who worked for the railroad.
Item of interest
Harley A. Wilhelm was born on a farm near Ellston. He was the Manhattan Project chemist who invented the Ames Process for purifying uranium which made the atomic bomb possible.

Ellsworth (Hamilton)
(1983), (1989), (2012)
Ellsworth was platted in 1880. There have been at least three theories to how Ellsworth got its name.
- It has been stated in several historical references that Ellsworth was named for a railroad official who helped to survey the right of way through this territory.
- Another story is that the town was named to honor the memory of Colonel Elmer E. Ellsworth, who died in Virginia, the first Union soldier killed in the Civil War.
- Another source stated that it was named for a banker at Iowa Falls.

Elma (Howard)
(1987), (1996)

Elma was founded in 1886 and named for Lemuel Potter's youngest daughter Elma.

Elon (Allamakee)
(1977)
A post office was opened in Elon in 1850, and remained in operation until 1907.

Elvira (Clinton)
(1978), (1985), (1994), (2004)
Elvira is an unincorporated community platted in 1854. The town was named by W. H. Gibbs, the owner of the town site, in honor of his wife.

Elwood (Clinton)
(1994), (2004), (2012)
Elwood is an unincorporated community named in honor of Kinsey Elwood who platted the town in 1873.

Ely (Linn)
(1990)
Ely was laid out in 1872 and named for John F. Ely.

Emeline (Jackson)
(1991)
There are two stories as to how the town got its name.
- It was named after a woman who was a member of one the founding families.
- Another is that Emeline means work in German and the area had attracted many hard-working Germans.

Emerson (Mills)
(1986), (2003), (2009)
Emerson was incorporated in 1875. The town was named by a railroad official for Ralph Waldo Emerson (1803-1882) who was an American lecturer, philosopher and poet. The phrase "Build a better mouse trap and

the world will beat a path to your door" is attributed to Emerson. Emerson was a shipping point on the Chicago, Burlington, and Quincy Railroad.

EMMETSBURG (Palo Alto) (County Seat)
(1985), (1993), (2002), (2014)
Emmetsburg was incorporated in 1877. It was originally settled between 1845 and 1852 by Irish immigrants fleeing the Irish potato famine. It was named for the Dublin born Irish nationalist Robert Emmet, who was executed at the age of 25 for leading an 1803 rebellion against the British.

Enterprise (Polk)
(1984), (2000)
Enterprise is an unincorporated community which started with the discovery of a large vein of coal. The Des Moines Coal & Mining Company (later renamed Enterprise Coal Company) opened Enterprise Mine No. 1 in 1903. As more workers arrived, a town was quickly set up to accommodate the miners and their families. In 1914, the Enterprise Coal Company was ranked as one of the top 24 coal producers in the state. The vein would eventually run dry, and in 1919 the mine was shut down and Enterprise was no longer a coal mining town. Many of the workers moved and began new lives farming the surrounding area or working for stores in the town's center.

Epworth (Dubuque)
(1974), (1993)
Epworth was incorporated in 1879 and named for the town of Epworth, Lincolnshire, England. This was the birthplace of John Wesley who was an English cleric, theologian and evangelist who was a leader of a revival movement within the Church of England, known as Methodism. The societies he founded became the dominant form of the independent Methodist movement that continues today.

Essex (Page)
(1976), (1984), (1992), (2003), (2016)

Essex was platted in 1870 by R. B. Wood for the construction of the Chicago, Burlington & Quincy Railroad. It was name for Essex, Massachusetts, the home town of R. B. Wood.

ESTHERVILLE (Emmet) (County Seat)
(1982), (1996), (2005)
Estherville was incorporated in 1881 and named for Esther A. Ridley, one of the first white female settlers in the area.

Evansdale (Black Hawk)
(1974)
Evansdale began its existence in 1947, when the residents of the Home Acres and River Forest Area, which adjoined the city limits of Waterloo, were confronted with a common drainage problem. They formed the Home Acres Improvement Association and in August of 1947, petitioned for articles of incorporation as a town. The documents were presented to District Judge William T. Evans through a Parkersburg attorney. The town was named Evansdale for Judge William T. Evans who once owned the farm which is the current site of the city.

Everly (Clay)
(1982)
Everly was founded in 1884 as Clark, but there was already a town named Clarke so its name was changed to Everly. It is believed to be named for a Chicago, Milwaukee & St. Paul Railroad conductor or a surveyor when the land was surveyed and platted in 1884.

Exira (Audubon)
(1989) (2000), (2008)
Exira was founded in 1857 and named for Exira Eckman, daughter of Judge John Eckman from Ohio. He agreed to purchase a lot of property in the town if it was named for his daughter.
<u>Item of interest</u>
Perk Smith told of a memorable tale that happened in Exira. A man named Nelson was burning bricks in a kiln when one evening John R. Thacker and some of the boys met there. It was suggested that the fires

in the kiln offered a fine opportunity to roast chickens. Thacker agreed and said that Deacon Bush had some chickens. He proposed that some of the boys procure the chickens while he and Van Gorder prepare mud for roasting the chickens. The process consisted in covering the chicken, feathers and all, with a casing of soft clay and placing the mass in the hot fire until cooked. They would then remove the chickens from the fire, remove the crust of clay with feathers and skin then have a feast. The boys returned with a sack full of chickens, which were cooked and the feast was enjoyed. Thacker wondered what the Deacon would say in the morning upon missing his chickens. That never happened. When Thacker went home, he found his own chicken house empty. He considered himself the victim of a dirty, unpardonable trick, and treated his late companions with unmitigated scorn and contempt. He failed to see the joke!

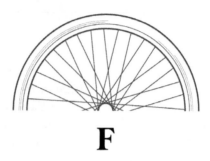

F

Fairbank (Buchanan and Fayette)
(2007)
In 1854, the village was laid out and platted by F. J. Everett and C. W. Bacon and called Fairbank. Initially they called the village Alton but changed it to Fairbank in honor of Bacon's grandmother, whose name was Fairbank.

FAIRFIELD (Jefferson) (County Seat)
(1979), (1984), (1988), (1997), (2013), (2019)
The area now known as Jefferson County was first settled in 1836 with the new community of Fairfield. The name was suggested by Nancy Bonnifield, one of the settlers, because it described the fair fields of the area. Susan Welty suggests it was a play of words on her own name (Bonny field).

Item of interest
Fairfield is a unique, eclectic community with a reputation for arts, entertainment, and music. It is known as "America's Most Unusual Town."

The city was the site of the first and second Iowa State Fairs.

It claims to have more restaurants per capita than San Francisco. Art lovers will find something to gaze at in more than its 25 art galleries.

Fairfield is home to the Maharishi University of Management. Since 1974, it has been referred to as "the world's largest training center" for practitioners of the transcendental meditation technique.

Down the road from Fairfield is Maharishi Vedic City. Incorporated in 2001, it was inspired by Maharishi Mahesh Yogi who recommended that its development be based on the knowledge derived from the ancient Vedic literature. Vedic religion, also called Vedism's, was the religion of the ancient Indo-European-speaking peoples who entered India about 1500 BC from the region of present-day Iran. It takes its name from the collections of sacred texts known as the Vedas. It was one of the major traditions that shaped Hinduism. In Maharishi Vedic City, every building is designed according to Maharishi Vastu architecture, which provides the knowledge of how to create buildings that promote harmony and balance for those who live and work in them. The city is the home to the Institute for Natural Medicine and Prevention and The Raj, a world-class Ayurvedic health spa and vegetarian restaurant. The city also has many recreational trails, parks, and lakes.

Parsons College, now a defunct American private liberal arts college, was located in Fairfield. The school was named for its wealthy benefactor, Lewis B. Parsons Sr. It was founded in 1875 with one building and 34 students. Over the years, new buildings were constructed as enrollment expanded. The school lost its accreditation in 1948, but regained it two years later. In 1955, the school appointed Millard G. Roberts as its president which began a period of rapid expansion with the student population by 1966 rising to 5,000. There was a turning point in 1966 when Look Magazine published an article criticizing the college and its president. Later that year the school lost its accreditation and Roberts was asked to resign as president. Enrollment quickly declined and the college was $14 million in debt and closed under bankruptcy in 1973.

Fairview (Jones)
(1978), (2004), (2012)
The village of Fairview was laid out in 1841 and named after Fairview township where it is located.

Farley (Dubuque)
(1974), (1993)
Farley had its start in the 1850s with the building of the Dubuque and Sioux City Railroad through the territory. It was named for the superintendent of the railroad.

Farlin (Greene)
(1988)
Farlin was founded in the 1880s and named for Mr. McFarlin, an early prominent grain buyer.

Farmington (Van Buren)
(1981), (1992)
Farmington was incorporated in 1841 and named for Farmington, Connecticut.

Farnhamville (Calhoun and Webster)
(1998), (2012)
Farnhamville was incorporated in 1892 and named in honor of R. E. Farnham, a railroad official. Postal authorities refused to accept the name Farnham, so town was renamed Farnhamville.

Farragut (Freemont)
(1976)
Farragut started in 1870 with the building of the Burlington & Missouri River Railroad through the territory. It was named for Admiral David Farragut, a flag officer of the United States Navy during the Civil War. He was the first rear admiral, vice admiral and admiral in the United States Navy. He is remembered in United States Navy tradition for his order at the Battle of Mobile Bay where he said, "Damn the torpedoes, full speed ahead."

Farrar (Polk)
(1975)
Farrar is an unincorporated community which owes its development to the railroad line that came through the area in 1902-1903. It was named

in honor of one of the railroad employees involved in the creation of that line.

Farson (Wapello)
(1984), (2000)
Farson was laid out in 1902.

Faulkner (Franklin)
(1983)
Faulkner was platted in 1878. The town was named for James Faulkner, an early settler.

Fayette (Fayette)
(1980), (1996)
Fayette was incorporated in 1874. It was named for Marquis de la Fayette, a French hero of the Revolutionary War.

Fernald (Story)
(1986)
In 1901, the Rock Island Railroad was built across Richland township and in 1902 the town of Fernald was platted in the center of the township. A wealthy easterner named George Fernald said he would build a large store if the town would be called Fernald.

Fenton (Kossuth)
(2002),
Fenton was platted in 1899 and named for Reuben E. Fenton, a New York State governor and Senator.

Finchford (Black Hawk)
(1982), (1985)
Finchford was laid out by Lewis Goings in 1872. It was first named Newell's Ford, for the original settler family. It was later called Finch's Ford for J.L. Finch, who operated the first mill on the West Fork River. Finch's Ford eventually came to be known as Finchford.

Flagler (Marion)
(1984)
The first post office opened in 1876 as Flagers. The town was formed in 1877 by the Union Coal and Mining Company and named for the superintendent of the company. In 1892, Flaglers was renamed Flagler.

Fonda (Pocahontas)
(1979), (2015)
Fonda was founded in 1870 and originally called Marvin. Marvin was found to be too similar to nearby Mason and mail was being mixed up, so in 1874, town officials changed the name to Fonda for Fonda, New York. Fonda is derived from the Latin word which means a fountain.
Item of interest
Fonda is proud of its annual Cinco De Mayo Cultural Celebration on the weekend closest to May 5.

It is the birth place of Ruth Stafford Peale (1906–2008) writer and co-founder of Guideposts with her husband Norman Vincent Peale.

Fontanelle (Adair)
(2000), (2009)
Fontanelle was incorporated in 1878 and named for Chief Logan Fontanelle of the Omaha tribe. He was the son of French fur trader, Lucien Fontanelle, and an Omaha tribeswoman.

FOREST CITY (Hancock) (County Seat)
(1982), (1987), (2002), (2014)
Forest City was incorporated in 1878. It was formerly known as Puckerbruch, Big Brush, or Hill City. Robert Clark, the founder and surveyor, renamed it Forest City because it was literally cut out of a forest.
Items of interest
Forest City is home to Waldorf (College) University which was founded in 1903 as a result of "The Great Hotel War." There was a fierce competitive battle between the two first-class hotels, built simultaneously,

which left the beautiful Waldorf Hotel vacant only after four months of operation.

The Hotel War of 1900 nearly tore the citizens and businesses of Forest City apart. The new courthouse had been built and there were four banks and five trains that passed through town, two of which were passenger trains.

Bankers B.A. Plummer of the south bank and Charlie Thompson of the north bank both thought Forest City would be a great place for people to stop and spend the night, so each said they were going to build a hotel. There was a meeting of people interested in the downtown district. At that meeting, Plummer said the hotel should be near the courthouse, but Thompson said it should be on the north end of town because that was where they wanted the city to grow. After a discussion they left the meeting, and the next thing the people read in the paper was that Plummer was going to build a hotel called Waldorf.

When Thompson heard that Plummer was going to build the Waldorf, he decided he would build his own hotel called the Summit. The two started building within six months of each other and finished within four months of each other at the cost of around $70,000 each.

The Waldorf, the south hotel, had a white theme with white table cloths, white horses, white carriages and, white uniforms for the servants. The Summit, the north hotel, had a black theme with black table cloths, black horses, black carriages and, black uniforms for the servants.

When staff of the hotels went down to the depot to pick up passengers, the passengers had a choice of black or white. Each hotel had chefs from the east coast to cook the meals. They each had 53 rooms renting for $1 a night, with room service it was $2.

People doing business on the south side of town were expected to stay in the Waldorf and people doing business on the north side of town were expected to stay at the Summit. Otherwise, they wouldn't do business with them. It really split the town. After a little over a year it became apparent there was not enough business to support both men, so the two bankers met and agreed to put a bid in for the other's hotel. Whoever had the highest bid would own both hotels. Thompson won the bid with $43,000 for the Waldorf, which he immediately shut down for a year while the Summit stayed open.

C.S. Salveson, a Lutheran pastor, with a dream of opening a higher standard school, got together with the town to buy the Waldorf. They bought it for $18,000, of which $6,000 came from the city, $6,000 from the Lutheran Association, and the remaining $6,000 from Salveson himself, who mortgaged his family farm in North Dakota.

The college opened in 1903 with about 20 students. Classes were taught in farm and management and basic skills such as secretarial courses. Waldorf University grew from these beginnings and still calls Forest City home.

Thompson continued to run the Summit until around 1909, when he left Forest City and sold the hotel to Plummer. Since then the top half of the hotel burned in 1915. It was known as the Plummer hotel.

Forest City holds an annual tractor ride which travels through north Iowa's country roads and small towns. All tractors must be a 1960 or older and capable of traveling 50 to 70 miles.

Forest City also hosts an annual Steam Threshing Festival held the third weekend of September.

Fort Atkinson (Winneshiek)
(1996), (1999), (2005)

On May 31, 1840, a camp was made on the site of the future fort. The camp was named Atkinson in honor of the commanding officer in charge of the Winnebago resettlement efforts. The fort was essentially complete in 1842 and included 24 buildings and a stockade wall. Outside the 11'9" wall were 14 additional buildings.

Fort Atkinson was built to keep the Winnebago Indians on neutral ground (a 40-mile-wide strip of land established by the Treaty of 1830) after their removal from Wisconsin in 1840. It provided protection for the Winnebago Indians from the Sioux, Sauk, Fox and white intruders on Indian land.

On June 20, 1846, the regular army troops were pulled out of Fort Atkinson to fight in the war with Mexico. Iowa volunteers staffed the fort and continued to carry out their duties. In June of 1848, the Winnebago

Tribe was removed from Iowa just as they had been from Wisconsin. With their removal, there was no longer a reason for the fort and it was abandoned.

FORT DODGE (Webster) (County Seat)
(1973), (1987), (1995), (2004), (2015)

Fort Dodge was founded in 1869. Fort Dodge traces its beginnings to 1850 when soldiers from the United States Army erected a fort at the junction of the Des Moines River and Lizard Creek. It was originally named Fort Clarke, but because there was another fort with the same name in Texas, it was renamed Fort Dodge after Henry Dodge, governor of the Wisconsin Territory, which included Iowa at the time. The fort was abandoned in 1853. The next year a civilian storekeeper in Fort Dodge purchased the land and buildings of the old fort.

Items of interest

Fort Dodge is home to the Fort Museum & Frontier Village which showcases the frontier roots with a replica of the 19th century fort. It has a collection of thousands of artifacts ranging from military memorabilia to Native American art and tools.

Fort Dodge received national recognition for being the birthplace of the most famous American hoax. It was here that the idea was conceived and stone was quarried for the "Cardiff Giant," a supposed petrified human. Americans were fascinated during the late 1860s and 1870s by this hoax. It is now in the Farmers Museum at Cooperstown, New York. A replica of the giant is on display at the Fort Museum in Fort Dodge.

Another less famous hoax occurred when Mr. Freeman came to town saying he represented a wholesale house back east who sold pianos. Dr. Olney wanted a piano, so he gave Freeman a note for a piano. Freeman sold this note to Mr. Dwelle at a discount. The piano failed to arrive and it was determined that Freeman did not represent a wholesaler. Sheriff Walz went to Missouri on a fishing trip and brought back Freeman, who was indicted by the Grand Jury and went to jail.

Lew Anderson was born in Forest City. He was the last
Clarabell the Clown on the Howdy Doody show.

FORT MADISON (Lee) (County Seat)
(1975), (1988), (1997), (2003), (2013)
The city of Fort Madison was established near the site of the historic
Fort Madison (1808–1813), the first permanent U.S. military fortification
on the Upper Mississippi River. Fort Madison was named for the fourth
U. S. President, James Madison. Fort Madison was the site of the most
western battle of the War of 1812. **This war** was an armed conflict between
the United States and the British Empire. The British restricted American
trade fearing it would be harmful to their war with France. The Americans
objected to the British Empire restricting their trade and made American
sailors serve on British ships. The British promised to set up an Indian
state in the Midwest in order to maintain their influence in the region.
That is why 10,000 Native Americans fought on the side of the British
in this war. Fort Madison was the only fort in Iowa ever to be attacked
by Indians. **Americans** were eager to prove their independence from the
British Empire once and for all in this war.

Scholars who have studied Fort Madison generally agree that its
location was its greatest liability.

Items of interest

Fort Madison is home to the Iowa State Penitentiary, which is a
maximum-security prison for men. Stories are often told of actions by the
unruly inmates. A favorite tactic was to plug up a toilet and flood their cell.
Leonard Harvey, plant operations manager, navigated the walkway behind
the cell to get at the plug. When an inmate heard that pipes were being
uncapped, he flushed his toilet and sent fluids flying. This was worse than
getting spit upon, another inmate favorite. Lacking freedom, they used
body fluids as weapons.

In 1912, Walter A. Sheaffer took his idea of a pen-filling
apparatus that utilized a lever system to fill a fountain pen
with ink. Shaffer took his life savings and founded the W.

A. Sheaffer Company in Fort Madison. He began with just seven employees crowded into the small back room of his jewelry store. In 1997, The Bic Pen Company acquired the Sheaffer Company and in 2008, closed the Fort Madison facility and moved the operations off shore. The Sheaffer Company was the last company to make pens in the United States.

Franklin (Lee)
(2019)
Franklin was laid out in 1840 and first known as Franklin Centre. The city was named for Benjamin Franklin.

Fredonia (Louisa)
(2016)
Fredonia was platted in the 1840s. No one knows who gave it its name. It is believed to be named for Fredonia, New York or Fredonia. Pennsylvania. New Yorker's believe it is from "Free Donia" or "Free Lady" and Pennsylvania's believe it is from "Free Donia" or the Greek meaning "Free Gift."

Freeport (Winneshiek)
(1977)
A post office was established in 1854, and remained in operation until November 1905.

Fremont (Mahaska)
(2013)
Fremont was founded in 1848 by William M. Morrow and named for Captain John Charles Fremont. Fremont was an American explorer, politician, and soldier and in 1856 became the first candidate of the Republican Party for President of the United States. When exploring the west, his reports pointed emigrants to Oregon and helped inspire Mormons to settle near the Great Salt Lake. In his exploring, when he reaching the San Francisco Bay, he gave the harbor mouth the name of Golden Gate.

Item of interest

Freemont is the birth place of Steve Bales who is best known as the guidance officer on the Apollo 11 lunar landing.

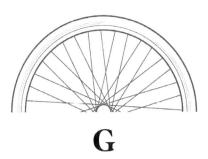

G

Galesburg (Jasper)
(1984), (1991), (2000)
Galesburg was platted in 1885 and was most likely named for Galesburg, Illinois.

Galland (Lee)
(1981)
The town is believed to be named for Isaac Galland, who was a merchant, postmaster, land speculator, and doctor. He is best known for selling large tracts of land around Commerce, Illinois in 1839 to Joseph Smith, founder of The Church of Jesus Christ of Latter-Day Saints.

Galva (Ida)
(1977), (1987), (1998), (2001)
Galva was incorporated in 1889. It was named for Galva, Illinois.

Garber (Clayton)
(1980), (1987), (2014)
Garber was first called East Elkport then renamed for John Garber who in 1872 surveyed the land and served as the first postmaster.

Garden Grove (Decatur)
(1981), (2016)
Garden Grove was the first temporary way station established in Iowa by the members of The Church of Jesus Christ of Latter-day Saints who left Nauvoo, Illinois because of persecution. This settlement was named Garden Grove because the entire grove was covered with wild onions as far as the eye could see. Within three weeks of their arrival, the pioneers planted 715 acres. They founded a village to assist those who did not have

sufficient means to continue their journey, as well as to support and supply future groups of pioneers.

The first winter at Garden Grove proved to be difficult because the last and most destitute individuals, who left Nauvoo in 1846, came to Garden Grove in October. These people were described as a miserable remnant consisting of about seven hundred people physically unfit and poorly equipped for their journey. They huddled down at a camp north of Montrose until wagons from Garden Grove arrived for them.

Supplies were very scarce the first winter. The difficult conditions forced the Saints to have Lyman A. Shurtliff and Brother Hunt to travel around the area pleading for assistance from the surrounding settlers who responded generously. Many of the Saints' lives were spared because of the kindness of their non-Mormon neighbors. However, death was a significant part of the experience at Garden Grove. One of the first causalities was President Samuel Bent, president of the Garden Grove Branch. His counselors, in a letter to the Quorum of the Twelve Apostles, described his passing as follows:

"Garden Grove is left without a president, and a large circle of relatives and friends are bereft of an affectionate companion and friend and the Church has sustained the loss of an undeviating friend to truth and righteousness. The glory of his death is that he died in the full triumphs of faith and a knowledge of the truths of our holy religion, exhorting his friends to be faithful, having three days previous to his death received intimations of his approaching end by three holy messengers from on high."

Through the winter of 1846/47, about 600 Latter-day Saints resided in Garden Grove. By 1852, the Mormon settlers had moved on to Utah, selling the property and improvements to other American frontiersmen.

Gardner (Audubon or Guthrie)
(1983)
Gardner was named for a member of the Gardner family who were early settlers.

Garnavillo (Clayton)
(1996), (2005)

Because of the rich farm land in the area, the town has been called the "Gem of the Prairie."

GARNER (Hancock) (County Seat)
(1985), (2010), (2017)
Garner was incorporated in 1881 and named for Col. W. W. Garner, a civil engineer on the Rock Island Railroad.

Items of interest

In 1895, the famous evangelist Billy Sunday held his first revival meeting in Garner where nearly 100 people accepted Christ during a week of meetings.

William Ashley "Billy" Sunday was an American athlete who, after being a popular outfielder in baseball's National League during the 1880s, became the most celebrated and influential American evangelist during the first two decades of the 20th century. Born into poverty in Iowa, Sunday spent several years at the Iowa Soldiers' Orphans' Home in Glenwood, before working odd jobs and playing for baseball teams. His speed and agility provided him the opportunity to play baseball in the major leagues for eight years.

After he converted to evangelical Christianity in the 1880s, Sunday left baseball for the Christian ministry. He became the nation's most famous evangelist. Sunday held widely reported campaigns in America's largest cities where he attracted the largest crowds of any evangelist before the advent of electronic sound systems. He also made a great deal of money and was welcomed into the homes of the wealthy and influential. Sunday was a strong supporter of prohibition, and his preaching almost certainly played a significant role in the adoption of the Eighteenth Amendment in 1919. (See Glenwood)

Each year Garner celebrates "Duesey Days," which gets its name from Frederick and August Duesenberg. The Duesenberg brothers had their beginning in Garner as bicycle mechanics, but went on to found the Duesenberg Motors Company (sometimes referred to as "Duesy.") They gained fame for building a luxurious, powerful, and fast vehicle known as the Duesenberg in the 1920's and

1930's. The cars used fine woods, leathers, and fabrics, and were sold for between $12,750 and $25,000. Any remaining Duesenberg cars today are extremely valuable.

Garrison (Benton)
(1978), (2012)
In 1872, Garrison was laid out and first called Benton. Because there was already a Benton, its name was changed to Garrison for Nelson Garrison. Garrison owned the land and was a farmer who ran the post office out of his home. Garrison was incorporated in 1880.

Items of interest
In 1994, Garrison was one of the top 5 communities in a nationwide contest to be named "The Best Little Small Town in America."

In 1911, the town was almost destroyed by fire. A total of twenty-six buildings were burned, which included nineteen businesses. Garrison never fully recovered from this disaster.

Garryowen (Jackson)
(1999), (2007)
Garryowen was founded by Irish immigrants in the late 1830s. It was part of a wave of Catholic settlements encouraged by the Bishop of Dubuque. His associate missionary founded a log church in 1840 with funds from Society for the Propagation of the Faith. The town was first called Makokiti but it was changed to Garryowen to reflect the community's Irish heritage.

Garryowen is a neighborhood in Limerick, Ireland. The word Garryowen is a transliteration of the Irish meaning "the garden of Owen. " It relates to the association in the 12th century, between St John's Church and the Knights Templar whose house in Limerick was dedicated to John the Baptist. In medieval times, Garryowen was located just outside the walled city of Limerick.

Garwin (Tama)
(1986), (2004), (2012)
The post office called Garwin has been in operation since 1880. The town was named for a railroad employee.

Geode State Park (Henry and Des Moines)
(2009, (2019)
While the geode is Iowa's state rock, few can be found in the park. The prime attraction is the 1,640-acre park and Lake Geode, a 187-acre lake built in 1950.
Item of interest
On Saturday, July 25, 2009, a RAGBRAI participant died from injuries sustained in a crash at the bottom of the hill near the Geode Lake dam at Geode State Park.

George (Lyon)
(1985), (1999), (2007)
The railroad official who was in charge of laying the tracks in the area had two children named George and Edna. It was at his request that two towns be named for his children. The coming of the railroad was the determining factor in the establishment of the town of George.

Often the supervisor of the railroad decided where new towns were to be located. They generally attempted to have the route go through established towns, and when a town was by-passed by the railroad, it was called an "inland town" and soon died out or was relocated. When the tracks were laid, the official in charge gave orders to lay a side track and place a box car for a depot. This was the beginning of the town of George. The first train went through George on December 25, 1887.

Germanville (Sioux)
(2009)
Germanville was settled in 1840 when a few families of Germans came to Jefferson County.

Gifford (Hardin)
(1986), (2004)

Gifford was laid out in 1875 and named for C. T. Gifford, who was instrumental in bringing the railroad to the town. By 1880, Gifford was at the junction of two railroads.

Gilbert (Story)
(1976)
Gilbert was first settled in 1855 and incorporated in 1904. It was named for George Gilbert, who owned the land upon which the town was built.

Gilbertville (Black Hawk)
(1974), (1985), (2010)
Gilbertville was platted in 1856 by John Chambaud, a Frenchman who had great plans for the town. Chambaud went out east and told exciting stories about the new western city to men who had lots of money. Chambaud did a booming business selling lots and then sailed to France with the investors' money. When the buyers arrived in Gilbertville, they discovered the well-advertised town was just a frontier settlement and the lots they purchased were sandy patches of ground. That is why Gilbertville might also be called the "Sand-Hill City."

Many European immigrants were from Luxembourg who spoke French as well as German and or Letzeburgesch. Gilbertville was often called Frenchtown.

Gillett Grove (Clay)
(1979), (1993), (2007), (2017)
Gillett Grove was laid out in 1899 when the railroad was extended and named for brothers George and Isaiah Gillett, who were pioneer settlers.

Gladbrook (Tama)
(1974), (1995)
A post office called Gladbrook has been in operation since 1880. A railroad official gave the town its name.
<u>Items of interest</u>
On March 21, 1910, the Green Mountain train wreck occurred between Gladbrook and Green Mountain, where a derailment killed 52

people riding on the Chicago, Rock Island and Pacific Railroad train. Early that morning there was another train wreck causing the Rock Island Railroad trains to be diverted from Cedar Rapids to Waterloo over the Chicago Great Western tracks. This resulted in two trains being combined into a ten-car train and two locomotives travelling backwards. The new combined train now had two wooden cars sandwiched between the locomotives, a steel Pullman car, and other steel cars.

Between Green Mountain and Gladbrook, the lead engine left the tracks, hit a clay embankment, and came to a sudden stop. The steel cars sliced through the two wooden coaches, a smoking car and a ladies' day coach which contained many children. One of the uninjured passengers said "I saw women in the coach crushed into a bleeding mass, their bodies twisted out of human shape. I have seen what I shall see all my life when I dream." A relief train arrived two hours after the accident. It was later reported, "The sight was one of horribly crushed, mutilated, and dismembered bodies." There were no fatalities in the Pullman cars.

Although it was the worst train wreck in Iowa history, no official cause was ever released for the wreck, nor were any charges of neglect made. The crash did result in the introduction of new safety procedures.

Pat Acton's Gladbrook home is the location of the Matchstick Marvels Museum, the world's largest collection of tiny matchstick mega-art. Here Pat Acton has methodically glued together matchsticks since 1977. "It's not something I normally bring up in conversation," said Pat with a laugh. "I learned years ago that if you tell people you make stuff out of matchsticks, the eyeballs roll."

Pat's painstakingly detailed creations are often called miniatures, but there's nothing miniature about his USS Iowa battleship, which is 13 feet long, or his U.S. Capitol, which is 12 feet wide. A recent sculpture, "Plane Loco," contains **over one million matchsticks**, each one individually shaped and glued by Pat. He has also created a model of the Notre Dame Cathedral in Paris, where it took him 20 months to glue together nearly 300,000 wood

matchsticks into what may be the best version of Notre
Dame that tourists can see until the real one hopes to
reopen in 2025.

GLENWOOD (Mills) (County Seat)
(1980), (1984) (1989), (1992), (2003) (2011), (2016)
Glenwood was established in 1848 by L. T. Coons, a Mormon, as
Coonsville, but in 1851 was renamed Glenwood, for the Presbyterian
minister Glenn Wood.
Items of interest
In 1876, the State Veteran's Orphan's Home at Glenwood became
the Iowa Asylum for Feeble-Minded Children (IAFMC), the 7th such
facility in the country and the first located west of the Mississippi River.
The Glenwood facility rapidly expanded with the treatment of mental
retardation and acceptance of eugenic (the sterilization of people
considered to be inferior). This process was developed largely by Francis
Galton as a method of improving the human race, it fell into disfavor only
after it was used by the Nazis. By 1925, the Glenwood IAFMC was the home
of 1,555 inmates categorized between idiots, imbeciles and morons. The
IAFMC became the Glenwood State-Hospital School in 1941 and during
the early 1950s covered 1,185 acres with 310 staff members responsible for
the 1,968 patients.
The deinstitutionalization of Glenwood began in the late 1950s,
especially after the November 17, 1957, Des Moines Register revealed that
Mayo Buckner had spent 59 years confined to Glenwood with an IQ of
120. National attention came to Buckner and the Glenwood State-Hospital
School in the December 9, 1957 issue of Time Magazine and the March
25, 1958 issue of Life Magazine. The transformation from traditional ward
buildings into group home styled cottages was largely completed during
the 1970s. The facility is now known as the Glenwood Resource Center.

After World War II, Glenwood became a meat-packing
center and during the early 1950s became home of one
of America's largest kosher packing houses. Most of its
products were shipped to New York and the East Coast.

William Ashley "Billy" Sunday as a child, lived in the Iowa Soldiers Orphans home in Glenwood. (See Garner)

Glidden (Carroll)
(1981)
Glidden was laid out in 1866 and named either for Capt. W. T. Glidden, a railroad promoter, or in honor of Joseph Farwell Glidden, the inventor of barbed wire.

Goodell (Hancock)
(1990)
Goodell was platted in 1884. Goodell was first call Cashman for the man who built a grain elevator. The town later changed its name to Goodell after John Goodell, who was one of the financial backers of the railroad.

Goose Lake (Clinton)
(1978), (2004), (2012)
Goose Lake was platted in 1889, and incorporated in 1908. It is named for nearby Goose Lake, which was named for the many wild geese seen there by early settlers.

Gowrie (Webster)
(1998), (2012)
A post office called Gowrie has been in operation since 1871 and named after Gowrie, Scotland.

Graettinger (Palo Alto)
(1985), (2014)
Graettinger had its start in the 1880s with the building of the Burlington, Cedar Rapids and Northern Railroad through that area. The land was originally owned by Dr. Alois Graettinger, a German physician, who gave the land to the railroad under the condition that the town be named for him.

Graf (Dubuque)
(2010)

Graf was founded around 1886, when farmer, Christian Graf, donated land to the Chicago Great Western Railroad for a depot. A coal chute and water tower was erected to serve the coal trains. A helper engine was kept in Graf to assist the trains up the incline to Farley. Graf was incorporated in 1933.

Grafton (Worth)
(1996)
Grafton had its start in 1878 with the building of the Chicago, Milwaukee and St. Paul Railroad through that area. The town was originally called Rock Creek, but the site didn't have rocks or a creek. The railroad renamed it Grafton after a man associated with the railroad.

Grand Junction (Greene)
(1976), (1994), (2008), (2018)
Grand Junction was incorporated in 1873 and took its name from the junction of the Keokuk, Des Moines and Chicago and Northwestern Railroads.
<u>Item of interest</u>
Grand Junction is the home of the Lincoln Highway museum.

Grand Mound (Clinton)
(1994)
Grand Mound was platted in 1866. The town was to be called Sand Mound for the nearby sand mound, but as a result of a spelling error it became Grand Mound.

Granger (Dallas and Polk)
(1974), (1984), (2000), (2006)
The town was surveyed and platted in 1885. It was named for C. T. Granger, a railroad man.
<u>Items of interest</u>
Granger is well known for having two water towers, with one labeled HOT and the other labeled COLD.

In early 1906, just two miles from Granger, Fred Buchanan established winter quarters for his Yankee Robinson Show, a Midwestern travelling circus. He built a large two story house and several outbuildings. The quarters were perfect for grazing circus animals. The land was also along the railroad and Buchanan added a side track that held five train cars. By 1926 there was a total of 20 out buildings. The circus was permanently closed in 1930 because of the depression. Granger may be the only town in Iowa to claim an elephant graveyard.

Granville (Sioux)
(1975), (1993), (1996), (2002), (2005), (2012), (2016)
Granville was platted in 1882 and named for Richard Grenville, an English explorer. The "e" in Grenville was changed to an "a."
Item of interest
Granville is known for "that black Iowa dirt," the same fertile dirt that made Iowa the top choice for pioneering farmers back in the 1800s.

Gravity (Taylor)
(1992)
Gravity was incorporated in 1883; however, the name came from a nearby landmark at the time, called the "Old Gravity Post Office." The origin of the name gravity is obscure.
Item of interest
Gravity is the only town in the United States called Gravity.

Greene (Butler)
(1985), (1999), (2014)
Greene was incorporated in 1879 and first called Elm Springs. In 1871, its name was changed to Greene in honor of Judge George Greene, president of the Burlington, Cedar Rapids and Minnesota Railroad. Judge Greene gave generously of land and money for the new town.

GREENFIELD (Adair) (County Seat)

(1981), (1984), (2000), (2009)

The plan for the town of Greenfield was created in 1856 when the land was purchased by Milton C. Munger. Greenfield is named for Greenfield, Massachusetts.

Item of interest

Greenfield is home to The Iowa Aviation Museum which is located at the Greenfield Municipal Airport and is dedicated to preserving Iowa's aviation heritage. The Iowa Aviation Hall of Fame is also located at the museum. It honors Iowans who have contributed significantly to the growth of aviation. The Iowa Aviation Museum has eleven civil aircraft on display, including some rare examples of early flying machines from the 1920s, 1930s and 1940s.

Green Mountain (Marshall)

(1974), (1979), (1986), (2008)

The town of Green Mountain was established in 1883 and named by early settlers from Vermont. It was named after Green Mountain, Vermont.

Items of interest

On March 21, 1910, Green Mountain was the site of the Green Mountain train wreck, which killed 52 people. This is known as the worst train wreck in Iowa history. (See Gladbrook)

Grinnell (Poweshiek)

(1976), (1991), (2001), (2011)

Grinnell was founded as a "Yankee" town by settlers from New England who were descendants of English Puritans. In 1854, four men including Josiah B. Grinnell, a Congregationalist from Vermont, founded the town. It was to be named "Stella," but Grinnell convinced the others to adopt his name, describing his name as rare and concise. Grinnell was incorporated in 1865.

Items of interest

Grinnell was a stop on the Underground Railroad. One of the most famous events occurred in February of 1859 when abolitionist John Brown and 12 slaves that he was helping escape to freedom, were hosted by J.B. Grinnell and several other community residents.

Grinnell is home to Grinnell College, which was founded in 1854 by Josiah B. Grinnell and was the first college established west of the Mississippi River. Grinnell College is a private liberal arts college and is known for its rigorous academics, innovative teaching, and commitment to social justice.

Grinnell has been named one of the "Top Ten Coolest Small Towns in America!" By Budget Travel.

Griswold (Cass)
(1989), (2011)
Griswold was named for J. N. A. Griswold, a railroad director. The town was incorporated in 1885.

Gunder (Clayton)
(1987), (2005)
Gunder is an unincorporated community.

GUTHRIE CENTER (Guthrie) (County Seat)
(1974), (1983), (1986), (1995), (2001), (2006), (2013)
Guthrie Center was incorporated in 1880. It was named for Capt. Edwin B. Guthrie, who was the commanding officer of a company of Iowa volunteers in the Mexican War.

Guttenberg (Clayton)
(1980), (1987), (1996), (2005), (2014)
Guttenberg was incorporated in 1851. Prairie La Porte, meaning "the door to the prairie," was the first name given to Guttenberg by French explorers in 1673. The German immigration began in 1845, and by 1850 the town was nearly all Germans. The city takes its name from Johannes Gutenberg, the inventor of the printing press. A replica of a Bible he printed is on display at the public library.
Item of interest
The area was the campground site for the Sac and Fox Native Americans until 1823.

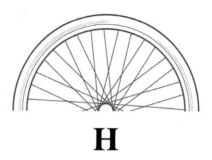

H

Hale (Jones)
(2012)
Hale was platted in 1876 and named for Hon. J. P. Hale.

Hale Village (Jones)
(1994)
(See Hale)

Hamilton (Marion)
(1984), (2000)
Hamilton was surveyed in 1849 and incorporated in 1900. It was first called Jacobs Ruin after Jacob Hendricks, but was later named for Hamilton, Ohio, where the original founders were from.

<u>Item of interest</u>
In 1873 Hamilton had a popular saloon where the men of the community would hang-out. The ladies of the town thought they would do something about the saloon. Armed with clubs and whatever else they could use, they paid a visit to the saloon. After the ladies were done, there was not much left of the saloon. Doors and windows were broken, chairs and tables were wrecked, and glasses and bottles were shattered. This ended the saloon in Hamilton.

Hamlin (Audubon)
(1974), (1976) (1983), (2013)
Hamlin was laid out in 1872 and named for Nathaniel Hamlin, a pioneer settler.

HAMPTON (Franklin) (County Seat)
(1990), (2007)

Hampton was founded in 1855. It was originally named Benjamin in honor of Benjamin Franklin, but, because there was already a town named Benjamin, the name was changed to Hampton for Hampton Roads, Virginia.

Items of interest

In the 1950s, St. Patrick Catholic Church of Hampton had two priests called Father Norton. Father Claude Norton was actually the son of Father Patrick Norton. After Patrick Norton's wife died he because a Catholic Priest. Father Patrick Norton had received all Seven Sacraments of the Catholic Church. (Baptism, Confirmation, Holy Communion, Reconciliation also known as Confession, Marriage, Holy Orders or Ordination, and Anointing of the Sick also known as Last Rites)

Nearly twenty years after the end of the Civil War, the people of Franklin County wanted to build a memorial honoring the Union war heroes. The G.A.R. Memorial Hall is the only building west of the Mississippi River built to honor Civil War soldiers. G.A.R. stands for the Grand Army of the Republic.

To construct the memorial, the Iowa General Assembly voted to allow each county to levy a tax, not to exceed $3,000, for a memorial or a building. The people of Franklin County decided they wanted a building. The City of Hampton provided the site and, with addition private contributions, the Franklin County Soldiers Memorial Hall was completed in 1890.

The building is a unique octagon-shaped structure in the Gothic Revival style. It houses ten marble tablets with the names of Franklin County Civil War soldiers engraved on them. Each of the seven arched stained glass windows has a different motif incorporating Civil War themes relating to weaponry and soldiers' gear used in the war. On top of the building is a Union Soldier statue made of white zinc, which was purchased for $170 from the Graves Registration Bureau in Washington, D.C.

Before the police car in Hampton had a two-way radio, the telephone switch board operator had to flip a switch to turn on a red light atop the water tower to inform the night policeman on patrol to contact the operator to find out where he was needed. When a call came in about a fire, the telephone operator would turn on the fire siren to alert the volunteer firemen who would then contact the operator to determine the location of the fire.

> The 1926 Hampton Bulldog girls' basketball team out-scored their opponents 1,235 to 334 during their 27-0 season. They also won the state girls basketball championship that year.

The Franklin county jail and sheriff's house was built in 1880 and is listed as a National Historic Landmark. The jail was used for 108 years and closed in 1988. At one time after the jail had closed, you could have been a "Guest" at the jail and played the role of an inmate. You would have been:

- Arrested and an officer will read you your rights
- Handcuffed and your legs will be shackled
- Searched
- All personal property will be taken and locked in a safe place
- Have a mug shot and fingerprinted
- Questioned and issued an inmate uniform
- Go to your cell in chains
- Life will be controlled and you would follow the jail routine

Hancock (Pottawattamie)
(1974), (1991), (1997)
Hancock started in 1880 with the building of the Rock Island Railroad through the territory. The town was named for its founder, F. H. Hancock.

Hanley (Madison)
(1991)
Hanley is an unincorporated community first settled in the 1850's.

Hanover (Allamakee)
(2012), (2015)
Hanover is located in Hanover Township and was organized in 1855, but it is no longer a town.

Harcourt (Webster)
(2012)

Harcourt was platted in 1881 and named for William Vernon Harcourt. a British statesman.

Hardy (Humboldt)
(1987)
Hardy started in 1881 with the building of the Cedar Rapids, Iowa Falls and Northwestern Railroad through the territory.

HARLAN (Shelby) (County Seat)
(1976), (1983), (1994), (2000), (2008), (2013)
Harlan was incorporated in 1879 and named for one of Iowa's early US Senators, James Harlan.
Item of interest
Harlan is home to the Shelby County Speedway, where the Tiny Lund Memorial Race is held each fall to honor Tiny Lund, who in 1963 won the Daytona 500.

Harper (Keokuk)
(1986), (2018)
Harper was incorporated in 1879.

Harper's Ferry (Allamakee)
(2017)
Harper's Ferry is not to be confused with Harpers Ferry, West Virginia.
Harpers Ferry was platted as Vailsville and in 1851 changed to Winfield; but, in 1860 the name was again changed to Harper's Ferry (with an apostrophe-s). It was named for David Harper, a leader in development of the town who operated a ferry on the Mississippi River.

Hartley (O'Brien)
(1979), (1999), (2007, (2017))
Hartley had its start around 1880 with the building of the Chicago, Milwaukee & St. Paul Railroad through the territory and was named for John Hartley, a railroad official.

Item of interest
In 1897, Hartley had two expert cigar makers who made the well-known brands of cigars: License, Cuban Star, Virginia, and Defender.

Harvey (Marion)
(1988)
Harvey was laid out by M. F. Marshall in 1876, and named for James Harvey. The town is located between the two railroads. The town was incorporated in 1903.

Havelock (Pocahontas)
(2007)
Havelock was platted in 1881 and named for Henry Havelock, a British general.

Haven (Tama)
(1979)
In 1854, the village of Eureka was founded and in 1874 the name was changed to Haven.

Hawarden (Sioux)
(1975), (1985), (1998)
Hawarden was incorporated in 1887 and named for Hawarden Castle, the Welsh home of William Gladstone, a British statesman, and liberal politician. In a career lasting over 60 years, he served for 12 years as Prime Minister of the United Kingdom, spread over four terms beginning in 1868 and ending in 1894. He also served as Chancellor of the Exchequer four times.

Hawkeye (Fayette)
(1996)
Hawkeye was established in 1879. The name came from either the 1826 novel, The Last of the Mohicans or the Sac Chief Black Hawk.

Hayesville (Keokuk)
(1992), (2016)

Hayesville was named for Joel Winthrop Hayes, an early settler who donated the land for the railroad depot. Hayesville was incorporated in 1916.

Hayfield (Hancock)
(1977), (1999)
Hayfield was platted in 1891. The town was named for the chief industry of the area, which was baling and shipping prairie hay in carload lots. Hay presses were used to make 125-pound hay bales

Hazleton (Buchanan)
(1990)
The town was incorporated in 1883 and named "Hazelton" because the community was in a hazelnut tree grove.
<u>Item of interest</u>
The Hazleton Old Order Amish Community is recognized as the most conservative in Iowa. With 800 residents and nearly 50 Amish businesses open to the public, it's also a popular destination for handmade furniture and homemade baked goodies.

Hedrick (Keokuk)
(2009), (2013), (2016)
Hedrick was incorporated in 1883 and named for General Hedrick who was a Civil War General.

Henderson (Mills)
(1980), (2003), (2009)
Henderson was platted in 1880 and named for Henderson county, Illinois.

Hiawatha (Linn)
(1994), (2004), (2015)
In 1946, Fay Clark, an entrepreneur of several ventures, had a vision of houses and a highway running through a new city. In 1950, Clark and 45 residents signed a petition seeking to become the 17th incorporated

town in Linn County. The town was named Hiawatha, for Clark's trailer company.

Item of interest

Hiawatha is home of Prairie Woods Franciscan Spirituality Center, which opened its doors in July of 1996 as a ministry of the Franciscan Sisters of Perpetual Adoration located in La Crosse, Wisconsin. The foundational vision for this center is the integration of spirituality and ecology, based on the new story of the universe and the writings of Thomas Berry, Brian Swimme, and similar authors.

High Amana (Iowa)
(1976), (1991)
(See Amana)

Hills (Johnson)
(1990), (2018)
Hills was incorporated in 1906. The town was first known as Hillssiding and later shortened to Hills. It was named for an early settler named Thomas Hill.

Item of interest

After WWII, there were 3 to 4 taverns operating in Hills, each having slot machines which were illegal. The "Feds" would raid taverns on a regular basis. When the local law enforcement got word of the raids, they would warn local taverns who then were able to get the machines out of the tavern prior to the raid. Sometimes tavern owners would allow themselves to be "raided" and pay the fine to avoid any suspicions.

Hillsboro (Henry)
(2003)
Hillsboro was laid out in 1840. Hillsboro (or Hillsborough) was originally called Washington, but changed the name when it was discovered there was already a Washington, Iowa.

Holbrook (Iowa)
(2006)
Holbrook was settled in 1850. It was named for Mr. N. B. Holbrook who was a surveyor and president of the Marengo Saving Bank.

Holland (Grundy)
(1978), (1983), (1989), (1995)
Holland was incorporated in 1897. B. Van der laf named the town because the areas terrain reminded him of his place of birth.

Homer (Hamilton)
(1995)
Founded in 1853 and named for the Greek poet Homer. Homer is the legendary author of the *Iliad* and the *Odyssey*, two epic poems that are the central works of ancient Greek literature.
Item of interest
In August of each year, Homer holds an annual threshing bee. Originally, local people worked together to get the season's threshing done. Today the original purpose is largely obsolete, but the festival tradition lives on.

Homestead (Iowa)
(1976), (2008), (2011)
(See Amana)
Item of interest
A meteorite struck the town in 1875.

Honey Creek Resort (Appanoose)
(2019)
Honey Creek State Park Resort opened in 2008 and is Iowa's first state-run resort. It has more than a hundred guest rooms, an 18-hole golf course, and an indoor water park. It is on Rathbun Lake, one of the largest lakes in Iowa. The lake was constructed to control flooding, provide recreation opportunities, abate stream pollution, fish, and maintain minimum stream flow on the Chariton, Missouri, and Mississippi Rivers.

Horton (Bremer)
(1982)
Horton was platted in 1856. It was named for George Horton, one of the first settlers. Horton is an unincorporated community.

Hospers (Sioux)
(1990)
Hospers was founded in 1872 when the St. Paul and Sioux City Railroad was extended to that point. The town was named for Henry Hospers, an Iowa banker and developer who got many Dutch immigrants and Dutch settlers from other parts of the country to relocate to Sioux County.

Houghton (Lee)
(1975), (1992), (1997), (2019)
Houghton was incorporated in 1962. It was once the junction of two rail lines. It was named for L. E. Houghton and his wife who owned the land.

Hudson (Black Hawk)
(1974), (1978), (2010), (2015)
Hudson was platted in 1857. The town was originally name Greenfield but because there was another town named Greenfield, it was renamed Hudson, after the Hudson River in New York.

Hugo (Dubuque and Jackson)
(1999)
Between 1892 and 1895 Hugo was the site of a creamery where Mr. Hugo was the butter maker. This resulted in the town being named after him.

Hull (Sioux)
(2014)
Hull was first named Winland then Pattersonvile for John G. Patterson. In the 1880s the name was changed to Hull for John A. T. Hull, a U.S. Representative from Iowa. Hull was a longtime Republican politician, an experienced government man who served as a representative of the state's 7th district in Congress for 20 years. He also served two terms as the Lieutenant Governor, and two as Iowa's Secretary of State.

Humboldt (Humboldt)
(1978), (1985), (2007)

In 1863, Stephen Harris Taft founded what is now Humboldt. The town was originally called Springvale because of several natural springs found near the Des Moines River. Taft had very big plans for the community, and expected many intellectuals from the East to move to his new community. Springvale was renamed Humboldt in honor of the German explorer and naturalist Alexander von Humboldt.

Taft had five goals for his idyllic community.

- The town shall be surrounded by trees and forests.
- The town shall be free of the sale of intoxicants.
- The town shall be founded upon a saw mill and grist mill on the Des Moines River
- The town shall have the moral fortitude of a solid church and good schools, and that it shall become a town of thinkers and beauty.
- The town shall grow with a college of university importance, and have a church that will not dissent into factions.

Items of interest

Between 1799 and 1804, Friedrich Wilhelm Heinrich Humboldt travelled extensively in both North and South America. His description of the journeys was written up and published in an enormous set of volumes over 21 years. Humboldt was one of the first people to propose that the lands bordering the Atlantic Ocean were once joined (South America and Africa in particular). This important work also motivated a holistic perception of the universe as one interacting entity. In 1831, based on observations generated during his travels, he was the first person to describe the phenomenon of human-induced climate change.

The First National Bank of Humboldt and its shareholders were the primary victims of what the Des Moines Register described as "one of the most spectacular white-collar crimes in state history." In 1982, Humboldt native Gary Vance Lewellyn, then a Des Moines stockbroker, attempted to pump up the value of the stock of a high-tech company by singlehandedly creating phony market demand for the stock. To carry out the scheme, he illegally obtained access to bonds of the First National Bank of Humboldt valued at $16.7 million, and secretly pledged the Bank's bonds as security for his personal orders of the company's stock through a Wall Street investment firm. When Lewellyn missed his margin calls on his stock purchases, the firms obtained the bonds. Suspicious federal regulators closed the Humboldt Bank when it could not account for its missing bonds, consideration was given to, but rejected, to the idea of liquidating the bank. Its accountholders were protected by federal insurance but the shares in the bank became worthless. For his crime, Lewellyn was sentenced to twenty years in prison, but served only five years. Lewellyn died in 2012.

Humeston (Wayne)
(1981), (2016)
Humeston was named after Alva Humeston who owned the land where the town is located. Humeston was incorporated in 1881.

Hutchins (Hancock)
(1985), (2010), (2017)
Hutchins was platted in 1893. The town was named for John Hutchins who settled in the area around 1887.

Huxley (Story)
(1994), (2001)
Huxley was incorporated in 1902. Before the town was formed, the land was purchased by S. S. Merrill, who was the president of the Milwaukee Land company. The village was named Huxley by Merrill's uncle, Thomas Henry Huxley who was a British biologist and defender of Darwinism. Thomas Huxley was a nineteenth century author and biologist and the grandfather of Aldous Huxley, the twentieth century author.

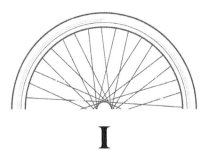

I

Iconium (Appanoose)
(1997), (2009), (2016), (2019)
In 1853, a post office was established and the community was named after the ancient city of Konya, Turkey. Konya in Latin is Iconium.

IDA GROVE (Ida) (County Seat)
(1977), (1988), (2001), (2006)
Ida Grove was founded in 1871 and incorporated in 1878. It was named for Mount Ida, Greece. The town was first known as "Old Ida Grove" and was located on the north side of the river. When the railroad was built on the south side of the river, Ida Grove relocated to the south side of the river.

The first surveyors chose the name Ida because Native Americans camped on a high hill west of Ida Grove, where they had fires burning on top of a hill drying their strips of meat over green sapling frames to preserve it for the winter months. Those fires were so constant and visible all night, that it reminded them of the fires of Mount Ida in Greece.

Imogene (Freemont)
(2016)
Imogene was incorporated in 1881. There are several thoughts on how Imogene got its name. Some believe it was named for the daughter of Captain Anderson, but there is no record of Captain Anderson having a daughter named Imogene. Other Imogenes in the town were Imogene Anderson, who was daughter of the town site manager and Imogene Blanchard who was the railroad superintendent's daughter. There is no evidence that can correctly source the name.

Item of interest
On July 4, 1886, August Werner, Imogene's furniture maker, attempted to be the first person to fly a heavier-than-air machine off

the ground. Some witnesses said he was able to get 4 feet off the ground while other witnesses disagreed. August had success in building model helicopters. He kept increasing their size, but on July 4th his attempt to fly to Washington and then to Germany failed. This aviation visionary spent the rest of his life as a carpenter at the Clarinda Mental Institute. Some of his furniture was used in the state capitol in Des Moines.

INDEPENDENCE (Buchanan) (County Seat)
(1982), (1989), (2007), (2014)
Independence was founded in June of 1847, and given the name because of the approaching July 4th celebration.

Items of Interest

The Independence State Hospital was built in 1873 as the second asylum in the state. The original plan was to relieve crowding at the hospital at Mount Pleasant and to hold alcoholics, geriatrics, drug addicts, mentally ill, and the criminally insane. The hospital has had many names include: The Independence Lunatic Asylum, The Independence State Asylum, The Independence Asylum for the Insane, The Iowa State Hospital for the Insane, and The Independence Mental Health Institute. The hospital has a system of underground tunnels which connects every building. Like most asylums of its time, it had a gruesome and dark history. Remnants of its dark history are the graveyard, hydrotherapy tubs, and lobotomy equipment.

For a few years in the late 1880s and early 1890s, Independence was nationally known as a horse-racing center, sometimes referred to as the "Lexington of the North." This came about as a result of Charles W. Williams financial success. In 1885, with no experience in breeding horses, Williams purchased two mares, each of which within a year gave birth to a stallion. These two stallions, which Williams named Axtel and Allerton, went on to set world trotting records. Williams' earnings enabled him to publish the racing horse newspaper, The American Trotter, to build a large three-story hotel, and an opera house called The Gedney. He also constructed a figure-eight shaped race track on the western edge of town along with a magnificent horse barn. Williams went on to raise other record-breaking horses, but lost much of his fortune in the panic of 1893.

INDIANOLA (Warren) (County Seat)
(1997), (2009), (2019)
Indianola was incorporated in 1863. The town's name was taken from a newspaper account of a Texas town named Indianola.
Items of interest
Indianola is home to the Buxton Park Arboretum, which is a 5.4-acre arboretum and botanical garden that was donated to the town in 1906 by William and Francis Buxton. It contains formal botanical gardens with twelve flowerbeds, an arboretum, a fountain, and a gazebo.

There are only two hot air balloon museums within the United States. One is located in Indianola and the other is in Albuquerque, New Mexico.

Indianola is home to Simpson College, a four-year, coeducational, liberal arts college affiliated with the United Methodist Church. George Washington Carver attended Simpson College before attending Iowa State University in Ames. (See Ames)

Ionia (Chickasaw)
(1977), (2017)
Ionia was the first named Dover, but there was some confusion with the town of Devan, so the name was changed to Chickasaw Station. The Railroad confused the towns of Chickasaw with Chickasaw Station. The town needed a unique name. The story is that in 1883 a railroad man talked about this to one of the locals who said, "I don't care what you call it, I own the lumberyard, I own that land, I own that building," which resulted in the railroad man saying "We'll call it Iona!"

Another thought is that the name Ionia came from the ancient region of the central Anatolia's shore in Asia Minor, one of the most important centers of the Greek world.

Iowa Center (Story)
(1986)
The founders of Iowa Center thought they were at the geographical center of the state and hoped the town would be the State Capitol of Iowa.

IOWA CITY (Johnson) (County Seat)
(1973), (1976), (1990), (1995), (2001), (2006), (2011), (2015), (2018)
Iowa City was created by an act of The Legislative Assembly of the Iowa Territory on January 21, 1839. This fulfilled the desire of Governor Robert Lucas to move the capital out of Burlington and closer to the center of the territory. This made Iowa City the second capital of the Iowa Territory and the first capital city of Iowa when it became a state in 1846.
Items of interest
Founded in 1847, Iowa City is home to The University of Iowa. It is recognized as one of the nation's top public universities, offering more than 100 areas of study for its 29,000 students. The institution's Writers' Workshop is internationally acclaimed, having fostered the creative talents of Ray Bradbury, Flannery O'Connor, Jane Smiley, and Kurt Vonnegut. The University also includes one of the largest university-owned teaching hospitals in the nation, providing patient care within 16 medical specialties. The University of Iowa Hospitals and Clinics have been named one of "America's Best Hospitals" by U.S. News & World Report.

The Old Capitol building is a National Historic Landmark in the center of the University of Iowa campus. While Iowa City was selected as the territorial capital in 1839, it did not officially become the capital until 1841, after construction on the capitol building had begun. The capitol building was completed in 1842, and the last four territorial legislatures and the first six Iowa General Assemblies met there until 1857, when the state capital was moved to Des Moines. Iowa City was compensated for its loss of the state capital with the establishment of the University of Iowa.

Iowa City has long been involved in politics. With the election of Moses Bloom in 1873, they had the first Jewish mayor of any American city, and with the election of Emma J. Harvat as mayor in 1923, they had the first woman elected mayor in a city with more than 10,000 inhabitants.

The 1970 riots made news nationwide and the Spring of 1970 was a tumultuous time on many college campuses. On April 30, President Richard Nixon announced that United States forces would invade Cambodia. Students around the country protested this escalation of the Vietnam War. On May 4, the National Guard fired on students at Kent State University in Ohio, killing 4 and wounding 9. This ignited protests all over the country. Anti-war protests were not new to Iowa City or elsewhere in Iowa. Protests had been occurring throughout the 1960s, but the Spring of 1970 was different.

After the Kent State shootings, University of Iowa students marched on the National Guard Armory and downtown businesses breaking windows. The City Council gave the mayor curfew powers. On May 6, there was a student boycott of classes. That night about 400 people had a "sleep-in" in front of the Old Capitol on the campus and about 50 people broke into the Old Capitol and set off a smoke bomb. The protesters left voluntarily when asked to do so. Around 2 am Friday, University President Boyd requested the highway patrolmen arrest students on the Pentacrest (the Pentacrest is the Old Capitol and a collection of four buildings that surround the Old Capitol on the campus of the University of Iowa). By the next day, he regretted the mass arrests and said he had received faulty information. On May 8, President Boyd cancelled the 89th annual Governor's day ROTC observance that was to be held the following day. On Friday and Saturday, a National Guard helicopter circled the Pentacrest.

In the early morning hours of Saturday May 9, the Old Armory Temporary, also known as "Big Pink," which housed the writing lab, was burned down. By Sunday morning, President Boyd tried to bring an end to protests by giving students the option to leave and take the grade they currently had or stay and attend classes.

During this time, there was also a strong ROTC presence on campus. Their presence and the academic credit they received for their service was called into question by both students and faculty, but Boyd said he could not abolish the ROTC. Eventually protest ceased and calm returned to campus.

> On September 2, 2017, a tradition started at the University of Iowa's Kinnick Football Stadium. At the end of the first quarter, all the players and fans in the stadium turn and face the University of Iowa Stead Family Children's Hospital, which overlooked the stadium, then they waved to the families and children looking out the hospital windows. The tradition continues today.

In the Oakland Cemetery, there is a Black Angel that, according to a legend, if touched at midnight on Halloween will bring death within seven years.

> Iowa City is home to The Grant Wood Art Colony which celebrates the life and legacy of Iowa's most famous artist. Grant Wood painted one of the most recognizable images in the world which he called American Gothic. At one time, Wood was also on the faculty of the University of Iowa.

On June 11, 2008, the Iowa River caused major flooding. Water exceeded the emergency spillway at the Coralville Reservoir outside of Iowa City, resulting in the city and the University of Iowa being seriously affected by unprecedented flooding. There was widespread property damage and forced evacuations in large sections of the city.

> Janet Guthrie was born in Iowa City. She is a retired professional race car driver and the first woman to qualify and compete in both the Indianapolis 500 and the Daytona 500.

Iowa Falls, (Hardin)
(1978), (1995), (2004)

Iowa Falls was platted in 1856 and named for the falls on the Iowa River.

Item of interest

Iowa Falls is home to Ellsworth Community College which was founded in 1890 by Eugene S. Ellsworth. Originally a private business academy, it later became a four-year college, a music conservatory, and a public junior college before being absorbed into the Iowa Valley Community College system.

Ira (Jasper)
(2001)
Ira was platted in 1883 and originally named Rippey and then Millard.

There are two theories of how the town got the name Ira. One theory is it was named after a railroad superintendent. The other theory is that it was named after a resident named Ira.

Ireton (Sioux)
(1998)
Ireton was platted and named for Henry Ireton, who served under Oliver Cromwell during the English Civil War.

Iron Hill (Jackson)
(1991)
Iron Hill was platted in 1859. It is believed that the town got its name from the iron deposits found in the area.

Irwin (Shelby)
(1994), (2001)
Irwin was incorporated in 1892 and named for E. W. Irwin, the property owner.

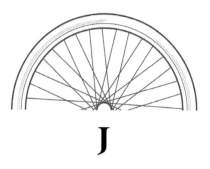

J

Jackson Junction (Winneshiek)
(1987), (2005)
The town is located in Jackson township and was first known as Alba then later New Alba and on December 7, 1891, the name was changed to Jackson Junction. This was a stop on the Milwaukee Railroad where passengers would transfer to another train.

Jacksonville (Shelby)
(1983)
Jacksonville was established in 1897 and originally mainly settled by the Danish. It was named after Jackson township.

JEFFERSON (Greene) (County Seat)
(1976), (1989), (1994), (2008), (2018)
Jefferson was incorporated in 1872. It originally was named New Jefferson after Thomas Jefferson but later dropped the "New."
<u>Items of interest</u>
Jefferson is the home of the Mahanay Memorial Bell Tower, a 168-foot tall structure, located on the town square, and visible for miles. The tower is named for Floyd Mahanay, a businessman, philanthropist, and former resident. It has a 47-bell carillon at the top which is operated by a digital piano used for weddings, birthdays, funerals, and even the local high school's fight song after games. For many years, the tower provided the current time with a recording of the Westminster Chimes. An elevator in the tower takes visitors to the observation deck for stunning views where they can see cornfields in 5 different Iowa counties.

The city is the birth place of George Horace, an American pioneer of survey sampling techniques. He created the

Gallup Poll, a successful statistical method for measuring public opinion.

Jefferson is home to the 1875 Historical Furniture Shop and Museum where master furniture maker Robby Pedersen has more than 20 years of experience building historically accurate furniture using only the tools, techniques and finishes used in 1875.

Jerico (Chickasaw)
(1987)
The town is named for Jericho as described in the Hebrew Bible as the city of palm trees. It is an unincorporated town.

Jesup (Buchanan and Black Hawk)
(1989), (1998)
Jesup was founded in 1858 and was named for Morris Ketchum Jesup, president of the Dubuque and Sioux City Railroad.
Item of interest
Jesup was once considered a dry town and became known as the "Banner temperance town of the country."

Jewell (Hamilton)
(1983), (1989), (2012)
Jewell was founded in 1880. Originally known as Jewell Junction which was named for D. T. Jewel, the original owner of the town site. The town slogan is "A Gem in a Friendly Setting."
Item of interest
In 1893, the Jewell Lutheran College Association established a college with the majority members being Scandinavian Lutherans. In 1903, the main college building burned killing two students. In February of 1904 two new buildings were built. The college closed in 1925.

Johnston (Polk)
(1988)
Johnston was established in 1905 as a station on the railway between Des Moines and Perry, known as Johnston Station. It was named for the railroad's freight supervisor, John F. Johnston.

Joice (Worth)
(1987), (1996)
Joice had its start with the building of the Chicago and North Western Railroad through the territory. Joice was incorporated in 1913 and named for R. M. Joice, a local banker.

Jolley (Calhoun)
(1979), (1995), (1998
Jolley was incorporated in 1895. The town was named for a railroad lawyer named O. J. Jolley.

Jubilee (Black Hawk)
(2010)
Jubilee is an unincorporated community.

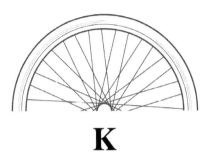

K

Kalo (Webster)
(1995)
In the 1880's, Kalo was founded by the Kalo Coal Mine Company. The word Kalo is Greek for beautiful.

Kalona (Washington)
(2018)
Kalona was established by the railroad in 1879. The name was suggested by a Mr. Myers, who owned a bull named Kalona. The town remained unincorporated until 1890.

Item of interest
An Amish settlement in the Kalona area began in the 1840s, placing them among the first Europeans in the area. These immigrants came to America from Switzerland and settled first in Pennsylvania. As their numbers increased they moved west to Ohio and then Iowa. They have an interesting history and practice unusual customs. Their history dates back to the Protestant reformation of 1525. They and the Amish Mennonites began with similar customs but through the years have divided mostly along lines of acceptance to change. Kalona was settled by the Old Order Amish who have changed little since that time. The less conservative Amish Mennonites split with the Old Order Amish in the 1880s and later assimilated in the community and lost their identity. Today there are 5 main degrees of conservativism in Kalona: Old Order Amish, New Order Amish, Beachy Amish, Conservative Mennonite, and Mennonite. The differences are usually recognized by the way they accept modern conveniences. The Old Order still use horses to farm and travel and also accept the Ordnung (rules for living), forbidding the use of color in their dress or homes. They have no electricity which means no TV, phones or electric appliances. The Beachy Amish can only drive tractors with steel wheels and black cars. Most Mennonites enjoy a modern way of life while

practicing traditional religious beliefs. The Amish have their own schools which are supervised by the consolidated district of Mid Prairie Schools. Many Amish are bilingual or tri lingual. Among themselves they speak Low German (similar to Pennsylvania Dutch), High German is reserved for church services, and English is spoken with outsiders.

Most Amish have religious objections to being photographed. The Amish in Kalona still practice shunning, a sad happening in a family when one breaks rules of living causing them to be cut from eating or talking with their family. The most important thing to remember about this unusual group is that they are people of faith whose practices reflect their beliefs.

Kalona Historical Village is made up of 15 restored historical building filled with interesting and informative displays, depicting the years the pioneers settled the Iowa prairies. The site includes two nationally-known quilt galleries, one strictly for Amish textiles and the other displaying a themed group of quilts. The Village houses the United States' premier collection of spool cabinets, as well as a collection of gems and antique glass and other collectibles.

Kamrar (Hamilton)
(1983), (2012)

Kamrar was platted in 1881 and named in honor of Judge J. M. Kamrar, a prominent lawyer of the area, who served as an officer of the Chicago & Northwestern Railway Company.

Kanawha (Hancock)
(1987), (1990)

Kanawha was platted in 1899 when the newly constructed railroad arrived from Belmond. Kanawha's founder, George Casper Call, petitioned Congressman J.P. Dolliver requesting a post office and proposing a town name of "Luzon." Luzon was rejected because it was thought to be too close to Luzerne in Benton County. Faced with having to find another name, a railroad engineer and West Virginia native suggested Kanawha, which is a county in West Virginia named for an Indian tribe.

Kellerton (Ringgold)
(1981), (1992), (2003), (2016)

Kellerton was incorporated in 1881 and named in honor of Judge Isacc W. Keller, one of the leading Ringgold County citizens. The site of Kellerton was purchased on high level ground where, on a clear day, one can see Mount Ayr to the west and Leon to the east.

Kelley (Story)
(1973), (2011)
A post office was established in 1875 and once called Hubbell, for a railroad contractor. The city was renamed for J. T. Kelly, who was the land owner. The "e" was added by the Post Office Department.

Kellogg (Jasper)
(1976)
Kellogg was laid out in 1865. It has had four names since its beginning: Manning Station; Jasper City; Kimball for A. Kimball Esquire who was a railroad superintendent; then Kellogg for Judge Abel Avery Kellogg.

Kensett (Worth)
(1987), (1996)
Kensett was platted in 1872, shortly after the railroad was built through the territory. It was named for a Baltimore oyster packer named Thomas Kensett, who promised to build a church in town if it was named for him. He never fulfilled his promise.

Item of interest
Kensett was home to Hans Langseth, who was credited with holding the world's record for the longest beard at 17 feet and 6 inches. He was born in Norway in 1846, then immigrated to the United States as a young man and settled in Kensett. He stopped shaving at the age of 19, entered a beard growing contest and decided to keep it. Hans spent much of his life as a farmer, but for a while, he traveled with a circus, known as King Whiskers, exhibiting his beard to the public. He got tired and left the circus for having numerous nonbelievers yank at his whiskers to see if they were real. When Hans died, he left his surviving children with a final wish. After his open-casket funeral, he wanted to have his beard cut off and stored for posterity. His son acquiesced, lopping off his father's beard before the

casket was buried. The beard sat tucked away in an attic box for decades before his son donated the beard to the Smithsonian.

KEOKUK (Lee) (County Seat)
(1981), (1992, (2019)
Keokuk was incorporated in 1848. It is named for Chief Keokuk, a chief of the Sac and Fox Indians. Keokuk is located at the junction of the Des Moines and the Mississippi Rivers, in the extreme southeast corner of the state on bluffs approximately 200 feet high. Much of the city's history centers on the life of Chief Keokuk. He was born in 1788 to a mother who was allegedly a French half-breed. His bones were brought to Keokuk in 1883 from Kansas and reinterred in Rand Park beneath a massive stone pedestal topped by a life-sized statue of the Indian chieftain. On the east side of this monument is embedded the marble slab taken from the grave in Kansas which says, "Sacred to the memory of Keokuck, a distinguished Sac chief born at Rock Island in 1788. Died in April, 1848." Keokuk, "The Watchful Fox," was not a hereditary chief, but raised himself to dignity by the force of talent and enterprise. He was a man of extraordinary eloquence in council and never at a loss in an emergency. He was a noble looking man about six feet tall, weighing over 200 pounds. He had an eagle eye, dignified bearing, and a manly, intelligent expression of approval. Keokuck advocated for peace with the white settlers

Items of interest

In 1820, the US Army prohibited soldiers stationed along the Mississippi River from having wives who were Native American. Dr. Samuel C. Muir, a surgeon stationed at Fort Edwards, resigned his commission rather than leave his Native American wife, then crossed the river to resettle. He built a log cabin at the bottom of the bluff, and became the area's first white settler.

The settlement was part of the land designated in 1824 as a Half-Breed Tract by the United States Government for allotting land to mixed race descendants of the Sauk and Fox tribes. Children of European or British men (fur traders and trappers) and Native women, were often excluded from tribal communal lands because their fathers were not tribal members. Native Americans considered the settlement neutral ground.

Rules for the tract prohibited individual from selling the land, but the US Congress ended this provision in 1837, creating a land rush and instability.

During the Civil War, Keokuk became an embarkation point for all of Iowa's soldiers. 80,000 Iowans were temporarily in Keokuk on their way to participate in the war. Five large hospitals were established to care for the wounded who were brought north on the river. As a result, Keokuk now has the only national cemetery for Iowans who died in the Civil War.

KEOSAUQUA (Van Buren) (County Seat)
(1981), (1997), (2003), (2013)
Keosauqua (kee-e-saw-kwe) The word Keosauqua is derived from the Meskwaki and Sauk name for the Des Moines River. "Ke-o-saw-qua", which literally translates as "Bend in the River." It was incorporated in 1855.

Items of interest
Overlooking the Des Moines River is Lacey-Keosauqua State Park with 19 mounds where Indians buried their dead. The park was originally named Big Bend for the curve in the river, but was renamed to honor Iowa congressman John Lacey, who campaigned for conservation decades before Teddy Roosevelt took up the charge. Lacey-Keosauqua is one of the largest state parks in Iowa. It was built by the Civil Conservation Corps during the Great Depression.

The Honey War was fought south of Keosauqua in what is now Lacey-Keosauqua State Park. A dispute over the state boundary between Missouri and Iowa almost caused a honey of a war. Only a matter of timing kept both state militias from expanding a legal dispute into a real war. In the late 1830s, Missouri claimed a strip of land nearly 13 miles into what many settlers considered Iowa territory.

When Missouri tax collectors cut down valuable bee trees as payment for taxes that settlers refused to pay, more than 1,200 Iowans lined up along the disputed border with pitchforks for revenge. History marks what is known today as the Honey War of 1839 as Missouri's most significant boundary dispute. There were no casualties. Bee trees might not seem worth fighting over, but our ancestors relied on honey because sugar was so scarce. Taking a supply of honey was almost as bad as stealing a horse.

The Van Buren County Courthouse is the oldest courthouse in Iowa and is the second oldest in continuous use in the United States.

The Pearson House is a stone and brick home built in 1847 that was a station on the Underground Railroad for runaway slaves. Officially, slavery never existed in Iowa and was generally viewed as an economic evil, but few settlers were willing to share with African-Americans the rights and privileges enjoyed by most white men. Among the people in Iowa who violently opposed slavery were Quakers, who were convinced that all people should have equal rights. Quakers throughout northern America and thousands of other settlers from New England joined in forming a network known as the Underground Railroad that funneled former slaves from deep within the south to freedom in Canada. Evidence exists in both Bentonsport and Keosauqua participated in this noble effort.

Keosauqua once had a higher percentage of black people than any other town or city in Iowa. Iowa was assembled as a free territory, but southern settlers and government officials brought in a few slaves, and laws were soon passed addressing the situation. For example, on April 1, 1839 a law was passed which stated that no "black or mulatto" was permitted to settle in Iowa Territory unless he could present "a fair certificate of actual freedom" under the seal of a judge, and provide a $500 retainer bond as surety against becoming a public charge.

In Keosauqua, on the banks of the Des Moines River, is Hotel Manning which is a classic example of Steamboat Gothic architecture that has welcomed guests continuously since 1899. As she enters her second century, this beloved historic Iowa landmark is more than ever the belle of

Van Buren County, an irreplaceable link between Iowa at the turn of the century and our country as we experience it today.

Keota (Washington)
(1986), (2018)
Keota was incorporated in 1873 and there are two theories of how the town got its name:

- One is that Keota was derived from a Native American word meaning "gone to visit" or "the fire is gone out."
- Another is that Reverend D. V. Smock suggested the name Keoton, being the first and last letters of Keokuk and Washington Counties, but either the Rock Island Railroad or Post Office Department changed to Keota.

Item of interest
In 2012, Keota was named the most extroverted city in the United States.

Kesley (Butler)
(2007)
A post office in Kesley has been in operation since 1900. The community was named for Kesley Green, a local farmer.

Keswick (Keokuk)
(1975), (1979), (1988), (1995), (2018)
The town was surveyed in 1879 and named for Keswick, England, the home town of a local woman who had offered lodging to the railroad track-laying crew.

Keystone (Benton)
(2004)
Keystone was platted in 1881 when the Chicago, Milwaukee, and St. Paul Railroad was extended to the town. The real reason for selecting the name of Keystone has never been definitely settled. Some believe that it is almost the central point between the Chicago and Omaha railroad line, thus the name represents the central part or the Keystone of the line. Another theory is that the land company, finding a considerable German

element among the early residents, erroneously concluded that they were "Pennsylvania Dutch" emigrants and named the town from the nickname of Pennsylvania, the Keystone State. Keystone was incorporated in 1894.

Item of interest

Home of the Darold Sindt Antique Museum which features approximately 200 tractors and implements, plus riding lawn mowers, pedal tractors and other interesting collectibles.

Kilduff (Jasper)
(1991)

Killduff is an unincorporated community with a post office that opened in 1883.

Kimballton (Audubon)
(1974), (1976), (1980), (1983), (1986), (2008), (2011), (2013)

Kimballton was founded in 1883 and incorporated in 1908. It was named for a railroad employee, Edward Kimball.

Items of interest

Since 1978, a replica of the famous Little Mermaid statue that is located in Copenhagen, Denmark has sat in the fountain at the city park. Hans Christian Andersen's famous tale is about a young mermaid who was willing to give up her life in the sea as a mermaid to gain a human soul.

The Danish villages of Elk Horn and Kimballton are the two largest rural Danish settlements in the United States.

The art of Danish folk dancing has long been a part of Kimballton's rich heritage and continues today. Some 100 persons, from kindergartners through grandparents are involved in the folk-dance program.

Kingsley (Plymouth)
(1973), (2001), (2010), (2015)

Kingsley was originally known as the village Quorn and named after Quorn Hunt, England. The village was later relocated a mile to what is now Kingsley, due to a railroad not going through Quorn. In 1883, every business, except for a mill, moved to Kingsley.

It was founded in 1884 and named for Nahum P. Kingsley, who laid out the city in 1883. At a celebration of the town's centennial, former United States President Ronald Raegan wrote: "The spirit which has built and sustained your community reflects the energy which has forged America into a land of wonder."

Item of interest

Kingsley is known for its black squirrels which has been the town's trademark for many years. Black squirrels have a genetic mutation caused by a faulty pigment gene (a black pigment) which causes them to be black.

Kingston (Des Moines)
(1979), (2000)
Kingston was founded in 1885 and named for its founder, W. King.

Kirkville (Wapello)
(2003)
John Kirkpatrick laid out the town and on 1848 it was named for him.

Kiron (Crawford)
(1987), (2001), (2004)
Kiron was platted in 1899 and was supposedly named for a place in China.

Klinger (Bremer)
(2007)
Klinger was first settled around 1855. It was named for its founder, Francis Klinger. Klinger is an unincorporated community.

Knierim (Calhoun)
(1995), (2004)
The city was founded by William and Wilhelmina Knierim in 1899 and incorporated in 1901.

Item of interest

Texas outlaws Bonnie and Clyde and members of their Barrow Gang were suspects in the holdups of at least three Iowa banks. One of those banks was the State Savings Bank in Knierim on February 1, 1934. A woman thought to be Parker, who was often reported to be the driver of the get-away car, was thought to have been seen in Knierim. The car used in the Knierim robbery had the same Arkansas license plate found on the abandoned car in Louisiana in which Bonnie and Clyde were killed by Texas and Louisiana Peace officers on May 23, 1934.

Knox (Clarke)
(1992)
Knox is an unincorporated community.

KNOXVILLE (Marion) (County Seat)
(1988), (1991), (1992), (2000), (2013)
Knoxville was incorporated in 1855 and named for General Henry Knox to commemorate his service in the American Revolutionary War.
Items of interest
Knoxville is home of the National Sprint Car Hall of Fame and Museum located next to the famous Knoxville Raceway dirt track.

Knoxville is home of Dixie Cornell Gebhardt, who, was a leader of the Daughters of the American Revolution in Iowa during World War I and designer of the Iowa's state flag.

Lake Red Rock, which is the largest lake in Iowa, is located some six miles north of Knoxville. The town of Red Rock ended in 1968/1969 when it was flooded by the creation of the Red Rock Dam and Lake. The dam was built by the Army Corps of Engineers as a flood and erosion control reservoir.

Kossuth (Des Moines)
(2000)
Kossuth started in 1835 and named for Louis Kossuth (1802-1894), the Hungarian patriot and exile leader of the revolt of 1849. He was a marvelous linguist and a very effective public speaker. Kossuth made a tour of the United States in 1851-52 where he delivered many eloquent addresses on behalf of Hungarian independence.

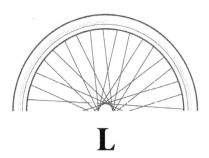

L

Lacona (Warren)
(1997), (2003), (2009), (2019)
Lacona was incorporated in 1881 and originally known as Jefferson, but changed its name to Lacona in 1857 because there was already another Jefferson, Iowa. The name Lacona possibly comes from Greek Laconia, the region of Greece ruled by the Spartans. The modern English word "laconic" comes from the same source.

Ladora (Iowa)
(1976), (1986), (1991), (2006), (2011)
Ladora was incorporated in 1879. When deciding upon a name, Mrs. General Scofield, a music teacher, conceived of taking the musical syllables "la," "do," and "ra" thus spelling Ladora.

Lake Ahquabi State Park (Warren)
(2019)
Ahquabi means "resting place" in the Fox Language. The lake is a 115-acre man made reservoir.

Lake City (Calhoun)
(1975), (1981), (2012)
Lake City was founded in 1856 and took its name came from Lake Creek, which flowed out of a nearby lake.
<u>Items of interest</u>
The sign coming into town proudly proclaims that Lake City has "Everything but a Lake."

Lake Mills (Winnebago)
(1996), (2005)

Lake Mills was incorporated in 1880. The town was first called Slaunchville, but in 1864 was renamed to Lake Mills for its grist mill.

Items of interest

In 1862 and 1863 settlers from the surrounding countryside demanded a grist mill which could be used the entire year. Most of the water mills were either dry or frozen almost every winter, requiring people to carry their grain about forty miles to get it transformed into flour. In 1864, a grist mill was constructed using water flowing out of nearby Rice Lake.

Lake View (Sac)

(1975), (1981), (1995), (2004), (2012)

Lake View was first called Fletcher but in 1887, when the town was incorporated, changed its name to Lake View for the scenic view of Black Hawk Lake named for Chief Black Hawk.

Items of interest

Black Hawk Lake is the southernmost natural glacial lake in the United States.

It's fitting that Lake View's 9–foot concrete statue of the Sauk Chief Black Hawk has a steel spine. The man it honors resisted white settlement for decades, conceding his homeland to the United States government only in the last few years of his life. Chief Black Hawk said. "It [the land] is now yours. Keep it as we did. It will produce good crops," he told a crowd in Fort Madison on July 4, 1838, a few months before his death in October at the age of 70 or 71.

Lambs Grove (Jasper)

(1975), (1984), (2000), (2006), (2018)

Lambs Grove was founded in 1927 and named for Richard Lamb. It was incorporated on December 29, 1952.

LaMoille (Marshall)

(1994)

The town was platted in 1867 and named LaMoille after the LaMoille, River in Vermont.

Lamoni (Decatur)
(1981)
The city was named after Lamoni, a king mentioned in the Book of Mormon. The area was first settled in 1834 to 1840 by people who thought they were settling in the slave-owning State of Missouri. It was only after the Sullivan Line, which separating Missouri and Iowa, was formally surveyed and when Iowa became a state in 1846, that it was realized the slave owning settlers were in non-slave-owning Iowa. In 1816, The **Sullivan Line** originally marked three quarters of the border between Missouri and Iowa with an extension of it forming the remaining border line. The line was initially created to establish the limits of Native American territory where they would not be permitted south of the border. Disputes over the boundary were to erupt into the Honey War. (See Keosauqua for Honey War)

Items of interest
In 1870, Joseph Smith III authorized the Order of Enoch to purchase over three thousand acres to form a community of the Reorganized Church of Jesus Christ of Latter Day Saints (RLDS Church). Smith lived at Liberty Hall which is now a museum.

Graceland University was established as Graceland College in 1895 by the RLDS Church. The main campus is in Lamoni. The name "Graceland" was selected by Col. George Barrett, the land surveyor for the college, for the graceful slope of the hill upon which the college was built.

Lamont (Buchanan)
(1993), (1999), (2007), (2014)
Lamont was first settled in 1852 and first called Erie, then Ward's Corners. The railroad changed the name to Lamont, according to some authorities.

La Motte (Jackson)
(1999), (2007)
La Motte was planned in 1873 and incorporate in 1879. It was named for Alexander La Motte, one if its founders.

Lanesboro (Carroll)
(1975), (1988), (1994) (2011)
Lanesboro had its start in 1901 with the building of the Mason City and Fort Dodge Railroad through the territory. It was named for Julius Lane, an early settler.

Lansing (Allamakee)
(1977), (2017)
Lansing was platted around 1851 and named because the first settler was a native of Lansing, Michigan.

Item of interest

Lansing is home to the River History Museum, which has a collection of antique commercial fishing gear, boat motors, button-making industries equipment and much more.

(See Waukon for county seat battle)

La Porte City (Black Hawk)
(1983), (2015)
La Porte City was platted in 1855 and named for La Porte, Indiana, the former home of one of its founders.

Items of interest

Legend has it that at the time of the town's beginning, surveyors were lured into town by strategically placed jugs of whiskey along the route between Cedar Falls and Cedar Rapids.

In the 1880's it was customary for the bride and groom to take some wedding cake and other treats to the printer's office, then he (the printer's devil) would toast the happy couple and write an article about the wedding. Sometimes the writer would get carried away and almost forget to tell about the wedding.

In an 1872 list of rules for teachers found in La Porte City stated the following:

"Teachers each day will fill lamps, clean chimneys and trim wicks. Each teacher will bring a bucket of water and a scuttle of coal for the day's session. After ten hours of school, the teacher should spend the remaining time reading the Bible or other good works. The teacher who performs his labors faithfully and without fault for five years will be given an increase of 25 cents per week in his pay if the Board of Education approves."

Laurens (Pocahontas)
(1977), (2007)
Laurens was platted in 1881 and named in honor of father and son Henry and John Laurens, French Huguenots who were patriotic and loyal to the Colonial cause during the Revolution.

Lawler (Chickasaw)
(2017)
Lawler was first called Crane Creek but renamed Lawler for John Lawler, who was an early settler instrumental in bringing the railroad to the settlement. The town was incorporated in 1871.

Leando-Douds (Van Buren)
(2019)
Douds was platted in 1866 by brothers Eliab and David Doud and originally called Doud's Station. Douds was never officially incorporated. On the southern bank of the Des Moines River lies Douds' "Twin City," Leando. Leando is the older but smaller town. It was settled in the 1830s and originally called Portland. Until the construction of the first iron bridge in 1898, the towns of Douds and Portland saw much rivalry. Now Douds and Leando are considered as one community.
Items of interest
In the original deed, it was stipulated by the Doud brothers that there was to be no buying or selling of intoxicating liquors in the town. This was upheld until the 1990s when Rob Moore began selling alcohol in his grocery store.

Douds is home to Douds Stone Inc. which operates one of the largest underground limestone mines in the state.

The Farmers and Traders Savings Bank, founded 1910, is located in Douds and was one of the few banks to survive the Great Depression.

> Douds is the birth place of John Fremont "J.F." "Grandpa" McCullough who in 1938, with his son Alex, developed the soft-serve ice cream formula. They convinced a friend and loyal customer of his dairy business to offer the product at his ice cream store in Kankakee, Illinois. On the first day of sales within two hours, Noble dished out more than 1,600 servings of the new dessert. In 1940, Noble and the McCulloughs opened the first Dairy Queen store in Joliet, Illinois.

Lebanon (Van Buren)
(1981), (1997), (2003), (2019)
In 1850, the Lebanon post office was first established under the name of Indian Prairie and later changed to Lebanon. It is an unincorporated community.

Le Claire (Scott)
(2008)
The city takes its name from Antoine Le Clairea, a trader of First Nations-French Canadian descent who originally owned the land. Although the city's official name is "Le Claire," it is often spelled "Le Claire," and has also been recorded as "Le Clare." It was incorporated in 1855.
Items of interest
Le Claire is known as the site of the reality television series American Pickers.

> Le Claire is the birthplace of William Frederick Cody, aka Buffalo Bill Cody. The Buffalo Bill Museum is located in Le Claire and contains memorabilia from his Wild West Show.

Tugfest is an annual three-day-long event held in early August in which a rope is stretched across the Mississippi River from Le Claire, Iowa to Port Byron, Illinois, for a tug off. There are 10 men's teams of 20 and one woman's team of 25, who tug against each other. The team which pulls the most rope wins and then the state wins the Tugfest.

From December to March at Lock and Dam 14 on the Mississippi River, Le Claire offers some of the best bald eagle photography opportunities in the continental United States. The migrating eagles congregate at the lock and dam area to catch fish.

Ledges State Park (Boone)
(2018)
The area was designated one of the first of Iowa's state parks in 1924, and today is one of its most visited parks. The park contains a sandstone gorge carved by Pea's Creek, a tributary of the Des Moines River. The gorge is 100 feet deep in places.

Leeds (Woodberry)
(2015)
Leeds was established in 1889. Leeds was built as a manufacturing suburb of Sioux City that included a flourmill, a stove works, a shoe factory and an engine and iron works factory. At the turn of the 20th century, Leeds began to evolve into the residential area as it is known today. It was named after Leeds, England which is also a manufacturing town.

Le Grand (Marshall and Tama)
(1979), (1994), (1995), (2008)
Le Grand was incorporated in 1891. It was named for Le Grande Byington, the original owner of the town site.

Lehigh (Webster)
(1973), (1995), (2012)

Lehigh was first settled in 1855. The town is divided by the Des Moines River, which was unusual for such a small town. Originally the two halves of Lehigh were two separate towns. While the town on the west side of the River was always called Lehigh. The east town was called Slabtown because slabs scrap from the saw mill were used in construction. Both towns were later named Lehigh which came from comparing it to the local coal veins of those in Pennsylvania's Lehigh Valley.

Le Mars (Plymouth) (County Seat)
(1982), (1993), (1998), (2005)
Le Mars was platted in 1869 and first called St. Paul Junction. Railroad magnate John I. Blair hosted an excursion of the new town and asked the ladies to rename the town. The towns name was based on the first initial of **L**ucy Ford, **L**aura Walker, **E**llen Cleghorn, **E**lizabeth Underhill, **M**artha Weare, **M**ary Weare, **A**deline Swain, **R**ebicca Smith and **S**arah Reynolds. (Some letters represent more than one person) Delmar was similarly named.

Item of interest

During the Great Depression in 1933 when banks foreclosed on many farmers, Le Mars caught the attention of the nation, according to an account by historian Arthur Schlesinger, Jr., when over five hundred farmers crowded the Le Mars court room. The farmers were there to demand that Judge Charles C. Bradley suspend foreclosure proceedings until a recently passed laws could be considered. Judge Bradley refused. One farmer remarked that the court room wasn't his alone and that the farmers had paid for it with their taxes. The crowd rushed the judge, slapped him, and placed a rope around his neck and a hub cap on his head. However, they did not lynch him.

In 1913, Fred H. Wells opened a milk route in Le Mars. By 1925, Wells and his sons had opened an ice cream manufacturing plant. The plant and the Wells name was purchased by Fairmount Ice Cream in 1928. In 1935, Fred and his sons sought to begin selling ice cream again, but could no longer use their name. They therefore sponsored a "Name That Ice Cream" contest in the Sioux

City Journal. The winner of the $25 prize suggested "Blue Bunny," because his son had enjoyed seeing blue bunnies in department store windows at Easter.

Dominating the skyline of present-day Le Mars is Wells' Blue Bunny Dairy's, a 900,000-square-foot plant with a 12-story refrigeration tower called the "South Ice Cream Plant," named because it is on the south side of town. The plant is a major employer in the area and each year the plant produced 150 million gallons of ice cream. The plant can also produce 1 million ice cream sandwiches a day. The milk comes mainly from three large Iowa dairy farms. Each hour on average, 365 days a year, the factory unloads one tanker truck of milk. The size of this plant has led to speculation that the company is the world's largest family-owned and managed dairy processor and the world's largest manufacturer of ice cream at one location, resulting in Le Mars claiming to be the "Ice Cream Capital of the World." Wells is best known for its various sweet products, including Blue Bunny, Bomb Pop, Blue Ribbon, and Chilly Cow. Le Mars is home to the Ice Cream Capital of the World Museum.

LEON (Decatur) (County Seat)
(1981), (1992), (2003), (2016)
Leon was incorporated in 1858 and first named Independence, but there was already a town name Independence so in 1854, by act of the legislature, the name was changed to Leon. The name of Leon was suggested by W. H. Cheevers who found a liking to the name while serving as a soldier in the Mexican War.

Item of interest
The earliest settlers who came from 1834 to 1840, thought they were settling in Missouri. In those days, many had intense feelings and marked division over the slavery issue. Several settlers located in Missouri because it allowed slave holding. They miscalculated by a few miles on the boundary and found they could not hold slaves in the Iowa Territory.

In 1940, after a gypsy queen died, a wake was held and, according to custom, thieving ceased until after the burial.

Letts (Louisa)
(2016)
Letts was established in 1855. It was first called Lettsville for Madison Letts, but later renamed Letts. Madison Letts was a pioneer who owned about 4,000 acres of farmland.

Lewis (Cass)
(1989), (2011)
Lewis is located in Cass County and was named for Lewis Cass. The town took his first name for their towns name, leaving the last name for the county. The town was incorporated in 1874.
Item of interest
Lewis Cass was an American military officer, politician, and statesman. He represented Michigan and served in the Cabinets of Presidents Andrew Jackson and James Buchanan. He was also the 1848 Democratic presidential nominee and a leading spokesman for the Doctrine of Popular Sovereignty, which held that white people in each territory should decide whether to permit slavery

> The Lewis home of Reverend George B. Hitchcock was a welcome place for runaway slaves and abolitionists who traveled through the state. A minister of the Congregational Church, Hitchcock was an ardent abolitionist and an agent for the Underground Railroad. From his house, Hitchcock carried out his Underground Railroad activities, providing shelter to fugitive slaves on their way northward.

In 1927, Edwin Elijah Perkins, who was born in Lewis, invented the powdered drink mix Kool-Aid.

Liberty (Clarke)
(1992)
The town of Liberty was laid out by Alfred Rhodes in 1855. Liberty is an unincorporated community.

Liberty Center (Warren)
(2019)

Liberty Center is an unincorporated community laid out in 1875. It was named after Liberty township and is at the center of that township.

Libertyville (Jefferson)
(2019)
Libertyville was platted in 1845. It was originally known as "The Colony," but 300 people gathered on July 4, 1842 to witnessed the raising of a flagpole. Some of the men celebrated by firing anvil salutes, (bottles of powder wrapped in twine), and even fired some flintlock muskets. It was there that it was proposed to rename the community Libertyville, which was unanimously adopted.

Lidderdale (Carroll)
(1988), (1994) (2011)
Lidderdale: was incorporated in 1906 and named for Lord Lidderdale, who was one of the shareholders of the railroad.

Lime Springs (Howard)
(2005)
The old town of Lime Springs was platted in 1857. After the railroad was built in the area, the town relocated to be nearer the railroad tracks. The new town was then called Lime Springs Station after a spring that produced fresh water.
Item of interest
Lime Springs was noted for its milling industry and the historical site of Lidtke Mill. The mill was famous for its buckwheat flour and in the 1870s produced 100 barrels of flour a day.

Liscomb (Marshall)
(1979,
Liscomb was platted in 1869 and named for H. P. Liscomb, an official of the Iowa Central Railroad.

Lisbon (Linn)
(1991), (2008), (2015)
Lisbon was laid out in 1851 and named for Lisbon, Portugal.

Item of interest
The Lisbon Cemetery has a 4 ton bolder that came from Gettysburg, Pennsylvania. It was placed in remembrance of those who served our nation in the Civil War.

Littleton (Buchanan)
(1982)
Littleton was platted in 1855 by Moses Little and named for him.

Livermore (Humboldt)
(1985), (1993)
Livermore was founded in 1879 and incorporated in 1882. It was first called Washburne.

Lockridge (Jefferson)
(1979), (1984), (2009)
Lockridge was incorporated in 1913. The town was founded in 1837 by William G. Coop who named it Lockridge, because of the two ridges that looked as if they interlocked as they sloped toward Wolf and Lick Creeks.

Lohrville (Calhoun)
(1979), (2012)
Lohrville was platted in 1881 when the railroad was extended to that point. It was named for Jacob A. Lohr, who owned the land where the town is located.

Lone Rock (Kossuth)
(2002), (2014)
Before any settlement took place, an unusual 175-ton boulder was used as a landmark for travelers. Lone Rock was platted in 1899 when the railroad was built through the area.
Item of interest
In 1970, the lone rock was moved to its new location by blasting it into four pieces and reconstructing the pieces inside the community.

Lone Tree (Johnson)
(1986)
Lone Tree was platted in 1872. The Lone Tree name came from a giant elm tree that grew nearby. In the pioneer era, the tree served as a prairie landmark.
Items of interest
Local legend has it that the tree was so large, buffalo grazed under its expansive branches. It escaped prairie fires because of the lack of grass around the tree. The tree succumbed to Dutch Elm disease in the 1960s, although valiant efforts were made to save it. The wood from the tree was used to make a sign to note the tree's home on the hill southeast of the city limits.

The town had an incident during the economic crisis of the 1980s. On December 9, 1985 a local farmer, Dale Burr, became distraught over his growing debt. He shot his wife Emily in their home. He then went to Hills Bank & Trust in the neighboring town of Hills and attempted to cash a check, but when denied, he returned with a shotgun and killed bank president John Hughes. Next on his list was his neighbor Richard Goody, who had recently won a court settlement against Burr's son. When Burr was pulled over by Johnson County sheriff's, he fatally shot himself. This story is captured in Bruce Brown's book, Lone Tree.

Lorimor (Union)
(1997)
Lorimor was platted in 1887 and founded by and named for J. S. Lorimor.

Lost Nation (Clinton)
(1985), (1994), (2004), (2012)
Lost Nation was platted in 1872. Lost Nation is the only city in the United States named Lost Nation.

There are several stories of how Lost Nation was named:

(1) It was the second town started at this site; the first "lost" town had been decimated by disease.

(2) A tribe of Native Americans pitched their camp where the town site now stands because of the natural advantages: deer, bear and wild turkey abounded in the woods to the north; buffalo, antelope and prairie grouse on the south; and only a short march to the river where fish were plentiful. The camp was located in the center of a rich area and became rich in ponies, pelts, and population. This prosperity awakened envy and jealousy. Many tribes wanted their hunting ground and several tried to take it by force. The chief, a crafty leader, when in danger of attack would take his band to the inaccessible cliffs around Bear Creek, where he and his warriors hid until the invaders could be safely surrounded and defeated. This strategy succeeded a number of times. They were left in peace and the tribe became known as the Indian word for "Boss Nation." When the first settlers arrived, a friendly Indian told this story of the tribe, which had since migrated west. The original name of "Boss Nation," became "Lost Nation" in the retelling of the story because of the disappearance of the tribe. The Lost Nation name still lives to this day.

(3) Another legend is that a German named Baum was looking for relatives near this point. When asked where he was going, he said he was looking for a lost nation.

(4) Another story tells that people from the Nation River in Canada found the folks they were looking and remarked, they had found the lost nation.

Item of interest

Lost Nations claims to have the best water in the nation.

Lovilia (Monroe)
(1984), (2000)
Lovilla was laid out in 1853. It was first named Bremem. No one knows for sure how it got its name changed to Lovilia, some think it was named after a lady and other believe it was a family name.

Lowell (Henry)
(2003), (2009)

Lowell was settled in 1833. It was first called McCarverstown, but in 1843 was renamed by Edward Archibald after his hometown of Lowell, Massachusetts.

Luther (Boone)
(1973), (1975), (1983), (1988) (2011), (2018)
Luther was laid out in 1893 and named for Clark Luther, a local merchant.

Lu Verne (Humboldt and Kossuth)
(1985)
Lu Verne was platted in 1880 and named for Luverne, Minnesota.

Luzerne (Benton)
(1986), (2008)
Luzerne had its start with the building of the Chicago and Northwestern Railroad through that territory and was platted by the railroad in 1868. It was incorporated in 1895. The president of the railroad asked if the town had been named and found out it had not. Because of the beauty of the surrounding hills and valleys, it reminded him of Lucerne, Switzerland so he named the town Luzerne.

Lynnville (Jasper)
(1973), (1975), (2006), (2018)
Lynnville was incorporated in 1875 and named for a linden grove near the original town site. Linden trees are recognized by other names: Basswood and Lime. The tree is commonly found in Europe where they are called "Lime," though that is not a reference to the citrus fruit, rather, "Lime" is an altered form of Middle English "Lind."
Item of interest
The town was incorporated in 1875 to control the liquor traffic, which was found to be unmanageable under the general laws.

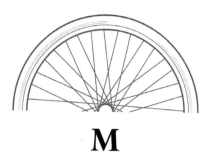

M

Macksburg (Madison)
(2009)
Macksburg was platted in 1873 and named for Dr. Joseph Hughes Mack, one of the original owners of the town site.
<u>Item of interests</u>
Macksburg was the home of Glenn Martin, inventor, designer, and manufacture of the Martin B-10 Bomber used in WWI. He was born in 1886. Shortly after his pioneering flight in 1909, he was nicknamed "The Flying Dude." By 1911 he was being mentioned, along with the Wright Brothers and Glenn Curtiss as one of the American leaders in powered flight.

Macksburg is home to the Annual National Skillet Throw Championship. This is a team sport where the players are awarded points for knocking the head off of a dummy, using an underhand throw of a skillet. Each player will throw 3 skillets at 3 different dummies from a line that is 30 feet from the dummies nose. This event is on the third weekend of June.

Madrid (Boone)
(1986), (1994), (1999), (2001)
Madrid was settled in 1846 by Charles W. Gaston who named it after Madrid, Spain.
<u>Item of interest</u>
Madrid gained a large Italian and Croatian population who worked in its coal mines during the 1920s and 1930s. In the winter, Madrid was a small coal mining community and in the summer, it was a farming community. Initially, coal was used locally for winter heating, which was

the reason it was considered a part-time job by most residents. Mining later became a larger part of Madrid's economy.

Magnolia (Harrison)
(1981)
Magnoila was platted in 1861 and named for a large native grove of Magnolia trees.

Mallard (Palo Alto)
(1977), (1990), (1993), (2017)
Mallard started about 1882 with the building of the Des Moines and Fort Dodge Railroad through the territory. The town was named by the railroad president, an avid hunter, who named it for the mallard ducks, which inhabited the area ponds.

Malvern (Mills)
(2016)
Malvern was founded in 1869 and originally named Milton. When it was discovered that another Milton existed, Dr. Brothers renamed the town Malvern for his old home town of Malvern, Ohio. Malvern, Ohio was named for Malvern Hills in England. Malvern started as a result of the Burlington and Missouri Railroad coming through the area.

MANCHESTER (Delaware) (County Seat)
(1983), (1989), (1993), (1999), (2007), (2010)
Manchester was founded in the 1850s and originally called Burrington after its founder, Levings Burrington, who settled there in 1852. In 1857, the town's name was changed to Manchester. It was incorporated in 1864.
Item of interest
On November 8, 1866, Mr. J. W. Meyers was jealous of his wife so he attempted to shoot her but missed. He then turned the gun on his Mother-In-Law who was holding their 4-month-old baby which killed the baby and badly wounded his Mother-In-Law. Next, he went to the barn and cut his throat three times which severed his jugular vein and wind pipe.

Manilla (Crawford)
(1994), (2001)
Manilla was primarily settled by Germans but the new town did not yet have an official name. In 1885, the community celebrated the Fourth of July. One of the events was a tug-of-war. The community decided to name the town at the tug-of-war contest. There were some who thought the town should be named for Les Paup for the person who owned the land before the railroad bought it. They wanted it called Paupville. Until this time, grain had been bound by hand, but the self-binder had just been invented. Mr. Blackburn's Hardware store was advertising the new twine, called Manila Binder Twine. Mr. Blackburn furnished a Manila rope for the tug-of-war and suggested the town be named Manilla. An additional "L" was added to the towns name.

Manning (Carroll)
(2006), (2011), (2018)
Manning was incorporated in 1882 and named for O. H. Manning, who was a school teacher, lawyer, newspaper publisher, and politician.
<u>Item of interests</u>
A German Hausbarn (farmer's house) was originally constructed in 1660 in Schleswig-Holstein, Germany and was dismantled, boxed, and shipped to Manning and in 1996. A German master carpenter worked with local volunteers to reconstruct the Hausbarn, or farmer's house. It is located at the Heritage Park at 12196 311th Street.

The Great Umbrella Ride is a story often told in Manning. Harold Reinke and Herbert "Hoopy" Hoover decided one day to parachute off of the train trestle. Harold used a tractor umbrella and Hoopy used his mother's umbrella. Hoopy jumped first and his umbrella inverted and down he went. Harold then jumped with his sturdier tractor umbrella and about half way down his umbrella inverted and down he went. At the bottom was a pile of sand that they were jumping into, but even with the sand, both Hoopy & Harold landed with a thud. Fortunately, they were able to walk away with only their pride hurt.

In 1969, an unknown saboteur used dynamite to bomb and derail a passenger train, hoping that it would fall into the Nishnabotna River below. Fortunately, the train came to a safe stop, but not until it derailed. The crime was never solved. No group ever claimed responsibility and no motive for the bombing was ever discovered.

In 1948, a gangland shooting hoax occurred on Main Street Manning. It was a first-class mystery because none of the four involved was known and the body was missing. Three or four witnesses saw the victim fall on Main Street after three blasts from a 20-gauge shotgun. The two assailants placed the "victim" in a 1946 Ford and drove off. The four 16-year old youths involved, admitted it was a fake affair. The boys were caught after a state-wide search and the case was turned over to the Juvenile Court.

Manson (Calhoun)

(2015)

Manson was platted in 1872 and incorporated in 1877. It was named for a high railroad official.

<u>Items of interest</u>

Manson is located near the site of the Manson Crater. It was formed 74 million years ago by a meteorite collision which measured more than 23 miles across. The crater's existence was first discovered during an oil-drilling wildcatting expedition in the 1930s. At one time, it was thought to be the biggest impact by an object from outer space in North America; however, subsequent studies revealed larger examples. The impact event was also once theorized to have contributed to the extinction of the dinosaurs. It was thought to be a fragment of the Chicxulub meteor, until tests by the U.S. Geological Survey in 1991 and 1992 proved that it was too old by 9 million years. Not much remain of the crater due to glacial deposits. It's undetectable at ground level; however, due to infilling, it is one of the best-preserved impact sites on Earth. The crater now sits approximately 200 feet below the City of Manson. The impact of the meteor significantly changed the geography of the area. As a result, the city of Manson was known for years as the "soft water capital of the world."

Mapleton (Monona)
(1977), (1981), (1995), (2004)
Mapleton was platted in 1857 and its name came from the nearby Maple River, which was named for the maple trees along its banks.

MAQUOKETA (Jackson) (County Seat)
(1978), (1994), (2004)
Maquoketa was laid out in 1838 and originally called Springfield. In 1844, it was renamed for the Maquoketa River. The river's name was derived from Maquaw-Autaw language, which means "Bear River" in Meskwaki. At that time, there was a great number of bears inhabiting its banks and streams that fed the river.

Item of interest

Maquoketa Caves State Park has more caves than any state park in Iowa and is one of Iowa's most unique outdoor attractions. Enormous bluffs tower throughout the park. A six-mile trail system winds through geologic formations and forests brimming with natural beauty. It was one of the state's earliest state parks, Maquoketa Caves has been a popular destination for picnickers and hikers since the 1860s.

Marathon (Buena Vista)
(1979), (2002), (2007)
Marathon was incorporated in 1892. The post office in Marathon has been in operation since 1882. The name of the city commemorates the Battle of Marathon.

The first Persian invasion of Greece, in an attempt to conquer Greece, was in 490 BC. The Persian forces landed in a bay near the town of Marathon. The Athenians asked for help from the Spartans but they were involved in a religious festival and could not help. The Athenians were able to turn back the Persian forces, then the Persian forces got into their ships and headed for Athens. After the battle, the Athenian army, with full armor, marched the 26 miles back to Athens to head off the Persian forces. They arrived in time to cause the Persian ships to turn away from Athens.

A later inaccurate version of this event is that after the battle, Pheidippides ran the 26 miles in full armor, from Marathon to Athens to announce the Greek victory. Legend also has it that he died from exhaustion upon arrival.

After the Battle of Marathon, Athens reached new heights and democracy blossomed and became the foundation of western civilization.

When the idea of a modern Olympics became a reality at the end of the 19th century, the organizers were looking for a great popularizing event to recall the ancient glory of Greece. The idea was to organize a "marathon race" in the first modern Olympics Games to be held in 1896 in Athens. This idea was heavily supported by Pierre de Coubertin, the founder of the modern Olympics, as well as the Greeks. This race would duplicate the legendary version of this event, with the competitors running from Marathon to Athens. This event was so popular that it quickly caught on and becoming a fixture in future Olympic games, with major cities staging their own annual marathon. The distance eventually became fixed at 26 miles 385 yards, though for the first years it was around 25 miles, the approximate distance from Marathon to Athens.

Marble Rock (Floyd)
(2014)
Marble Rock was incorporated in 1881. The town's name was derived from the presence of white limestone in the area.

Marcus (Cherokee)
(1975), (2002), (2012)
Marcus was incorporated in 1882. It was named by John Insley Blair, a railroad official, for his son Marcus L. Blair.

MARENGO (Iowa) (County Seat)
(1976), (1986), (1991), (2006), (2011)
Marengo was platted in 1847 and its name commemorates the Battle of Marengo, which took place on the plains of Italy, where Napoleon defeated the Austrian army.

Marion (Linn)
(1994)

Marion was first settled in 1839 and named for Francis Marion, a hero of the Revolutionary War. Francis Marion was referred to as the "Swamp Fox," for his ability to negotiate the swamps of South Carolina and out maneuver the British troops.

Item of interest

Each year during the last weekend of September, the city hosts the annual "Swamp Fox Festival," a celebration of Marion's heritage.

Marne (Cass)

(1986), (2019)

Marne got its beginnings in 1875 when German investors from Davenport filed papers and plotted the land that was purchased from Thomas Meredith. The city's name came from a city in Germany called Marne.

MARSHALLTOWN (Marshall) (County Seat)

(1974), (1994), (2004) (2012)

In 1851, Henry Anson found what he described as "the prettiest place in Iowa," located on a high point between the Iowa River and Linn Creek. In 1853, Anson named the town Marshall, after Marshall, Michigan, where he was a former resident. Another source indicated it was named of Chief Justice John Marshall, who served on the United States Supreme Court from 1755 to 1835. In 1862, the town changed its name to Marshalltown because another Marshall already existed.

Items of interest

Henry Anson and his fellow settlers became friendly with a local Native American Potawatomi chief named Johnny Green (Che Muese) who provided much needed help for early settlers to get established in the wilderness and in the young town. When Green died in 1868, members of this tribe and the grateful citizens of Marshalltown buried him on a high bluff overlooking the Des Moines River. Today, a large monument stands on the grounds of the Iowa Veterans Home in tribute to this Native American leader.

In 1880 before becoming a popular evangelist, Billy Sunday moved to Marshalltown where he launched his major-league baseball career. After a few years in the big leagues, when Sunday found religion to be most importance, left his career in professional baseball and began speaking to crowds nationwide. He became the country's chief evangelist. (See Garner)

David Lennox was an American inventor and businessman who in 1895 founded a furnace manufacturing business in Marshalltown. Today it is known as Lennox International. The headquarters are now located in Richardson, Texas.

Located near Marshalltown is The Big Treehouse, a huge structure with 12 levels towering 55 feet around a tree. It is complete with music, electricity, telephone, microwave oven, refrigerator, running water, grill, 14 porch swings, a spiral stairway and a Shady Oak Museum. The tree house is located at 2370 Shady Oaks Road.

Marshalltown is the birth place of Jean Dorothy Seberg, an American actress who lived half her life in France. Her performance In Jean-Luc Godard's 1960 film *Breathless*, immortalized her as an icon of the French New Wave cinema. She appeared in 34 films in Hollywood and Europe. She was also one of the best-known targets of the FBI COINELPRO project. (The project was aimed at surveilling, infiltrating, discrediting, and disrupting American political organizations.) Her targeting was a well-documented retaliation for her support for the Black Panther Party of the 1960s. Seberg died at the age of 40 in Paris, with police ruling her death a probable suicide.

Martelle (Jones)
(2008)
Martelle was platted in 1872 when the Chicago, Milwaukee, St. Paul and Pacific Railroad was built through the area. The town was incorporated in 1899.

Martensdale (Warren)
(1992), (2009)
Martensdale was founded in 1913 and name for John F. Martens, one of the founders.

Martinsburg (Keokuk)
(2009), (2013)
Martinsburg was founded in 1855 and named for Daniel Martin, an early settler.

<u>Item of interest</u>

In 1962 Martinsburg was the scene of a gruesome killing spree. On May 27, 1962, Gayno Gilbert Smith murdered Andrew McBeth, Dora McBeth, and their three children then confessed to the crime.

The McBeth family lived about four miles north of Martinsburg, where Gayno Smith had been living with them at the time. Another daughter, Patsy Lou, was wounded by Smith but escaped in the night and ran to a nearby farm for help. Kellogg's six-month old baby, Perry, was in a crib and left unharmed.

On the night of the murders, the McBeth children (Amos, Anna, and Donna Jean) had driven to Brighton for a dance. Donna Jean, as was her custom, had left her infant in the care of her parents. Smith remained at the dance a short time, then disappeared until midnight, according to court records. He came back to pick up the group after the dance ended. Thunder, lightning and heavy rain began as the five went to a truck stop for food. When they returned to their farmhouse, the lights were out. The children found flashlights and made their way around the house to investigate. Donna and Amos found the murdered bodies of their parents in the garage, where they'd been dragged. They tried to call for help but discovered the telephone lines had been cut.

Suddenly, Smith appeared before them with a flashlight and a gun. He shot Amos in the face, then Donna. He shot Patsy in the shoulder. Though badly wounded, Amos pleaded for his life but was shot again. Patsy escaped to another room where she found her older sister, Anna, already dead. Smith chased her to a ditch in the countryside. She played cat and mouse through the ditches, crawling and crouching to escape his roving flashlight through the early morning hours. She finally reached a nearby farmhouse, and called her uncle, Firman McBeth.

Smith went into hiding but was found four days later in a barn near Lake Wapello. After being arrested, he confessed both to the McBeth murders in Martinsburg and also to the murder of his stepmother, Juanita Smith, the previous October in Hedrick, Iowa. Smith was sentenced to five life terms for first-degree murder and one 50-year term for second-degree murder.

Infant Perry was adopted by his uncle Firman, Andrew McBeth's brother, and raised with Firman's nine biological children. Gayno Smith's body was cremated and buried in Mount Zion Cemetery next to the plot of his mother.

MASON CITY (Cerro Gordo) (County Seat)
(1982), (1985), (2014)

The region was first called "Shibboleth" and was the summer home to the Sioux and Winnebago nations. The first settlement was made at Shibboleth in 1853 at the confluence of the Winnebago River and Calmus Creek. The town had several names: Shibboleth, Masonic Grove, and Masonville, until the name of Mason City was adopted in 1855, in honor of a founder's son, Mason Long.

Items of interest

The city is often referred to as "River City." It is known for its musical heritage, consistently producing successful performers and educators. In 1951, the city's favorite son, Meredith Willson, began working on a musical story. Mason City is the River City of Meredith Willson's The Music Man. The story was about a salesman trying to convince the citizens of River City to start a boy's band. The musical played in several theaters in the East until Warner Brothers bought the movie rights and began producing it in 1961. On June 19, 1962 at the Palace Theater in Mason City, The Music Man premiered. The movie cast traveled to Mason City for the gala event, which was held in conjunction with the North Iowa Band Festival.

By 1934 the Great Depression hit north Iowa along with the rest of the country. Throughout the upper Midwest, John Dillinger and his gang were robbing banks and making a name for themselves. Dillinger became somewhat of a hero to the depression weary farmers of the Midwest, as he would often destroy foreclosure records during bank robberies. It was on March 13, 1934 that "public enemy number one" came to Mason City and robbed the First National Bank. Dillinger and his gang left with $52,000. Little did they know that the bank just happened to have more than $300,000 on hand that day. The First National Bank is now called the City Center and remains a historical treasure in downtown Mason City.

Masonville (Delaware)
(1989)
Masonville was laid out in 1858 and named for businessman R. B. Mason.

Maxwell (Story)
(1974), (1986), (2001)
Maxwell was incorporated in 1883 and named for J. W. Maxwell who had purchased the land on which the town is located.

May City (Osceola)
(1979), (1985), (1996), (2005), (2014)
The town was created in 1889.

Maysville (Scott)
(2008)
Maysville was platted in 1856 and named in honor of James May, who owned the land.

McCallsburg (Story)
(1979), (1986), (1998), (2012)
McCallsburg was founded in 1868 and in 1882 incorporated as Latrobe. One year later the name was changed to McCallsburg in honor T. C. McCall, who sold many of the lots to the early settlers.

McClelland (Pottawattamie)
(1974), (2019)
McClelland was established in 1903 as a watering stop and railroad station for the Great Western Railroad. The town was named in honor of W. H. McClelland, who had purchased the land where the town is located.

Mechanicsville (Cedar)
(1982), (2008)
Mechanicsville was platted in 1855. Several of its first settlers were mechanics, thus the name Mechanicsville.

Mediapolis (Des Moines)
(2000)
Mediapolis was founded in 1869. Media meaning "middle," and "polis" meaning "village," because Mediapolis is halfway between Wapello and Burlington.

Medora (Warren)
(1991), (1992), (2003)
Medora is listed on an 1875 map of Warren County.
Items of interest
Medora's claim to fame centers around a murder trial. On a moonlit Saturday night on December 1, 1900 in prosperous Warren County, Iowa, farmer John Hossack was murdered in his bed by two blows of an axe to his head. Four days later, Hossack's wife of 32 years, Margaret (Murchison) Hossack was arrested at her husband's funeral and charged with killing him. After two trials, Hossack's murder remains unsolved.

Margaret claimed to be innocent, but stories of domestic troubles and abuse provided prosecutors with a motive for the crime. Neighbors and family members were reluctant to talk about what they knew about the couple's troubled marriage.

Shep, the couple's 10-year-old dog, figured prominently in the trial, especially in the argument for the defense. During the first trial one newspaper headlined proclaimed "Defense hopes rest upon Hossack dog." Shep was said to be an active dog with a tendency to bark at stray cattle and strangers. On the night of the murder, Margaret testified that she

198 Eugene H. Schlaman

had heard Shep barking vigorously between 9 and 10 pm. Several family members and neighbors who saw the dog soon after the murder thought he was quiet and uncharacteristically listless, fueling speculation that the assailant had drugged the dog with chloroform. When the defense made this argument in court, the prosecution countered by claiming that Shep had witnessed Margaret killing her husband and that the dog's demeanor expressed shame and sorrow.

On April 11, 1901, after five days of testimony before an all-male jury, Margaret was found guilty and sentenced to life in prison. Her conviction was overturned a year later, and she was given a second trial. She was retried and that ended with a hung jury verdict; nine jurors found her guilty, while three held out and voted "not guilty." There was no third trial, and no one else was ever charged with the murder. Margaret refused to discuss the murder after the second trial.

Melbourne (Marshall)
(1976), (2018)
Melbourne was incorporated in 1895. The name of Wenselville was suggested for W. L. M. Wensel, the land owner, but he declined the honor so the town was named for a railroad employee named Melbourne.
<u>Item of interest</u>
In 1903 Melbourne suffered the worst disaster in the town's history when a fire consumed the whole business district and then in 1981 the southern end of town was destroyed by a tornado.

Melcher-Dallas (Marion)
(1991), (2003)
Melcher and Dallas were separate cities until they merged in 1986. Dallas was first called Ohio because many of the first settlers came from Ohio to work in the coal mines. Melcher was established in 1913 and named for a Rock Island Railroad executive. In 1913, there was a battle between these two towns. The railroad decided to name their depot Dallas, even though it was located within the incorporated city limits of Melcher. Later in that same week federal authorities changed the name of the post office from Melcher to Dallas.

Melvin (Osceola)
(1999), (2005), (2007), (2014)
Melvin started in 1900 with the building of the Gowrie branch of the Rock Island Railroad through the territory. It was named after an early settler named Melvin.

Menlo (Guthrie)
(1991), (2019)
Menlo was laid out in 1869 and first called "The Switch" and then "Guthrie Switch." It was finally renamed Menlo in order to prevent confusion with Guthrie Center. It was named for Menlo, Ireland.

Merrill (Plymouth)
(1993),
Merrill was incorporated in 1894 and named for the seventh Governor of Iowa, Samuel Merrill.

Meservey (Cerro Gordo)
(1990)
Meservey was founded in 1886. It was originally known as Kausville named for Karl and George Kraus, but renamed Meservey for the Meservey brothers, who were railroad employees.

Middle Amana (Iowa)
(1976), (1991)
(See Amana Colonies)

Middletown (Des Moines)
(2009), (2019)
Middletown was laid out in 1846 and named for Middletown, Pennsylvania, home of one of the early settlers.
Item of interest
The Iowa Army Ammunitions Plant is located in Middletown. The property belongs to the United States Army. The mission of the plant, established in 1940, has been to manufacture and deliver large caliber items for the Department of Defense. The plant is still in operation today.

Milford (Dickinson)
(1982), (1985), (1996), (2005), (2014)
Milford was incorporated in 1892 and its name was given by the Seymour Foster & Company.

Miller (Hancock)
(1977), (1999)
Miller was platted in 1895 and named for E. C. Miller, who owned the land.

Millersburg (Iowa)
(1973), (1986), (2001)
Millersburg was platted in 1852 and named for its founder, Reuben Miller.

Millerton (Wayne)
(1981), (1997), (2009), (2016), (2019)
In 1912, George Miller purchased a farm, laid out a town, and named it Millerton for himself.
<u>Item of interest</u>
A staple in any small town is a general store. Francis Fry opened a store in 1944. The Fry's Store in Millerton is well known to everyone in several counties. Farmers, electricians, plumbers, or anyone looking for that hard to find replacement part came to Fry's. If it was made or is still made today, Fry's probably has it somewhere in the recesses of that old building. The store is still open.

Milo (Warren)
(1997), (2009)
Milo started in 1878 with the building of the railroad through the territory. Its founder, Smith Henderson Mallory, named the town Milo for Milo, New York which was named for Milo of Croton, a famous athlete of Ancient Greece.

Milton (Van Buren)
(1997)

Milton was laid out in 1851 and was named Milton by its founders who were from Milton, Delaware

Minburn (Dallas)
(1974), (2013)
Minburn was founded in 1869. The name was derived from "burn," a Scottish word for brook or river and "min" meaning small; therefore, the name Minburn suited the small town located near the Raccoon River.

Item of interest

A memorable event in Minburn's history occurred in 1902. Thugs came into town and robbed four stores. A hitchhiker spending the night in the unlocked depot and the telephone operator, Lena West, both notified the night Marshall, Virgil, telling of what was happening. He along with two armed citizens headed to Shaw's Grocery. The thieves had taken a small amount of money from a nearby gas station plus 6,000 cigarettes and three tires. They had robbed the grocery store and were trying to break into a safe which was next door to the telephone company. As Marshall Virgil walked up the street he was shot multiple times. After shooting Virgil, the robbers raced to their car and headed toward Des Moines. Dr. Hinchliff gave Virgil first aid treatment and rushed him to King's Daughters Hospital in Perry where he died. The robbers were never caught.

Minden (Pottawattamie)
(2000), (2008), (2013), (2019)
Founded in 1877. Minden was named for Minden, Germany, the Fatherland of most of the industrious settlers.

Mineola (Mills)
(1986), (2009)
Mineola started as a small town with only a few people so the people decided to call the town Mineola. Mineola is an unincorporated community.

Mingo (Jasper)
(2001)
Mingo was platted in 1884 and named for Mingo, Ohio, a city that derived its name from an Indian chieftain, known as The Mingo Chief.

Mississippi and Missouri Rivers
Tradition on RAGBRAI (Registers Annual Great Bike Ride Across Iowa) is that the rear bike tire is dipped into the Missouri River and the front tire is dipped into the Mississippi River. The Ojibwe Native American word for the Mississippi River is "Misi-ziibi" meaning "long river." The Sioux Native American word for the Missouri River is Missouris meaning "town of large canoes."

Missouri Valley (Harrison)
(1981), (1991), (1997), (2008)
Missouri Valley was laid out in 1867 when the Chicago and North Western Railroad was extended to that point. The city was named for the valley of the Missouri River.

Mitchellville (Polk)
(1973), (1975), (1984), (2000), (2006) (2011)
Mitchellville was founded by Thomas Mitchell in 1856 and incorporated in 1875. The town was named for its founder.
Items of interest
Thomas Mitchell came to Iowa in 1840 and was the first white settler in Polk County. He was very friendly with the Native Americans. Upon learning that the railroad was coming to the area, he moved to the present area and founded Mitchellville. He was very active in the Underground Railroad.

The Iowa Correctional Institution for Women is located in Mitchellville.

Moneta (O'Brien)
(1999), (2007)
Moneta was platted in 1901. Its name is supposed to be a poetic form for the island of Anglesey, which is off the north-west coast of Wales.

Monmouth (Jackson)
(1978),

Monmouth was laid out in 1856. It took its name from Monmouth Township, which was named to commemorate the Battle of Monmouth in the American Revolutionary War.

Monroe (Jasper)
(1992), (2013)
Monroe was laid out in 1851 by Adam Tool and originally called Tool's Point. It was renamed Monroe for President James Monroe. Monroe was incorporated in 1867.

Item of interest

An interesting story told in Monroe is about how James White and Peter Bicklehaupt mistakenly drink carbolic acid for whiskey. In 1876 White went to the drug store to order a bottle of whiskey. The druggist was busy so White left the store. When White returned, the druggist nodded toward the rear of the store where White picked one of the two bottles that were close together. He went to meet Bicklehaupt and invited him to take a drink. Bicklehaupt took a big swallow followed by White, who then noticed that something was wrong. Bicklehaupt died in a few minutes in much pain. White was in critical condition for two days but did recover.

Montezuma (Poweshiek) (County Seat)
(1973), (1975), (2001), (2006), (2018)
Montezuma was laid out in 1848 and named to honor Montezuma, the Aztec emperor of Mexico.

Item of interest

Thomas Harris McDonald was a well-known civil engineer who grew up in Montezuma. He supervised the creation of 3.5 million miles of highways in the United States.

Monti (Buchanan)
(1998)
Monti was founded in the 1880s and platted in 1905. The town traces its roots to the late 19th century, when large numbers of Irish immigrants came to the state. The town's Catholic roots can be traced to these first Irish settlers. It is believed the town is name for Monti, a historical district in Rome.

Monticello (Jones)
(1974), (1985), (1998)
Monticello was founded in 1836 and incorporated in 1870. It was named by Daniel Varvel for the home of Thomas Jefferson.

Montieth (Guthrie)
(2006)
Monteith started in 1881 with the building of the railroad through that territory. Monteith is an unincorporated community.

Montour (Tama)
(1979), (1994), (1995), (2008)
Montour, originally called Orford but in 1873 was renamed Montour after Montour County, Pennsylvania. It was incorporated in 1870.

Montpelier (Muscatine)
(2018)
The original Montpelier was settled in 1834, several miles from the current town. The current Montpelier was established in 1881. Montpelier's first settlers were natives of Vermont who chose to name their town after the capital of Vermont. Montpelier in an unincorporated community.
Item of interest
In 1834, Benjamin Nye and his nephew, Stephen Nye built cabins on the opposite sides of Pine Creek, near where it meets the Mississippi River. Benjamin had a trading post where he sold goods to the Sauk and Meskwaki Indians who lived in the area.
A family dispute brought Nye's pioneering days to a sudden end. One of his employees, George McCoy, married Nye's daughter, Harriet. Nye did not approve of the union, so in 1836 the couple eloped, slipping across the river to marry in New Boston, Illinois. In 1849, McCoy went off to California in search of gold, leaving Harriet behind in the care of a respected member of the community, Judge Samuel Bissel. When McCoy came back to Iowa in 1852, Harriet had a young baby that obviously wasn't his. He was unhappy about that, so he rounded up his children and took them out of town.

On March 3, 1852, when Nye was in town on business, McCoy rode to Nye's house and retrieved his children. Nye soon arrived home and realized what was happening. He stormed after McCoy, confronting him on the road out of town. As Nye walked to the wagon to get his grandchildren, McCoy fired at him. Nye changed directions and went after McCoy. In the ensuing fight, McCoy pulled out a knife and stabbed Nye, mortally wounding him. McCoy turned himself in, but a Grand Jury refused to indict him, citing self-defense. McCoy promptly divorced Harriet and sent his children to live with his sister in Michigan, then went back to California, where he became a prominent early resident.

Montrose (Lee)
(1981), (1992), (2019)
The area around Montrose had been occupied continuously since the 1780s, when Quashquame's village was established nearby. Quashquame was a Sauk chief who was the principal signer of the 1804 treaty that ceded Sauk land to the United States government. The area was strategically important because it is at the head of the Des Moines River rapids, a major impediment to river traffic that caused large boats to land in this area and transfer freight overland to avoid the rapids. It was first called "River House" then named Mount of Roses because of the great number of wild roses on the hills and bluffs. It was later shorted to Montrose.

Item of interest
Montrose was the location of Fort Des Moines, a military post from 1834-1837. From 1839 to 1846 Montrose was the home to many members of the Church of Jesus Christ of Latter Day Saints (LDS). This was especially true in 1839 when many LDS members that lived in the abandoned barracks which served as a good short term residence, while homes were being built in Nauvoo, Illinois. Among Montrose's residents at this time were Brigham Young, Wilford Woodruff and Erastus Snow. Despite legends that the streets of Montrose were aligned to allow a direct view of the Nauvoo Temple across the Mississippi River in Illinois, the streets were actually aligned with the 1834 layout of Fort Des Moines.

Moorhead (Monona)
(1981), (2018)

Moorhead was platted in 1899 and was named for J. R. Moorhead, a first settler in the area.

Item of interest

In the early 1900's, the city moved to its current location because the location didn't satisfy the rail line. The town picked up and literally moved the buildings with horses to where the city now sits.

Morning Sun (Louisa)

(1979)

Morning Sun was laid out in 1851 by Cicero Hamilton.

Item of interest

Early settlers could not agree on a name for their new town until one night when Cicero Hamilton had a couple of oxen break out and wander away. He aroused some neighbors in the early dawn and started a search for the lost oxen. When the sun peeped over the horizon, a great and glorious idea hit Henry C. Blake, who was one of the men helping in the search. Blake cried out, 'I've got it! Let's name our town "Morning Sun."' The name Morning Sun was adopted and the city was incorporated in 1867.

Morrison (Grundy)

(1974), (1983)

Morrison was incorporated in 1884 and was named for Jefferson Morrison who gave the land for the town.

Moravia (Appanoose)

(1981), (1997), (2009), (2016)

Moravia is named for the Moravian Christian faith.

Item of interest

Moravian families left Salem, North Carolina in 1849 to start a colony in the west. Money was sent to purchase forty acres of land for a town site by several benevolent Moravian sisters. It was their wish that town lots be sold and the money used to build a Moravian Church. A church was built and dedicated in 1851. The early Moravian Families honored the customs of the Moravian Church, which was founded in the country of Moravia in 1597.

Several of these customs are remembered and celebrated today in Moravia's annual events and festivals. Christmas time was a time for Moravians to visit their neighbors and view their colorful Christmas decorations. This custom is remembered and practiced at Christmas time each year. Another Moravian custom at Christmas time is the love feast. The love fest is a traditional religious service with music that is provided by local talent. Moravian coffee and buns are also served at the love feast in the tradition of the early Moravians.

Morley (Jones)
(1982), (1994), (2004), (2008)
Morley was laid out about 1873 on the main line of the Chicago, Milwaukee, St. Paul and Pacific Railroad. It was first called Viroqua but in 1886 was renamed Morley.

Moscow (Muscatine)
(1973), (1982), (2001), (2006), (2011), (2015), (2018)
Moscow was laid out in 1836 by Henry Webster and Dr. Charles Drury. The town was named after Moscow, Ohio where some of the early settlers were from. Another story says it was derived from an Indian name "Moose Cow."
Item of interest
In early days Moscow was quite a business center, full of life and activity, although it bore the reputation of being a hard place. Regularly every Saturday, either a horse-race or a shooting-match took place. The prize ranged from one to three or more gallons of whiskey, which, according to rule, was to be drunk on the ground. In case of an excess of whiskey, the balance was reserved for a rainy Saturday. Fights were an every-day occurrence. Several of the best physical men in the neighborhood often make it lively for strangers if an opportunity presented itself.

Mount Auburn (Benton)
(2015)
Mount Auburn was platted in 1871 when the Burlington, Cedar Rapids and Minnesota Railroad was extended to that point. It was named for Mount Auburn, Illinois.

Item of interest
A cheese factory was established at Mount Auburn in 1873. In 1874, 27,484 pounds of cheese was sold for $3,591.44. It sold for a little over thirteen cents a pound.

MOUNT AYR (Ringgold) (County Seat)
(1992), (2003), (2016)
Mount Ayr was founded in 1875 and named in honor of poet Robert Burns' birthplace in Ayr, Scotland. Mount was added to indicate its location on the highest point of land in the area.
Item of interest
On March 6th of 1952, the branch office of the Security State Bank of Mount Ayr was robbed. The thieves broke into the office during the night and blew the safe open with liquid explosives. The entire interior of the bank was destroyed, but none of the townspeople heard or were awakened by the blast. The thieves made off with $2,871 in cash. It isn't known if they were ever caught.

Mount Carmel (Carroll)
(1988), (1994)
It was founded in 1868 with the construction of Our Lady of Mount Carmel Church from which the town took its name. Mount Carmel is located in Israel and in biblical times was considered a place of refuge.

Mount Hamill (Lee)
(1992)
Mount Hamill was first called Courtright after the surveyor, but renamed Mount Hamill when the post office was established.

MOUNT PLEASANT (Henry) (County Seat)
(1975), (1979), (1984), (1992), (2003), (2009)
Mount Pleasant was founded in 1835 by pioneer Presley Saunders and incorporated in 1842. It was named for its commanding elevation and pleasant shade trees.
Items of interest
Mount Pleasant was the site of the state's first courthouse in 1839.

On December 10, 1986, Ralph Orin Davis, a resident, walked into a city council meeting and shot Mayor Edward King and two council members. Mayor King died of his wounds after being shot point blank in the head. The 69-year-old gunman had attended previous meetings complaining about a backed-up sewer and wanting the city to pay for damages to his house.

Mount Pleasant is home to the Midwest Old Thresher's Reunion which attracts over 100,000 people during the five-day celebration which ends on Labor Day. The reunion dates back to 1950 and pays tribute to the agricultural heritage of the American Midwest in an extensive, highly interactive manner. The live action exhibitions centers on restored mechanical equipment, particularly steam engines, farm tractors, stationary gas engines, antique and classic cars, the narrow-gauge Midwest Central Railroad, and electric trolleys.

Mount Pleasant is the home of Iowa Wesleyan University which is rooted in the religious, educational and cultural aspirations of early settlers. Their aspirations were shaped by a vision and determination to build an institute of learning in the rapidly developing southeast corner of the Iowa Territory. The University is affiliated with the United Methodist Church.

Mount Union (Henry)
(1979), (1990), (2000)
Mount Union was incorporated in 1904, but in November of 2016, the city's residents voted 32 to 31 to be unincorporated.

Mount Vernon (Linn)
(1978), (1991), (2008), (2012), (2015)
Mount Vernon was originally known as "Hilltop." In 1847, it was changed to "Pinhook," for the wooden pins used in the stores to hang up

goods. Later in 1847, it was renamed Mount Vernon, after the estate of George Washington.

Items of interest

As a result of Chief Black Hawk's war with settlers along the Mississippi River and his flight into Illinois and Wisconsin, a large tract of land in Iowa was taken from his Sac and Fox tribes as partial payment for damages done. In 1832, a treaty at the end of the war opened up the Iowa territory for settlement. Mount Vernon is at the western edge of the required land cession.

In 1853, the Iowa Conference Male and Female Seminary was established in Mount Vernon. It later became Cornell College. It is the only college in the nation to have its entire campus listed on the National Register of Historic Places.

Munterville (Wapello)
(1984)
Munterville was founded in 1847 and first known as the Swedish colony of Burgholm. The name was changed to Munterville in honor of a Swedish school teacher named Munter.

MUSCATINE (Muscatine) (County Seat)
(1976), (1986), (1995), (2001), (2006), (2016)
Muscatine began as a trading post founded by representatives of Colonel George Davenport in 1833. It was incorporated as Bloomington in 1839 but the name was changed to reduce mail delivery confusion, as there were several towns named Bloomington in the Midwest. Before that, Muscatine had been known as "Newburg" and "Casey's Landing." The origin of the name Muscatine is debated. It may have been derived from the Mascouten Native American tribe which lived along the Mississippi River in the 1700s.

Items of interest

From the 1840s until the Civil War, Muscatine had Iowa's largest black community. They were fugitive slaves who had traveled the Mississippi River from the South and free blacks who had migrated from eastern states. One of the most prominent community leaders was Alexander G. Clark Sr., who was born free in Pennsylvania. He was a barber, a respected position at the time, and eventually became a wealthy timber salesman and real estate speculator. In 1848, he was among the founders of the local African Methodist Episcopal Church, which was established as the first independent black denomination in the United States.

He assisted fugitive slaves, and petitioned the state government to overturn racist laws before the Civil War. In 1863, Clark helped organize Iowa's black regiment, the 60th United States Colored Infantry (originally known as the 1st Iowa Infantry, African Descent), though an injury prevented him from serving.

In 1868, he gained desegregation of Iowa's public schools. He sued the Muscatine school board after his daughter Susan was turned away from her neighborhood school. Eleven years later, in 1879, his son Alexander Jr. became the first black graduate of the University of Iowa College of Law. At the age of 58, Clark Sr. enrolled in the college and became its second black law graduate five years later. He said that he wanted to serve "as an example to young men of his own race." Clark rose to prominence in the Republican Party, serving as a delegate to state and national conventions. In 1890, Clark was appointed ambassador to Liberia by President Benjamin Harrison.

In 1884, J.F. Boepple, a German immigrant, founded a button company that produced buttons that looked like pearls by machine-punching them from freshwater mussel shells harvested from the Mississippi River. Muscatine's slogan, "Pearl of the Mississippi," refers to the days when pearl button manufacturing by the McKee Button Company was a significant economic contributor. In 1915, Weber & Sons Button Co., Inc. was the world's largest producer of fancy freshwater pearl buttons. From that time forward, Muscatine was known as "The Pearl Button Capital of the World." Weber is still manufacturing buttons today.

Muscatine is also well known as the "Watermelon Capital of the World," a title that reflects the agricultural rural nature of the county.

In 1926, the Maid-Rite sandwich was created in Muscatine by Fred Angell. Angell was a butcher who combined a special cut and grind of meat with a selected set of spices to create the Maid-Rite sandwich. It is called a "loose meat" sandwich.

Mystic (Appanoose)
(1981), (2016), (2019)
Mystic was named after Mystic, Connecticut.
<u>Items of interest</u>
At the end of the 19th century, the valley of Walnut Creek was one continuous mining camp. The first coal mine in the Mystic area opened in 1857, on Little Walnut Creek. The Mystic coal seam was exposed on the surface and drifts were opened and abandoned over the next few decades, until the hills were honeycombed with mines. By 1893, there were 14 mines in Mystic.

Mining was a tough job performed by tough men. Sometimes arguments broke out and personalities clashed. Mystic coal miner Elmer Anderson, a 26-year-old Swedish immigrant developed foes. On Monday morning, March 29, 1897, Anderson's mangled body was found on the railroad tracks where, according to newspapers it was "ground into a hundred pieces." Despite the condition of the body, Anderson could be identified. Authorities told the public that Anderson was killed "by enemies in Mystic" and then placed on the railroad tracks to be run over.

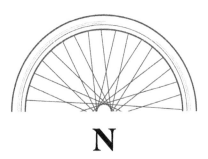

N

Napier (Boone)
(2018)
Napier was named for Robert Cornelius Napier, a British General. Another version is that Napier was the maiden name of Mrs. Crooks, whose husband gave 2 lots for the building of the Napier Church.

Nashua (Chickasaw)
(1982), (2002)
Nashua was incorporated in 1869 and named for Nashua, New Hampshire.
(Note: See Bradford for Little Brown Church)

Nemaha (Sac)
(1975), (1977), (1998), (2012)
Nemaha was platted in 1899 by the Milwaukee Land Company. The name Nemaha is from the Indian dialect.
Item of interest
In 1998, the idea of the Tractor Promenade was conceived with square dancing on tractors. Nemaha's gentlemen and their "lovely ladies" did their square dance with eight antique tractors from the 1950s. The show was complete with a square dance caller who directed them to swing their partners, promenade their ladies fair, grand right and left, and do-si-do.

Neola (Pottawattamie)
(2000), (2008), (2013), (2019)
Neola had its start in 1869 with the building of the Chicago, Rock Island and Pacific Railroad through the territory. The word "Neola" was given to the town by the Pottawattamie Indians. The word means "Lookout," a word that refers to the hillside that the town was built on overlooking the Mosquito and Neola Creeks.

NEVADA (Story) (County Seat)
(1976), (1994), (2008), (2018)
Nevada was platted in 1853 and named for the Sierra Nevada mountains.

Newell (Buena Vista)
(1977), (2015)
Newell was established in 1870 and named for an official with the Illinois Central Railroad. Newell was incorporated in 1876.
Items of interest
It was said about Newell in 1869: "This is a splendid location if it doesn't float away." There was so much swamp land surrounding the town that corn could not be planted in straight rows, because farmers had to go around the mud holes. Over time with improved drainage, ditches were hand-dug which allowed the fertile rich farm land to be tilled. The farming community constantly battled muddy streets, roads, mosquitoes and plagues of grasshoppers.

Newell was the home of George Allee, a Harvard graduate and fellow classmate of President Franklin D. Roosevelt. FDR invited the entire class to his inaugural celebration; but, George did not attend, since he did not smoke, nor drink and was not a Democrat.

George Allee was instrumental in the development of hybrid corn for Northwest Iowa and perfecting the "yield test" for small grain. This standard measurement is now used throughout the world. He was the first president of the Small Grain Growers Association, which evolved into the Iowa Corn Growers.

George's wife, Mary Kingman Allee was a true Victorian lady. She was well-educated but thought it was immoral to have a toilet in her new home. The outhouse remained for a period of time after the home was built in 1891.

Newhall (Benton)
(1994), (2004)
Newhall began in 1881 with the building of the Chicago, Milwaukee and St. Paul Railroad through the territory. There is no record of how the town got its name, but some believe it was named for John B. Newhall who was the Chamber of Commerce press agent for the Territory of Iowa.
Item of interest
In 1924, the Iowa High School Athletic Association decided that organized basketball was "unhealthy" for girls and announced their decision to eliminate the girls' state championship tournament. In response, female athletes statewide took action. Members of the Newhall team rode on horseback from farm to farm to win their neighbors' support. Those efforts paid off big for Newhall's players. In 1927, they won the first-ever girls state championship under the newly-founded Iowa Girls High School Athletic Union. On a breathless night, fans gathered at a Newhall restaurant to remotely follow the state championship that wasn't broadcast on the radio. The tournament plays were called out using a long-distance phone call. The whole town turned out the next morning to welcome their champions back home.

NEW HAMPTON (Chickasaw) (County Seat)
(1977), (2017)
New Hampton was founded about 1855 and named after New Hampton, New Hampshire, the native town of one of its founders.

New Hartford (Butler)
(2015

New Haven (Mitchell)
(1987)
New Haven was settled about 1883. It was originally known as Hell's Town. In the early days, there were two saloons. Fighting resulted from too much drinking and differences between the Irish and Germans. Because of the brawling, the village became known as Hell's Town. Finally, both saloons were closed as the result of the disturbances. When peace came to

the community, the residents began to call their village New Heaven which eventually was changed to New Haven, meaning a place of rest.

Newkirk (Sioux)
(1990), (2005)
Newkirk was first settled in 1870. Kirk is the Dutch word for church. The Dutch left the Netherlands in search of religious freedom which resulted in the town being named new church or Newkirk.

New Liberty (Scott)
(2008)
New Liberty was incorporated in 1909.

New London (Henry)
(2003), (2009)
New London was first settled around 1833. It was originally called Dover, after its founder Abraham C. Dover.

New Market (Taylor)
(2003)
New Market was incorporated in 1883. There is some question regarding the naming of the town. The old settlers wanted it to be called Stockton in honor of one of the earliest settlers of the township. Others wanted to call it New Memory. After the railroad painted the words "New Market" on the depot, the name remained.

New Providence (Hardin)
(1986), (1998)
New Providence was laid out in 1855 by E. Andrews, Dr. Eli Jessup and Daniel Dillion. It is located in Providence township and is where it got its name.

New Sharon (Mahaska)
(2018)
New Sharon was incorporated in 1871. The town was first called Schenefeld, which means pretty field, but the name was difficult to spell

and was rejected. The name of Sharon was selected but there was already a Sharon in Iowa, so the name was changed to New Sharon.

Item of interest

In the early days whenever smoke was spotted, the towns' people would start yelling and soon afterwards the men of the town would show up with pails and blankets to try to extinguish the fire. It is said that the first person to arrive at the scene of a fire would be the person in charge. He was the one who would coordinate the activities of everyone as they arrived at the site.

NEWTON (Jasper) County Seat)
(1975), (1984), (2000), (2006), (2018)

Newton was incorporated in 1857 and first named Newton City. It was named for Sgt. John Newton who was believed to be an American War Solider. Newton was from South Carolina who served under Major Francis Marion, AKA "The Swamp Fox."

Items of interest

In the late 19th century, Newton's growth was fueled by the development of coal mines in the region. In the 20th century, Newton was a manufacturing community with much of its growth derived from the washing machine industry.

Newton entered the national stage in 1938 when martial law was declared during a strike at the Maytag Washing Machine Company. The governor ordered the Iowa National Guard to protect the company against the workers with tanks and machine guns. With the backing of four troop companies, Maytag beat the strike and forced workers to return to work with a 10% pay cut.

Newton is home to the Iowa Speedway, a 7/8-mile race track purchased by NASCAR in 2014. It is the only short track owned by NASCAR west of the Mississippi River.

On August 30, 1969, world boxing champion Rocky Marciano died when his airplane crashed in Newton.

In 1941, Frederick Louis Maytag established the Maytag Dairy Farm, which manufacturers blue cheese and other cheeses. The cheese is still made entirely by hand in the small plant that Fred constructed more than 75 years ago in the shadow of the milking barn. The prize-winning herd is gone, but the barn remains and the company now uses fresh milk from local dairy farms. The hand-formed wheels are aged for approximately six months to reach their peak perfection. The Maytag Dairy Farms is owned by eleven members of the Maytag family.

Starting in 2002, Newton started to host the Iowa Sculpture Festival. This is an annual event held in June.

New Virginia (Warren)
(1991), (1992), (2003)
New Virginia was laid out in 1856 and named New Virginia because many of the early settlers were from Virginia.

New York (Wayne)
(2016)
New York was established in 1856, and named for the state of New York

Nichols (Muscatine)
(1986)
Nichols was established in the early 1870s. Its orginal name was "Railroad Addition," then later referred to as Nichols Station in
reference to the previous owner of the town. The town's name was then changed to Nichols by Benjamin F. Nichols, in honor of his father, Samuel Nichols, who was instrumental in bringing the railroad to the area.

Nodaway (Adams)
(1992), (2009), (2016)
Nodaway was incorporated in 1900 and is located on the bank of the East Nodaway River. It was first named East Nodaway but then a new name of Rachelle was proposed, adopted and recorded in Washington

D.C. during the 1870s. The name was unpopular and was changed to Nodaway again. The word Nodawa, as named by a party of Dakota Indians while traveling through this part of Iowa, means crossed without a canoe. The name Nodawa was recorded in the journal of Lewis and Clark during their 1804 expedition.

Nora Springs (Cerro Gordo)
(2002), (2014)
Nora Springs was founded in 1857 and incorporated in 1875. Its early name was Woodstock.

In 1857, Edward P. Greeley was persuaded by Edson Gaylord to come to Woodstock and make a substantial investment in the town. Mr. Greeley agreed, providing the towns name be changed to Elnora, the name of his lady friend in Vermont. Gaylord wanted the town to be named Springs for the many springs in the area. As a compromise, they agreed to rename the town Nora Springs. Upon returning to Vermont, Mr. Greeley was rejected by his lady friend.

North English (Iowa and Keokuk)
(1986), (1995)
North English was laid out in 1855. The town boasts three different name before being named North English. First it was called "Soaptown," based on the soap making business in town, then called Nevada but there was already a Nevada, and finally North English after the English River.

North Liberty (Johnson)
(2008),
The North Liberty area was first settled in 1838 by John Gaylor and Alonzo C. Dennison. It was originally known by early settlers as "Big Bottom" or "North Bend," in reference to its location near the bend of the Iowa River. It was later known as "Squash Bend." In 1857, the city was platted and officially named as North Liberty. It was incorporated in 1913,

NORTHWOOD (Worth) (County Seat)
(1996), (2005)

Northwood was laid out in 1857 and platted in 1858. The town was first name Gulbrand by Scandinavian settlers. On the side of Gulbrand was the south woods and the north woods. The first postmaster lived near the north woods, so the post office was renamed Northwood.

Norwalk (Warren)
(1992), (1997), (2019)

Norwalk was incorporated in 1900. The first settlers came to the Norwalk area about 1846. The town was first known as Pyra. Mr. Swan, who was born in Norwalk, Connecticut and was associated with a newspaper in Norwalk, Ohio, changed the town's name to Norwalk.

Items of interest

In 1937, Mrs. G. R. McAnich, 35, killed five of her seven children and then turned the gun on herself.

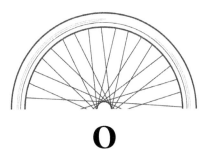

O

Oak Lake (Kossuth)
(1999), (2005)
Oak Lake is a lake located just 4.9 miles from Algona.

Oakland (Pottawttamie)
(1997)
First called Big Grove, Oakland began in 1880 with the building of the Chicago Rock Island and Pacific Railroad through the territory. Its name was changed to Oakland for the many oak trees in the area.
Items of interest
Oakland is home to the Nishna Heritage Museum.

Oakland Acres (Jasper)
(1991)
Oakland Acres was incorporated in 1875.

Oakland Mills (Henry)
(1975), (1992), (2003)
In 1833, thirty years after the Louisiana Territory was purchased from France, President Jackson gave settlers permission to cross the Mississippi River to buy land. In this early scramble, a small group of people made their way up the Skunk (Chicauqua) River and settled in an oak tree covered valley. They named the area Oakland.
Item of interest
By 1839, a wood-stone dam was built and a grist mill was being constructed. Next a saw mill built on the south side of the river and later a woolen mill. All this occurred before Iowa became a state on December 28, 1846.

Oakley (Lucas)
(1997), (2009)
Oakley was settled in the 1850s. It was named for the 40 acres of oak trees which covered the area.

Item of interest

In October of 1900, the Liberty Township Republicans gathered at Oakley to organize themselves into Lucas County's own incarnation of the Rough Riders. A mounted unit of some sixty volunteers, male and female, was formed to campaign for Republican candidates. The Rough Riders became legendary, thanks in large part to President Theodore Roosevelt.

Oakville (Louisa)
(1979)
Oakville was laid out in 1891 and incorporated in 1902. The town was known as Tater Island. It is believed that the name resulted from the area being shaped like a potato or that the area was perfect for growing potatoes; however, early settlers decided to call it Oakville after standing under a Burr Oak tree.

Ocheyedan (Osceola)
(1996)
Ocheyedan started in 1884 with the building of the Burlington, Cedar Rapids & Northern Railroad through the territory. In the early Dacotah (Sioux) dictionary compiled in 1852, there were two names, Acheya and Akicheya, meaning to mourn as for a dead relative. The Indians applied these to landmarks in the area to commemorate two Indian boys who were killed by a party of tribal enemies. Acheya (white settlers pronounced it Ocheyeda) is a mourning ground. An "n" was added and the name became "Ocheyedan."

Items of interest

Ocheyedan's name was declared the "most difficult to pronounce" in the State of Iowa by Readers Digest.

It was thought that the mound located near the town was an Indian burying ground. This was found not to be true when geologists found that it was a kame of glacial origin. Kames

are hills and ridges of stratified drift deposits by glaciers.
The mound is chiefly sand and gravel with small boulders,
including rocks of many different kinds.

Odebolt (Sac)
(1988), (1988)
Odebolt was incorporated on May 13, 1878. Odebolt was named for
Odebolt Creek, but the source of its name is in disputed. There are many
stories about the origin of Obebolt:

- It was name by a French fur trapper whose name was reportedly
  Odebeau, and his name was modified.
- Another story is that a German was crossing the creek when the
  king bolt dropped out of the wagon gear. It is alleged that he
  exclaimed, "O de bolt!" Consequently, the name "Odebolt" was
  given to the creek and from the creek, the towns name.
- Captain William Familron, an agent for the railroad, was out
  with a party of six men, including a Frenchman. As they were
  crossing the creek, which was wider because it had rained all
  day, the Frenchman noticed that the bolt fastening the wagon
  tongue was about to fall out and he shouted, "O de bolt!" and
  that is how the creek was named.
- Odebolt is an incorrect pronunciation of the French words "eau
  de beau" which is translates as "water of beauty" or "beautiful
  water." This pronunciation is thought possible for an uneducated
  half-breed fur trapper to mispronounce the words.

Oelwein (Fayette)
(1990), (2002), (2014)
In 1872, Oelwein was laid out by Gustav Oelwein and named for him.
Some years later the two dividing streets of Oelwein were named for his
sons, Frederick and Charles. Oelwein was incorporated in 1873 and again
in 1888.

Ogden (Boone)
(1976), (2008), (2018)

Ogden was incorporated in 1878 and named for William B. Ogden, a railroad official.

Items of interest

Ogden's main street was part of the famous Lincoln Highway, the first highway to cross the continent from New York City to San Francisco.

Ogden was the home of Brooklyn "Brookie" Supreme (April 12, 1928 – September 6, 1948), a Belgian stallion noted for his extreme size. It was thought that the horse may have been the world record holder for largest (but not tallest) horse. He was designated the world's heaviest horse. He stood 19.2 hands tall (about 7 feet) and weighed 3,200 pounds, with a girth of 10 feet 2 inches.

Okoboji (Dickinson)
(2014)

Okoboji was incorporated in 1922. The Dacotah Indians called East Okoboji Lake "Okoboozhy" and West Okoboji was named "Minnetonka," signifying big water. Since there was already a large popular lake in central Minnesota called Lake Minnetonka, Iowa renamed it West Okoboji. At one time, there was an attempt to be renamed it Lake Harriot in honor of Dr. Harriot and the east lake was to be named Rice Lake in honor of Senator Henry M. Rice, a U.S. Senator from Minnesota. However, the local people settled with the current names of West Okoboji and East Okoboji. There appears to be some confusion over the origin of the word Okoboji. Professor T.H. Macbride says the name means, "place of rest." Others believe the origin of the word means "and there are others" from the Dacotah Indian translation.

Olds (Henry)
(2000)

Olds incorporated in 1900.

Olin (Jones)
(1994), (2004)

Olin was incorporated in 1878 and named for D. A. Olin, general superintendent of the Chicago, Milwaukee, St. Paul and Pacific Railroad.

Ollie (Jones)
(1979), (1988)
Originally known as Hemingford, the town voted to change the name to Ollie in 1892.

ONAWA (Monona) (County Seat)
(1977), (1983), (1987), (1995), (2004), (2018)
Onawa was platted in 1857 and named for a character mentioned in the poem <u>The Song of Hiawatha</u> by Henry Wadsworth Longfellow which features Native American characters. The epic relates to the fictional adventures of an Ojibwe warrior named Hiawatha and the tragedy of his love for Minnehaha, a Dakota woman. Events in the story are set in the pictured rock area on the south shore of Lake Superior.

Onawa, which originated from Onaway, is found in Book XI of this poem. The musician Chibiabos recites a song in which he addresses an imagined lover named Onaway.

And the gentle Chibiabos
Sang in accents sweet and tender,
Sang in tones of deep emotion,
Songs of love and songs of longing;
Looking still at Hiawatha,
Looking at fair Laughing Water,
Sang he softly, sang in this wise:

"Onaway! Awake, beloved!
Thou the wild-flower of the forest!
Thou the wild-bird of the prairie!
Thou with eyes so soft and fawn-like!

"If thou only lookest at me,
I am happy, I am happy,
As the lilies of the prairie,
When they feel the dew upon them!

"Sweet thy breath is as the fragrance
Of the wild-flowers in the morning,
As their fragrance is at evening,
In the Moon when leaves are falling.

"Does not all the blood within me
Leap to meet thee, leap to meet thee,
As the springs to meet the sunshine,
In the Moon when nights are brightest?

"Onaway! my heart sings to thee,
Sings with joy when thou art near me,
As the sighing, singing branches
In the pleasant Moon of Strawberries!

"When thou art not pleased, beloved,
Then my heart is sad and darkened,
As the shining river darkens
When the clouds drop shadows on it!

"When thou smilest, my beloved,
Then my troubled heart is brightened,
As in sunshine gleam the ripples
That the cold wind makes in rivers.

"Smiles the earth, and smile the waters,
Smile the cloudless skies above us,
But I lose the way of smiling
When thou art no longer near me!

"I myself, myself! behold me!
Blood of my beating heart, behold me!
Oh awake, awake, beloved!
Onaway! awake, beloved!"

Items of interest
From 1944 to 1946 Onawa was the site of a Prisoner of War (POW) camp for captured German soldiers. Historical documents indicate there were never more than 50 POWs in camp.

In 1920, the Eskimo Pie was created in Onawa by Chris Nelson, a Danish schoolteacher and candy shop owner. He got the inspiration from a young Onawa boy who could not decide between chocolate candy and ice cream. Mr. Nelson experimented with this tasty treat and eventually worked with Mr. Russell Stover to bring the Eskimo Pie to market.

Onslow (Jones)
(1974), (1985)
Onslow was platted in 1871 and incorporated in 1888. It was noted that Onslow was named after a former governor of Maine; however, Maine did not have a governor called Onslow.

ORANGE CITY (Sioux) (County Seat)
(1975), (1993), (1996), (2002), (2005), (2012), (2017)
Orange City was founded in 1870 and first called Holland for the settler's country of origin. It was named for William of Orange of the Netherlands.
Items of interest
In the 19th century, there was a second Dutch migration to the New World and the Midwest. It brought immigrants who desired freedom of religious expression and opportunities. In 1847, the best-known settlements of the Dutch Reformed immigrants were in Holland, Michigan and Pella, Iowa. Most of these immigrants joined the Reformed Church in America. In the 1870s some Pella residents, led by Henry Hospers,

moved to inexpensive, fertile land in northwestern Iowa and named their main settlement Orange City, for William I, Prince of Orange, who in the mid 17th century led the Dutch revolt against Spain which resulted in independence for the Netherlands.

Thanks to its Dutch heritage, Orange City has been called one of the cleanest towns in America.

Orange City is home to Northwestern College, a Christian college in the reformed tradition dating back to the 16th-century Protestant Reformation and the works of John Calvin. Calvinist churches spread throughout continental Europe and the English-speaking world, including North America. Their best-known representatives were the Puritans and the Presbyterians.

In 1872, the one of the founders of what became Hope College in Holland, Michigan, desired to establish a Christian classical academy in Orange City to prepare students for college and ultimately for ministry in the Reformed Church in America. A grasshopper invasion and intermittent floods, hailstorms and droughts delayed fulfillment of that dream. After considerable economic hardship, the area's Dutch Reformed people incorporated the Northwestern Classical Academy on July 19, 1882, with the motto "Deus est lux" (God is light). The constitution called for establishing an institution of learning "for the promotion of science and literature in harmony with religion as expressed in, the doctrinal standards of the Reformed Church in America."

Orient (Adair)
(1981), (1984), (2000), (2009)
Orient started in 1878 with the building of the railroad through the territory and was incorporated in 1882. It was named for Orient township.

OSAGE (Mitchell) (County Seat)
(1987), (1993), (1996)
Osage started in 1854 by Dr. Moore and named for his eldest daughter Cora, but the name was never recorded. In 1855, Mr. Gibbs arrived from Massachusetts, representing wealthy capitalists in Massachusetts and Connecticut and prevailed upon Mr. Orrin Sage, a banker from Ware, Massachusetts to invest in this community. Later Mr. Sage gave $2,000 and 600 acres of land to the Library Building Fund. Because of his benevolence, the town's name was changed to Osage in his honor (Mr. O Sage).

OSCEOLA (Clarke) (County Seat)
(1992), (2003)
Osceola was laid out in 1851 and named after Chief Osceola of the Seminole Indian tribe.

OSKALOOSA (Mahaska) (County Seat)
(1988), (1992), (2003), (2013)
The town was platted in 1844 when William Canfield moved his trading post from the Des Moines River to Oskaloosa. Oskaloosa derives its name from Ouscaloosa who, according to town lore, was a Creek princess who married the Seminole chief Osceola. It means "last of the beautiful." (This interpretation of "last of the beautiful" may not be correct. "Oskaloosa" in the Mvskoke-Creek language means "black rain" from the Mvskoke words "oske" (rain) and "lvste" (black).

Items of interest
In the city's town square is a bronze statue of Chief Mahaska, the 19th-century leader of a Native American tribe for whom Mahaska County was named.

The first white settlers arrived in 1835 led by Nathan Boone, youngest son of Daniel Boone, who was acting on instructions to select the first site of Fort Des Moines. The Fort was located on a high ridge between the Skunk River and Des Moines River.

In the late nineteenth and early twentieth century, Oskaloosa was a national center of bituminous coal mining. The town was known for its coal-mining operations until an explosion in 1902 that killed 20 workers.

Oskaloosa is home to William Penn University founded in 1873 and named for the Quaker William Penn. In the 19th century, members of the Quaker Society from Pennsylvania made their way into Iowa looking to find new a life. Immediately, they began to plan for a place for their annual Friends Meetings. This area would soon become Mahaska County. More and more Quakers made their way into Iowa. Since education was very important to them, Quaker educational institutions were built to maintain and teach their way of life.

History buffs can pay respects to Becky and Jennie, the mule pair that now rest in peace at the Nelson Pioneer Farm Museum. During the Civil War, the mules pulled cannons before returning to the Nelson homestead, where they died years later at the ripe old ages of 34 and 42. "They're each buried with their head lying on a satin pillow," said Kelly Halbert, the museum's administrator and curator.

Ossian (Winneshiek)
(1993), (1999), (2017)

Ossian was platted in 1855 and named for its founder, John Ossian Porter. Porter's middle name has an interesting origin. Ossian is described as "A legendary Irish hero and bard (professional story teller) of the third century," the subject of a collection of poems by James MacPherson, published from 1760 to 1768. They were thought to be translations from the original Gaelic manuscripts of "Ossian." Legendary or not, Ossian the Bard was a well-known tradition in Ireland. Quite likely, Porter, though born in New York State, was of Irish ancestry.

Items of interest

In 1851, John Porter was delinquent in his taxes in the amount of $3.80. John McKay of Washington Prairie, who was thought to be the richest man in Winneshiek County, paid the taxes and was issued a tax deed to the Porter farm by the county treasurer for the additional sum of $119. Although Mr. Porter retained ownership, perhaps by delayed payment during a grace period, the title to his property remained cloudy. When the parcel of 32 acres was sold to Sarah Owens many years later, she demanded that the title be cleared. John McKay's widow and children agreed to sign off their claim for $1. That is how close Ossian first came to be called "McKaysville!"

Otterville (Buchanan)
(1982), (2014)
The village of Otterville was platted about 1857, by Robert T. Young, who owned the land. Otterville is located near Otter Creek from where it got its name. It has never incorporated.

Ottosen (Humboldt)
(1985), (1993)
Ottosen was founded in 1896 by Chris Ottosen, a grain dealer, and named for him. It was incorporated in 1909.
Items of interest
Much of the town was burned by a fire in the mid 20th century and has never rebuilt.

In 1978 Ottosen was ground zero for multiple sightings of a strange creature, considered by some to be Sasquatch or Bigfoot. Between July and September of 1978, twelve people either reported to the authorities that they saw a giant creature or heard strange howling sounds. Multiple farm animals were found dead and strange footprints were seen in the mud. Other reports in 1978 came from the Humboldt County communities of Hardy and Humboldt, as well as several from Marion, Mahaska, and Lucas Counties. The witnesses of Ottosen were considered to be the most credible. According to two residents in different statements, the creature was seen in town along Main Street.

OTTUMWA (Wapello) (County Seat)
(1984), (2000), (2009), (2016)

Ottumwa was laid out in 1843 during a land rush, when the region was opened to settlers. Originally called Appanoose Rapids before the name was changed to Louisville and then Ottumwanoc before being shortened to Ottumwa. Ottumwa is said to be derived from an Algonquian (Fox) word meaning "rippling waters," although it may simply mean "town."

Items of interest

In the 1880s Ottumwa had over 40 cigar manufacturers which employed 500 people. Some of the leading cigar manufacturers were located in Ottumwa. Julius Fecht, owned a tobacco plantation in Cuba. The tobacco was loaded onto ships and sent to Florida, then the valuable cargo would be hauled to Ottumwa by wagon train escorted by armed guards.

Ottumwa is called the "City of Bridges," even though there are only three main bridges. The bridges were small, and crossed over the Des Moines River.

Cpl. Walter Eugene "Radar" O'Reilly, the company clerk in the M*A*S*H television series mentioned Ottumwa as his hometown.

Oxford (Johnson)
(1976), (2011)

Oxford was platted in 1868. The name came from Oxford Township which takes its name from Oxford, New York. It was originally called "Tanktown" or "The Tank."

Oxford Junction (Jones)
(1985), (1994), (2004), (2012)

The town was laid out in 1871 and got its name from the junction of two rail lines.

Item of interest

It cannot be found on a street sign, but Oxford Junction had a "Goose Street." Main Street was called this because several early residents along the street raised geese for their eggs, meat, feathers, and fat (goose grease). Local lore has it that when the housewives were plucking geese, the breeze carried feathers over the street like a snow storm.

Oyens ((Plymouth)
(1993), (2005)
Oyens was platted in 1886 and incorporated in 1909.

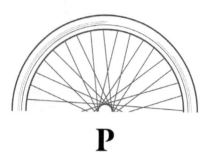

P

Packard (Butler)
(1999), (2014)
Packard was named for Joseph Packard, a local land owner.
<u>Item of interest</u>
In 1916, five persons lost their lives and a number were injured in the wreck of Rock Island Train No. 19 when the train went through a bridge at Packard. The wreck was caused by a storm which weaken the bridge and crippled wire service making it was impossible to obtain accurate information. According to information from various sources, the greatest loss of life was in the day coach, which toppled on its side under ten feet of water.

Packwood (Jefferson)
(1979), (1984), (1988), (2000), (2009), (2013)
In 1883, Samuel Packwood founded the village along the existing Burlington Western Railroad.

Palmer (Pocahontas)
(1987)
Palmer was first called Hanson which sounded too close to Manson so the town changed its name to Palmer. Palmer was the name of one of the railroad workers.

Palo (Linn)
(1994), (2004), (2012), (2015)
Palo was first settled in 1839. It was named for the battle of Palo Alta; however, it was shortened to Palo. In 1846, Palo Alta was the first major battle of the American Mexican war over disputed land which is now part of Texas.

Item of interest
Iowa's only nuclear plant is located north of Palo. The Duane Arnold Energy Center generates enough electricity to power 600,000 homes every year.

Panama (Shelby)
(1983)
Panama began in 1882 with the building of the Chicago, Milwaukee and St. Paul Railroad through the territory and was incorporated in 1886.

Panora (Guthrie)
(1974), (1986)
Panoea was established in 1851. When pioneers viewed the site of the present town from the hillside they exclaimed, "What a beautiful panorama!" Later, when the town was platted, the word "panorama" was shortened to Panora.

Paralta (Linn)
(1978), (1991)
Paralta was formed when the Chicago, Rock Island and Pacific Railroad came to the area.

Paris (Linn)
(1981), (1997), (2003)
Paris was first settled in 1841 and named for Paris, France.

Parkersburg (Butler)
(2010), (2015)
Parkersburg was incorporated in 1874 and named for Pascal P. Parker, a prominent settler and the town's first postmaster.
Items of interest
In 2008, a tornado hit Parkersburg killing seven people, injuring 70, and damaging over 400 homes.

In 2009, a disgruntled 24-year old former football player walked into the school's weight room, which had at least 20 students, then killed the high school's football coach.

Parnell (Iowa)
(1995), (2001)

Parnell was incorporated in 1891 and named for Charles Stewart Parnell, an Irish nobleman and statesman who came to America to plead the case of Ireland's impoverished peasants.

Item of interest

In 1884, the people of the little Irish town of Lytle City moved residences, stores, buildings and families three miles to Parnell so they would be near the railroad.

Paton (Greene)
(1975), (1979), (1989), (1998), (2011)

Paton (Pay-Ton) was incorporated in 1884. It takes its name from a wealthy pioneer land-holder who lived in New York City.

Paullina (O'Brien)
(1996), (2017)

Paullina was laid out in 1882 when the Chicago & Northwestern Railroad was extended to that point. It takes its name from a wealthy pioneer land-holders, Henry and D. Edward Paullin. The Paullin boys came from the east and were Harvard graduates. They came to the Iowa prairies and bought nearly 7000 acres of land in 1880. They were entrepreneurs and speculators looking to make money in the booming land business of the west. No doubt they had good information about the railroad, which was planning to build its tracks through that part of the country. In 1881, the Toledo and Northwestern Railroad laid track from Eagle Grove to Hawarden. Edward Paullin, being a shrewd businessman, offered a town site to the railroad free of charge if it would run the rail lines through his ranch property. The only stipulation was that the town site be named for him. The agreement was made and the town site was called Paullina, which was filed on December 31, 1881 and recorded on January 13, 1882.

Paullina is called "The Gem of the Prairie."

Pekin (Jefferson) (Keokuk)

(2009)

Pekin was first established in 1883 and was first known as Ioka Station, but renamed Pekin. Not much is left of the town and now it is the location of the Pekin Community School District office. The school is built on the former Linby Naval Outlying Landing Field which was built in 1974 for training purposes.

Pella (Marion)

(1984), (1991), (2000), (2013)

Pella was founded in 1847 when eight hundred Dutch immigrants settled in the area. The name "Pella" is in reference to the area of what is now known as Northwestern Jordon, where the Christians of Jerusalem found refuge during the Roman-Jewish war of 70. This was the decisive event in which the Roman army captured the city of Jerusalem and destroyed both the city and its Temple. The word "Pella" means City of Refuge. The name was selected because these immigrants were also seeking religious freedom.

<u>Items of interest</u>

Pella was the childhood home of Wyatt Earp. Before he became a soldier, buffalo hunter, bouncer, miner, saloon-keeper, boxing referee, and sharpshooter, Wyatt Earp was just one of the neighborhood kids. His boyhood home is part of the Pella Historical Village near the town square.

Wyatt Berry Stapp Earp (1848 –1929) was a city policeman in Wichita, Kansas and then in Dodge City, Kansas. He also served as a deputy sheriff and deputy United States marshal in Tombstone, Arizona. He is best known for his part in the gunfight at the O.K. Corral during which three outlaw were killed. The 30-second gunfight defined the rest of his life. Earp's modern-day reputation is that of being the Old West's "toughest and deadliest gunman of his day."

Pella is the headquarters of the Pella Corporation which manufactures windows and doors across the U.S.A and the Vermeer Corporation that manufactures agricultural, environmental and construction equipment.

Pella is the home of Central College, a private liberal arts college affiliated with the Reformed Church in America. Central College officially opened in 1854, with a class of 37 students. In 1916, Central was transferred from Baptist control to the Reformed Church in America.

In 1935, Pella's High School performed an operetta called "Tulip Time in Pella." This prompted a discussion about holding an annual festival to promote and commemorate Pella's Dutch heritage.

The first planned Tulip Time festival was too late in the year to have real tulips, so a local cabinet-maker made 125 four-foot-tall wooden tulips for the event. A committee then was formed to make sure that 85,000 tulips were planted that fall. The annual Tulip Time festival is the first weekend of May.

Peoria (Mahaska)
(2018)
Peoria was founded in 1853 and named for Peoria, Illinois.
<u>Item of interest</u>
The First World War sparked a wave of hyper-patriotism in the United States that had an impact on ethnic communities with German roots. The federal government, under President Woodrow Wilson, set off a campaign by having Congress create the War Propaganda Committee. Its purpose was to promote patriotism and identify "traitors" with pro-German sympathies. Since Dutch is a Low German language, it was confused with Duits or Deutsch (High German), and tended to be associated with Germany.

The Netherlands remained neutral during the war and this led some Americans to conclude that the Dutch were sympathetic to Germany. Dutch immigrants were also known to harbor anti-British sentiments lingering from the Anglo-Boer War (1899-1902). Many Dutch immigrants came to America in the last big wave before WW I and had not yet applied for American citizenship; therefore, they were exempt from the military draft. The Dutch prospered in the booming war economy while their neighbors went off to fight in the war. This created a lot of animosity. The Dutch not only prospered, but the Dutch farmers willingly paid a premium for nearby farmland to keep their adult children close. This angered the American neighbors, who resented in having to sell their land to the Dutch.

Twenty-seven states enacted sedition laws (most targeting Germans) far more severe than the national model. Iowa Governor William Harding in May of 1918 issued a "Language Proclamation" that prohibited the use of any tongue but English on the streets, in stores, in telephone conversations (all phones were then open party lines), and in all worship services. The worship service provision created the greatest hardship for the recent Dutch immigrants because most of their clerics could only preach in Dutch. Under the governor's edict, they had to struggle to use English or not preach. Most chose the former course and fumbled for words. The Iowa governor later offered one concession, the clerics could provide parishioners with English translations of their sermons.

Such conciliatory gestures did not assure hyper-patriots who were focused on rooting out disloyalty. War hysteria prevailed. In some communities, anti-Dutch sentiment boiled over into mob action. Ministers found burning crosses on their parsonage lawn and farmers lost barns to the torch. In the vicinity of Pella, several Christian schools were set fire in what became known as the "Hollander Fires." Supporters managed to extinguish the flames at the Sully Christian School, leaving only minor damage, but the Peoria Christian School and adjacent Christian Reformed Church burned to the ground. In nearby New Sharon, the Reformed Church was set ablaze and the pastor found dynamite under the parsonage that had failed to explode because of a defective fuse.

Events in Peoria took an ugly turn in May of 1918 when a young thug brutally beat the Christian school principal as he walked home from the village general store. The flash point apparently was the decision not to raise the American flag over the school, buy war bonds, or sign food pledges. The school was busting at the seams, due to the high birthrate among the Dutch, while four nearby public schools were "almost without pupils." The birth rate among the Americans was low because their men were off to war, but the Dutch birth rate was high. Following the attack, the school board immediately suspended classes and county authorities ordered the school to remain closed. Some weeks later, state education officials rescinded the order as illegal and allowed the school to reopen.

Dutch leaders saw the troubles rooted in "old and deep-rooted jealousy caused by the prosperity of the Holland-Americans." Dutch farmers around New Sharon received threatening letters in the mail to "leave or be burned out." American farmers, it was reported, hired thugs to set fires for $50 or $100 per "job." The big barns of two Dutch farmers who had two sons serving in the army were also burned down. Another Hollander lost a new house he was about to occupy. At the deepest level, it was a cultural clash between Dutch Reformed immigrants and Protestants, who lived in close physical proximity but in entirely separate social worlds.

Perry (Dallas)
(1980), (1983), (1986), (1994), (2001), (2013)
Perry was laid out in 1869 and named for Col. C.H. Perry, a railroad official.

Item of interest

What does Perry have in common with the Metropolitan Museum of Art in New York, the Victoria and Albert Museum in London, and the Smithsonian's National Museum of Art? A set of grand metal sculptures created by Albert Paley, a metal sculptor known around the globe for his inventive approach to form, development, and metal techniques. Made of farm equipment, mining tools, railroad items, and used pieces of metal donated by local residents, the silver Reconfiguration Arches were welded together into four 16,000-pound pieces. This was complemented by a poem written by Ted Kooser, a former United States Poet Laureate and consultant in poetry to the Library of Congress and Pulitzer Prize winner. The sculpture is located at the front and back of Soumas Court

Persia (Harrison)
(1994)
The town received its name in 1882 from a railroad construction crew member who was from Persia.

Peterson (Clay)
(1982)
Peterson was platted in 1881 when the railroad was extended to that point. The town was named for Adlie Peterson, an early settler.
Item of interest
The first settlement was made in 1856 and in 1862 a fort was built by settlers to defend against anticipated Dakota attacks during the Dakota War of 1862. The fort was never attacked. The blockhouse from this fort still stands near its original location at the corner of Second and Park.

Pierson (Woodbury)
(1978)
Pierson was named for Andrew Pierson, a pioneer settler. It was incorporated in 1891.

Pilot Grove (Lee)
(1997)
Pilot Grove was laid out in 1858 under the name of Overton, but in 1908 its name was changed to Pilot Grove. On a crest far removed from any forest growth, there was a beautiful grove of elm trees. In the midst of this grove stood a giant elm which towered above the stately trees that surrounded it. This grove could be seen for many miles across the prairies and served as a guide to the pioneer who journeyed over the plains. The name Pilot Grove resulted from the many early settlers who were guided to their destination by this friendly pilot.

Pilot Mound (Boone)
(1975), (1979), (1980), (1989), (1998), (2011)
Pilot Mound was laid out in 1881 and the community took its name from the prominent summit which gave a clear view of the surrounding area.

Pioneer (Humboldt)

(1973), (1978)

In 1881, the Hay Press Company purchased the property for its prairie grasses, which they baled and shipped to cities in the east. This is how the town became known as Pioneer.

Pisgah (Harrison)

(1981)

Pisgah was laid out in 1899. Members of the Church of Jesus Christ of Latter-day Saints (Mormons), established Pisgah as temporary settlement in central Iowa and chose the biblical name of Mount Pisgah. In the Book of Deuteronomy (34:1) God commanded Moses to climb up and view the Promised Land. "And Moses went up from the plains of Moab to Mount Nebo, to the top of Pisgah, which is opposite Jericho. And the Lord showed him all the land"

Like Garden Grove, Mount Pisgah was a campsite and temporary settlement in southern Iowa for members of the LDS Church traveling west from Nauvoo, Illinois to winter quarters. Mount Pisgah was established as a temporary way station for Mormons who crossed the plains from 1846 to 1852.

Pittsburg (Van Buren)

(1981), (1997), (2003)

Pittsburg was laid out in 1839, and was originally known as Rising Sun. It changed its name to Pittsburg for Pittsburgh, Pennsylvania.

Pleasant Hill (Polk)

(1988), (1992), (2013)

Pleasant Hill was incorporated in 1956. It was first called Youngstown. The town incorporated so that it could receive the property tax benefits of the Iowa Power & Light Company power plant, which is now within the incorporated city limits of Pleasant Hill.

Pleasant Plain (Jefferson)

(2009)

Pleasant Plain was first settled by Quaker farmers in 1836 and originally called Pleasant Prairie and was later changed to Pleasant Plain. The town was incorporated in 1900.

Pleasantville (Marion)
(1988)
Pleasantville was established in 1849 on land owned by William Wesley Jordan, who purchased it for one horse and $30. It was incorporated in 1872. Tradition has it that the name came from the first pioneers who referred to it in their letters as a pleasant place.

Plover (Pocahontas)
(1987), (2010), (2017)
Plover was platted in 1883 after the Des Moines and Fort Dodge Railroad was built through the territory. The railroad president named the town after the plover bird.

Plymouth (Cerro Gordo)
(2002),
Plymouth was platted in 1858 and incorporated in 1900. It is believed that the very large glacial boulder, found southeast of the existing town, reminded the settlers of The Plymouth Rock in Massachusetts, resulting in the town being named Plymouth.

POCAHONTAS (Pocahontas) (County Seat)
(2010)
Pocahontas was incorporated in 1892 and named for Pocahontas, a Powhatan woman from Jamestown, Virginia. She was the daughter of the chief of the Powhatan Indians. She married the English tobacco planter John Rolfe in Jamestown, Virginia. The marriage ensured peace between the Jamestown settlers and the Powhatan Indians for several years.

Polk City (Polk)
(1973), (1984), (1988), (2000), (2006)
Polk City was settled in 1846 and incorporated in 1875. It took its name from Polk county which was named for President James K. Polk, who served from 1845 to 1849.

Pomeroy (Calhoun)
(2015)
Pomeroy was platted in 1870 in anticipation of the railroad being
built through the settlement. It was named for Charles W. Pomeroy, a
landowner and congressman.

Popejoy (Franklin)
(1978), (2004)
Popejoy was platted in 1880 and incorporated in 1908. It was originally
called Carleton, but renamed Popejoy for John Isacc Popejoy, a prominent
citizen known as the "Cattle King."

Portland (Cerro Gordo)
(1982)
Portland was founded in 1878, and named by the Chicago, Milwaukee
& St. Paul Railroad Company.

Portsmouth (Shelby)
(1994)
Portsmouth was founded in 1882 when the Chicago, Milwaukee &
St. Paul Railroad Company platted the town. The town was incorporated
in 1883.

Postville (Allamkee)
(2017)
Postville was platted in 1853 and named for Joel Post, a pioneer settler.
Items of interest
Postville is known as the "Hometown to the World" because of
its many diverse cultural communities. The town has residents from
Guatemala, Somalia, Russia and the Philippines along with a large Hispanic
and Jewish population.

In 1987, a group of Hasidic Jews started a Kosher slaughterhouse
called Agriprocessors. The business remained in operation until it filed for
bankruptcy on November 5, 2008, after a series of complaints concerning
labor law violations and mistreatment of cattle.

Around 10 on a clear May morning in 2008, two black helicopters circled over Postville, a town of two square miles and fewer than 3,000 residents. Then a line of SUV's drove past Postville's Main Street and its worn brick storefronts. More than 10 white buses with darkened windows and the words "Homeland Security" on their sides were on their way to the other side of town. Postville's four-man police force had no forewarning of what was about to happen. Neither did the mayor. The procession of SUV's, buses and state-trooper cars were descending on Agriprocessors, the largest producer of kosher meat in the United States and Postville's largest employer, which occupies 60 acres on the edge of town.

Within hours of the raid, which Immigration and Customs Enforcement's (I.C.E.) had planned for months, based on evidence that large numbers of Agri's employees used suspect or false Social Security numbers and that plant managers hired minors and violated other labor laws. I.C.E. agents detained 389 undocumented workers, mostly Guatemalans. (Agri employed more than 900 workers, over three shifts.) The agents handcuffed the wrists of the men and women then loaded them into the Homeland Security buses. With one state-trooper vehicle in front of each bus and another behind, they drove to Waterloo where I.C.E. had transformed an 80-acre fairgrounds into a temporary processing center for the workers. For weeks and months afterwards, the public learned of the abuses of workers at the plant. They learned about women who were sexually assaulted by supervisors and of underage employees who were among those on the "kill" floor of the plant who worked 17-hour shifts, six days a week without overtime pay.

Neither the owner, Aaron Rubashkin, nor his sons Sholom and Heshy Rubashkin, who were in charge of the management of Agriprocessors, were convicted of immigration and labor law violations.

Prairieburg (Linn)
(1974), (1985)
Prairieburg was settled in 1867 and named by Henry Ward, a local postmaster and merchant.

Prairie City (Jasper)
(1973)

In 1856, Prairie City was first called Elliott for its founder. Later it was changed to Prairie City because there was already a town named Elliott in Iowa.

Item of interest

The Prairie City Bank Robbery That Ended In An Iowa Cornfield.

It was about 1:30 in the morning on October 28, 1902, when Prairie City dentist, Dr. S. B. Gidford, woke up in his room across the street from the bank. As he stuck his head out a window, a "loaded 44-caliber Colt" was "presented to his face" by a stranger who told him his life was "worth less than 30 cents." That was enough to convince Gidford to retreat to his room.

Other town folks were awakened too. But most, like Dr. W.P. McConnaughy, heard the disturbance and thought it was a group of young men who were known to run down to Pella occasionally, where they became "more or less intoxicated." They typically rode the midnight train back to Prairie City after their night of carousing. And they usually created a disturbance as they made their way to their homes. So, most residents ignored the sounds and went back to sleep. But there was plenty of activity taking place at some local businesses, and it wasn't the antics of the local boys.

Night Marshal Alex Erskine had been overpowered by a gang of men who locked him in Little & Gill's hardware store. Pointing loaded revolvers at him, they warned him to keep quiet or risk losing his life. Then they unloaded five shots into the air, just to let him know they meant business.

As three men stood vigil, two others broke into the depot and the blacksmith shop gathering up crowbars, drills and tongs. They made their way to the bank and set to work. It took three hours of work and eight attempts with explosives; but eventually the robbers broke open the vault, safe and cash box. They made off with about $4,000. They left 81 cents behind but took a box with $10.50 worth of pennies.

The marshal never got a look at the men, so he wasn't able to provide a description. But a witness said they were unmasked and one was a "tall, well-dressed" fellow with a "magnificent physique." Harry Taylor, the town shoemaker, said he saw the men hurrying out of the bank; and one said, "We will camp at the water tank west of the depot." They took off on foot.

When bank officials heard about the robbery, they used telephones and telegraph to spread the news to local communities. But locals were slow in pursuing the robbers. Several hours after news of the robbery spread throughout the town, two buggies with two men in each headed south and southeast out of town to see if they could catch sight of the robbers. But they returned several hours later. People suspected the robbers were hiding along the river where there was dense growth and thick timber. It was said to be "one of the wildest pieces of country" in the state.

By evening a pack of bloodhounds had arrived from Knoxville. They followed scents from the bank, across the public square, to the edge of town. Then the dogs stopped. Heading back to the bank, the hounds rested a bit, had supper and returned to the hunt. But they were never successful in tracking down the robbers.

A couple days later, locals heard a stranger had been seen in a cornfield outside town. The marshal put together a posse. Surrounding the field, the marshal and his helpers flushed out the man and hauled him to the town jail. He wasn't talking at first. But the marshal said he was adopting the "sweating process" to convince the suspect to open up. He expected more information would be forthcoming.

Meantime, bank officials worried residents had lost faith in the bank. They feared a run on the bank, so cashier Albert Meller was dispatched to Des Moines to get some cash to shore up the Prairie City bank. Accompanied by a detective, Meller brought back $10,000 to handle "emergencies" that might come up at the bank.

It's unclear if the robbers were ever caught. Residents of Prairie City believed they had escaped over the border into neighboring Missouri.

"Courtesy of Cheryl Mullenbach"

By Cheryl Mullenbach/Iowa History September 9, 2017

Sources

"A Bank Robbery at Prairie City," Des Moines Register, Oct 29, 1902.

"Burglars Loot Iowa Bank and Escape With Booty," Daily Times (Davenport), Oct 28, 1902.

"Happenings in Hawkeyedom," Humeston, New Era, Nov 5,1902.

"Robber Found in Cornfield," Perry Daily Chief, Oct 30, 1902.

"Robbers Have Escaped, "Sioux Valley News, Nov. 6, 1902.

Prairie Grove (Des Moines)
(1984)
The schoolhouse site was on the prairie with a small grove of trees nearby. This is how the locally descriptive name of Prairie Grove was selected.

Prescott (Adams)
(1984), (1997), (2009), (2016)
Prescott was platted in 1870. With the building of the Burlington Northern Railroad in 1868. The settlement of Prescott was then known as Motley and later Glendale. Around 1869 the towns name as changed to Prescott, in honor of one of the men who helped build the railroad.

Items of interest

Prescott is home to the Kline Museum which is a showcase of one man's treasure, lovingly restored one piece at a time. This collection includes a wide variety of farm machinery, family heirlooms, and community memorabilia. The prize of the collection is the fully-restored 1911 Carter Automobile, one of only 500 ever manufactured.

For Allen Taylor, January 15, 1919 was just another day on his farm near Prescott. That is, until his 15-year-old neighbor Irene Hoskins came stumbling down the lane with a gash on the side of her head.

Young Irene told Allen that her father, John Hoskins, had murdered her stepmother, Hulda, and her two stepsiblings, Roy and Gladys.

Allen raced to the telephone and called for help. Chester Wood, another close neighbor, arrived soon thereafter. Together they rode to the Hoskins farm. The men had known John for some time, and wouldn't have thought him capable of something like this.

John Hoskins was a widower with two children, Merlin and Irene. In 1915, he had married Hulda Campbell, a widow from nearby Nevinville, Iowa. She had two children—Roy, 12, and Gladys, 18. John and Hulda had appeared to be happy together, and the family was well liked in the area.

When Wood and Taylor arrived at the Hoskins farm, they could see Hulda's bloodied body on the back porch. John stood nearby, grasping a straight razor. He told them not to come any closer, or he would attack.

By the time law enforcement arrived, John had slit his own throat, as well as one of his wrists. He lay in a pool of blood, just inside the back door of the house. One of the responders, a doctor, inspected the wounded man, declaring him beyond saving.

But then, John began to twitch. They lifted him up and carried him inside the house to treat his wounds.

A horrific sight awaited the responders once they entered the back door into the kitchen. On the floor were the bodies of Roy and Gladys. Blood covered the room in a grisly red mosaic. Merlin was nowhere to be found.

The doctor kneeled down to more closely examine John. It became clear that his wounds were superficial; the damage to his wrist was minor, and his throat had been cut too high to cause any fatal injury. The sheriff ordered Hoskins to be treated and then transported to the county jail in Corning, Iowa.

With John Hoskins in custody, the investigation commenced. At the coroner's inquest, several of those who had been present that day were called to testify. A grim timeline emerged, based largely on the testimony of Irene and Merlin, who it turned out, had witnessed some of the bloodshed before fleeing to his uncle's house. Irene said that she and Gladys had slept in until nearly 6:30 that morning, which was much later than John had wanted. The family planned to go see John's parents that morning.

The delay apparently put John in a foul mood and soon began arguing with Hulda. According to the children, this was far from an isolated event. Indeed, earlier that same year, an enraged John had grabbed Roy by the throat and began strangling him. When Hulda and Irene tried to break it up, John attacked them. The quarrel subsided without further injury, nevertheless it told of the violence to come.

As John argued with his wife, the children sat down at the kitchen table and began eating breakfast. Soon John joined them while Hulda went outside to the separating house to get some lard.

In the middle of the meal, John stood up and walked to the back door. He reached outside and grabbed a piece of wooden buggy axle that he used for mixing hog feed.

Without a word, John then walked over and clubbed Gladys in the head. She crumpled to the ground. John swung again, this time striking Roy. Irene and Merlin both ran, afraid for their lives.

John ran after Irene, catching her easily in the front yard. She begged her father to stop, but John swung the axle. Blood seeped from the gash left in her head as John turned away from his bleeding child.

He next spotted Merlin running across the yard, and called out to him. The boy froze in place. John ordered Merlin to take his horse and ride to his uncle's farm. He wanted Merlin to tell his uncle what had happened that morning. Petrified, Merlin obeyed. He ran to the barn, saddled up his horse, and prepared to go off to his uncle's house.

John then returned to the kitchen, where he finished off Gladys and Roy with additional blows to the head. It was at this point that Hulda returned to the main house. Upon entering, she discovered her children dead on the floor. John then struck her in the face with the axle. Hulda stumbled out the back door and into the yard. John followed her, smashing her in the head, then leaving her for dead.

Meanwhile, Irene had come to her senses. The first thing she saw was her stepmother in a heap in the back yard. She staggered over to the injured woman. Hulda was badly hurt, but still alive. She told Irene to run away and find help. Irene complied, and went straight to Allen Taylor's farm.

With the last of her strength, Hulda crawled onto the porch, and died.

By the end of the inquest, the entire region knew what John Hoskins had done. He showed absolutely no remorse about his crime, even relating details of that day to his jailers.

Local authorities brought Hoskins to trial almost immediately, and by March 1, 1919, he had pled guilty to murder. He was sent to Iowa State Penitentiary in Fort Madison, Iowa, to serve out a life sentence. Irene and Merlin were sent to live with their grandparents in Nevinsville.

In 1959, forty years after the murders took place, a 78-year-old John Hoskins was granted parole after his original sentence was commuted. Surprisingly, he went to stay with Irene, who was now living in California. Life outside prison didn't suit John, however, and he asked to be returned to Iowa. The state obliged, and a parole officer escorted Hoskins back to Fort Madison.

He died there in 1963. John's headstone is plain, and makes no mention of the heinous crimes he committed on a cold January day in 1919.

This account was written by John Brassard Jr.

Preston (Jackson)
(2004),
Preston was founded in 1870 and named for one of its founders, I. M. Preston. It was incorporated in 1890.

PRIMGHAR (O'Brien) (County Seat)
(1990), (1993), (2005) (2017)
Primghar was settled in 1872 and its name was derived from the names of eight early settlers who laid out the town. A poem was written to mark that event.

The only Primghar in the World
Pumphrey, the treasure who drives the first nail
Roberts, the donor, is quick on the trail
Inman dips slightly, the first letter in,
McCormack adds M, which makes a full PRIM
Green, thinking of groceries, gives the G
Hayers drops the H without asking a fee,
Albright, the joker, with his jokes all at par
Rereick brings up the rear and crowns

Item of interest
A brief history of O'Brien County, states: "the courthouse location in (the village of) O'Brien in the extreme southeast corner of the county became a growing issue. To resolve the matter, an election was held on November 11, 1872, to determine the location of the courthouse." A total of 360 votes were cast, with 307 voting to move the courthouse to the exact geographical center of the county. Another historian wrote, "Probably the only case in Iowa, perhaps anywhere, where a bare spot of raw prairie was

actually voted to be the county seat." This eventually became the town of Primghar.

Prole (Warren)
(1992), (2009)
Prole started in 1884 and first called Spencerville. It was named for Albert Western Prole, a pharmacist.

Protivin (Chickasaw) (Howard)
(1977), (1996), (2005), (2017)
Protivin was platted in 1878 and incorporated in 1894. Early settlers named the town for the Bohemian town of Protivin, which is now in the south Bohemian Region of the Czeck Republic. The first Czech settlers arrived around 1855 and settled here because the landscape reminded them of their home. The community was predominately Catholic and they built their own church in 1878, which was the town's first structure.

Item of interest
Protivin holds an annual weekend Czech Days festival each August.

Pulaski (Davis)
(1997)
Pulaski was founded in 1856. It was named for Casimir Pulaski, a Polish nobleman, soldier and military commander who fought in the Revolution War. He has been called, "the father of the American cavalry."

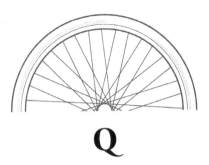

Q

Quasqueton (Buchanan)
(1982), (1990), (1998), (2002), (2010)
Quasqueton is located where several Native American trails intersected. The site was a well-known river crossing. The name Quasqueton means "swift running water." It was first settled by Euro-Americans in 1842.

Items of interest

In 1858, the Quaqueton Mutual Protection Company was organized to prevent horse thievery. In 1904, most of Quasqueton was destroyed in a fire.

Quasqueton is home to the Lowell and Agnes Walter House at Cedar Rock. It is a signature home designed by Frank Lloyd Wright. The house is located at 2611 Quasqueton Diagonal Blvd.

Quimby (Cherokee)
(1973), (1978), (1998), (2001), (2010), (2015)
Quimby was founded in 1887. It was first called Wendall, but was renamed Quimby after locals decided that Wendall sounded "too Republican." The name Quimby honored F. W. Quimby, who was the assistant superintend of the Illinois Central Railroad.

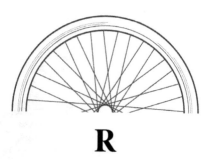

R

Radcliffe (Harden)
(2015)
Radcliffe was laid out in 1880 when the railroad was extended to that point. It was named after the 1853 novel <u>The Heir of the Redclyffe</u> by Charlotte Mary Yonge. The towns name was modified to its current spelling.

Randalia (Fayette)
(1996),
Randalia was founded in 1881 and named for A. J. F. Randall, an early settler.

Randall (Hamilton)
(1989,
Randall was founded in 1881 and named for Samuel J. Randall, a member of the U.S. House of Representatives from Pennsylvania.

Randolph (Freemont)
(1989), (2016)
Randolph was platted in 1877, shortly before the completion of the railroad through that territory. Agriculturalist Frank Peavy named the town for Lord Randolph Churchill, father of Winston Churchill.

Rathbun (Appanoose)
(1981), (2016)
Rathbun was established in 1892 as a mining town and incorporated in 1897. It was named for Charles H. Rathbun, a mining official.
<u>Items of interest</u>
The Star Coal Company of Streator, Ill. operated the Rathbun Mine, which had an 82-foot-deep shaft. This mine was in operation in 1895 and

by 1908 it was considered one of the best equipped longwall mines in the county.

Rathbun Lake was constructed and is operated by the U. S. Corps of Engineers. It is one of the largest lakes in Iowa. The lake was constructed to control flooding, provide recreation opportunities, abate stream pollution, fish and wildlife enhancement, and maintain a minimum stream flow on the Chariton, Missouri, and Mississippi Rivers.

Reasnor (Jasper)
(1973), (1975), (1984), (2000), (2006), (2018)
Reasnor was platted in 1877 and named for its founders, Samuel and Mary Reasoner.

Redding (Ringgold)
(1992
Redding was incorporated in 1882. It was first called "New Redding" but when there was no longer an "Old Redding," the "New" was dropped from its name. It is believed to be named after Redding, Pennsylvania.

Redfield (Dallas)
(1984), (2000), (2006)
Redfield was settled in 1855 and first called New Ireland. In 1860, the name was changed to Redfield in honor of Lieutenant Colonel James Redfield, an early settler who served in the 39th Iowa Infantry of the Union Army during the Civil War.

RED OAK (Montgomery) (County Seat)
(1976), (1986), (1997), (2009)
In the 1850s, the first settlers arrived in the area and in 1869 the community was founded when the Chicago and Quincy Railroad arrived. Red Oak got its name from Red Oak Creek which flows through the community and was noted for the red oak trees on its banks. The community was first named Red Oak Junction by the railroad, but in 1901, "Junction" was dropped from the name.

Items of interest

Red Oak has a spectacular collection of turn-of-the-century homes which reflects the wealth that the railroad brought to the area from 1870 to 1916. Because of the railroad, building materials such as wood, stone, marble, and granite could be delivered from other parts of the country. The size of the home made a statement as to the financial success of its owner.

Red Oak was the home of Thomas D. Murphy, the first person to successfully develop advertising art calendars. He was responsible for the creation, development, and expansion of the art calendar industry.

Reinbeck (Grundy)
(1983)

Reinbeck was settled around 1866 and incorporated in 1876. There were several names suggested for the town. Finally, Reinbeck was decided upon because the Blackhawk Creek, a clear running stream, is just north of the town. "Rein" means clear and "beck" means streams or brook in the German language.

Rembrandt (Buena Vista)
(2002)

Rembrandt was founded in 1899 and incorporated in 1901. The town got its start with the construction of the Minneapolis and St. Louis Railroad. The community was named for the noted Dutch painter Rembrandt Harmenszoon van Rijn. His many paintings include The Night Watch, which is on display at the Rijksmuseum in Amsterdam.

Remsen (Plymouth)
(1998)

Remsen was platted in 1876 and incorporated in 1889. Remsen was named for Dr. William Remsen Smith. Smith had a good friend who suggested the town be name Smithville, but Smith thought that there were too many Smiths in the world and chose to give the town his middle name.

Item of interest

During prohibition, Remsen was a major player in the brewing, transporting, and sale of illegal alcohol. Its location being near larger mid-western cities with vast farmlands between homes, made it a perfect location for making moonshine. Much of the moonshine produced ended up in the towns of Sioux City and Pocahontas.

Renwick (Humboldt)

(1987), (1993)

Renwick had its beginning in 1880 and 1881 with the coming of the Toledo branch of the Chicago and Northwestern Railroad. The town did not have a name until the first train made its water stop. One of the train's crewmen was a Mr. Renwick, who suggested the town be named for him.

Riceville ((Howard and Mitchell)

(1993), (2005)

Riceville was platted in 1855 and incorporated in 1892. It was named for the three Rice brothers (Leonard, Dennis, and Gilbert) who founded the town.

Richland (Keokuk)

(1992), (2000)

Richland was platted in 1840 by Pryor C. Woodward. The first name proposed for the town was Frogtown because after a heavy rain, they could hear frogs in the standing water. The town settled on the name Richland because of the rich soil in the area. The town was incorporated in 1869.

Ridgeport (Boone)

(1980)

Ridgeport was platted in 1854 and originally called Mineral Ridge. The town later changed its name to Ridgeport, taking its name from the ridge upon which the town site is located.

Ridgeway (Winneshiek)

(1977), (1999)

Ridgeway started in 1866 when the Chicago-Milwaukee and St. Paul Railroad passed through the community.

Item of Interest
In 1874, a fire destroyed about 80 percent of Ridgeway's businesses. The story is told that two 4-year old boys started the fire when lighting a cigar.

Rinard (Calhoun)
(1998)
Rinard was platted in 1904 and incorporated in 1914. It was named for a railroad man named Rinard.

Ringsted (Emmet)
(1982), (1996), (2005), (2014)
Ringsted was platted in 1899 and named for Ringsted, Denmark, the native home of an early settler.

Rippey (Greene)
(1980), (1994)
Rippey began in 1870 with the building of the Des Moines Valley Railroad through the territory and first named "New Rippey." It received its name from the pioneer village of Rippey, which was established about fifteen years before New Rippey was formed. The name New Rippey lasted until 1957, when the town voted to use the abbreviated Rippey, since Old Rippey had disappeared from all the maps. The town was named for Robert M. Rippey, an early settler.

Rising Sun (Polk)
(1988)
Rising Sun was founded in 1854 by Lewis Barlow. The community declined when the Railroad bypassed the community.

Riverside (Washington)
(1986), (1990), (2018)
Riverside was established in 1872 and incorporated in 1882. Its name was suggested by Dr. Mott, because it was located alongside the English River.

Items of interest
Riverside claims to be the future birthplace of Captain James T. Kirk, a fictional character in the television series Star Trek. Gene Roddenberry, the author of the book <u>The Making of Star Trek</u>, had the character of James Tiberius Kirk being born in the state of Iowa. Riverside contacted Gene Roddenberry who agreed that Riverside could claim to be the birthplace of Captain Kirk. Riverside then quickly changed its town slogan from "Where the best begins" to "Where the Trek begins," and changed its annual summer festival from River Fest to Trek Fest.

Trek Fest is an annual celebration of everything Star Trek and is held the last full weekend in June. There are activities for Trekkie and non-Trekkies; Star Trek costume contests, viewing of Star Trek Movies, and one of the largest parades in the area.

The Voyage Home Riverside History Center is also referred to as the "Star Trek Museum," that houses Star Trek themed exhibits and memorabilia, including a time capsule, a Star Trek themed bathroom, and an exhibit about the women of Star Trek.

Robins (Linn)
(1990), (2015)
Robins was incorporated in 1910 and named for John Robins, an early settler.

Robinson (Delaware)
(1983)
Robinson was founded around the turn of the 20th century and named for the Robinson family of southwestern Delaware County. William B. Robinson operated the Farmers Savings Bank of Robinson and the Robinson Lumber and Grain Company.

Rochester (Cedar)
(1973)

In 1856, the site of Rochester was settled and named for Rochester, New York. It was known for its flour mills located on the Cedar River.

Rock Creek State Park (Jasper)
(2011)
Rock Creek State Park was dedicated in 1952 and has a 602-acre lake which is the third largest in the state.

Rock Falls (Cerro Gordo)
(2002)
Rock Falls was founded in late 1851 or early 1852 and first named Shell Rock Falls, for the near-by water falls on the Shell Rock River. The town retained that name until the railroad came to town and Shell was dropped from its name and then the town became Rock Falls.
Item of interest
Charles Johnson, a native of Sweden, was an early mail carrier. He was middle-aged when he began working in the Rock Falls area. One of his friends suggested it was time he got married. Gradually plans were made for Johnson, who thought of himself as being too unsocial to marry a local girl. On the appointed wedding day, all the guests turned out in their Sunday best but the bridegroom failed to show up. When friends went looking for Johnson, they found him wandering around the prairie very depressed. Apparently, he had gone out that morning to show a hired man where to mow his fields, carrying his wedding clothes in a bundle. He had set the bundle down and couldn't find it in the tall grass. Finally, after borrowing clothes, the wedding came off a little late but happily for all.

Rockford (Floyd)
(1977), (1982), (1993), (2010), (2014), (2017)
The first town settler arrived in 1851. Robert Mathews came to the area that year and purchased most of the current town site. In 1856, he sold the land to a group of men who called themselves The Rockford Company, which resulted in the town being named Rockford.
Items of interest
The Floyd County Fossil and Prairie Park Center is a nature center located just west of Rockford and is open to the public as a County Park.

What makes this location special is that the ocean-bottom sediment that was deposited here millions of years ago never turned to hard stone as it had done almost everywhere else in the region. This allows the fossils to weather as separate, often complete museum-grade specimens. This is one of the few geological preserves in the United States where admission is free and collecting fossils for private use is allowed.

Fred and August Duesenberg, who developed and manufactured the Duesenberg automobile, were born in Lippe, Germany and with their families immigrated to Rockford. (See Garner)

ROCK RAPIDS (Lyon) (County Seat)
(1979), (1999), (2007)
A post office has been in operation since 1871 and the town is located on Rock River, where it got its name from the rapids on the river.

Rock Valley (Sioux)
(1985), (2014)
Rock Valley was platted in 1879 by Col. Warren, a Civil War veteran. It got its name from the Rock River which runs by the town.

Rockwell (Cerro Gordo)
(1999), (2010), (2017)
Rockwell started in 1870. It was named by Charles C. Gilman, the first president of the Central Railroad of Iowa, in honor of George B. Rockwell, the owner of the land on which the town is located.

ROCKWELL CITY (Calhoun) (County Seat)
(1979), (1998), (2004)
Rockwell City was platted in 1876 and named for its founders, John M. Rockwell and his wife Charlotte M. Rockwell.
Item of interest
The North Central Correctional Facility is a minimum-security prison located Rockwell City. It opened in 1982 on the site of the 1918 Iowa Women's Reformatory.

Roland (Story)
(1979), (1983), (1998), (2012)

Roland was incorporated in 1891. John Evenson, who was the postmaster, gave Roland its name suggesting that it was easy to pronounce and easy to spell in both English and Norwegian.

Item of interest

In 1846, Torkel Henryson, a young school teacher in Norway, had the idea of gathering a group of people to immigrate to America. The following spring a group of 165 passengers (29 families and 15 single persons) chartered a ship and on May 11, 1847, left Bergen, Norway. Six weeks later after they landed in New York, then traveled by boat to Chicago. From there they used ox-drawn covered wagons and traveled to Lisbon, Illinois, their intended destination. However, they found no government land available in the Lisbon area. The land that was available was beyond the means of the immigrants. They heard rumors of good land that could be bought from the government west of the Mississippi River and decided to send a group of men to investigate.

This group left early in the spring of 1855, traveling by two horse-drawn covered wagons. Their route took them along the northern part of Story County, where they made their headquarters on Long Dick Creek. From there they traveled over the prairie, mostly eastward, to examine the land. They decided the land looked favorable and bought several large tracts from the government at $1.25 an acre, and smaller tracts from private owners for $10 an acre.

They returned to Illinois and based on their favorable reports, a group of 12 families and three single men left in May of 1856 for the new location using 18 covered wagons, one was horse-drawn and the others were pulled by oxen. They reached their destination in mid-June and settled on the east side of the Skunk River, the point where Roland is now located.

Rolfe (Pocahontas)
(2007), (2010)

Rolfe was platted in 1881. The city was named for the Englishman John Rolfe, who married Pocahontas in Jamestown, Virginia. (See Pocahontas) Several names such as Highland, Highland City, and Milton were associated with Rolfe before Rolfe became the final towns name.

Rome (Henry)
(1979), (1984), (2009)
Rome was first laid out in 1846.
Item of interest
Rome has an interesting story of a bank robbery. It was closing time on Friday, July 5, 1912, at the Rome Savings Bank when cashier F.W. Hileman was closing his accounts. He was alone in the bank when a stranger came in and pointed a gun in his direction, demanding money. Hileman quickly closed the door of the safe and as he turned back to face the robber, he was shot in both arms. Jumping over the counter, the bandit grabbed cash, gold and silver and headed for the door and got into his getaway vehicle, which was a horse and buggy. The streets of Rome were crowded with shoppers as he drove "at top speed" through town and disappeared into the woods. Hileman, despite his injuries, sounded the alarm.

It wasn't long before Henry County Sheriff C.B. Goe and his deputy W.P. Daniels formed a posse which was headed by local merchant James O'Laughlin. Automobiles were loaded with armed men who took to the chase. For several hours, the posse and lawmen scoured the countryside looking for the robber. Finally, he was spotted south of Mt. Pleasant. He had ditched his buggy near Salem. There are two different versions of the chase from this point forward.

One account describes the scene this way: The bandit rode a horse as the posse pursued him in their cars. The suspect repeatedly turned to fire at the men and reloaded several times as he galloped through the countryside.

Another version describes the robber abandoning the horse and buggy and ran into the woods. A number of shots was exchanged between the members of the posse and the bandit. According to this account, he carried four revolvers and emptied each one as he shot at the posse. Both versions end badly for the bandit. The robber was shot to death through his heart.

The stolen money was recovered, either in the robber's clothes or under the buggy seat. Depending on which news report readers chose to believe, the amounts reported stolen varies from $800 to $2,000.

Rose Hill (Mahaska)
(1992)
Rose Hill was first call Ornbaum for Jim Ornbaum, the owner of the land. The towns name was changed to Rose Hill because Ornbaum sounded too foreign. Rose Hill was selected as the new towns name because of the wild prairie roses that covered a hill west of town. Rose Hill was incorporated in 1877.

Rowley (Buchanan)
(1998), (2010)
Rowley was established when the Burlington, Cedar Rapids and Northern Railroad was built through this area in 1873. The town was named in honor of D. W. C. Rowley, who was secretary of the railroad company.

Royal (Clay)
(1990), (1993)
Royal was platted in 1871 and incorporated in 1900. It was name by the postmaster, Elisa Nelson, who said the town could only have a one word name. Some believe Royal was selected because of the rich soil in the area.

Ruble (Plymouth)
(1982)
Ruble was established in 1900.

Rudd (Floyd)
(1993), (2002)
Rudd was incorporated in 1900. It was first called Danville, but changed its name to Rudd for the name of a director of the railroad who insisted the town be named for him. He offered an inducement of $1,000 to the first church organized in the town, but when two churches were organized, he disgraced himself by saying he knew nothing about this promise.

Runnells (Polk)

(1988), (2013)

Runnells was platted in 1881 and incorporated in 1903. It was named for John S. Runnells, a former editorial writer for the Iowa State Register and private secretary for Governor Samuel Merrill.

Runnells has an interesting history. Its beginning can be traced to the demise of Lafayette, a town that was laid out in 1849. In 1850, the county's largest ever celebration took place at Lafayette. There were toasts, speeches, and a hint that Fort Des Moines (population 275), was about to be overtaken by the town of Lafayette (population 175). All the towns along the river were in competition with Fort Des Moines to become the trade center for Central Iowa and to be the state capital.

Unfortunately, on May of 1851 heavy rains caused the river to raise 22 feet above the low water mark. (The annals of Iowa records state that there were 74 1/2 inches of rain that summer, more than six feet in less than five months.) Flooding caused heavy loss of houses, cattle, horses, hogs, and sheep. Houses were either covered with water or completely swept away. The Des Moines River, at flood stage, was three miles wide and steamboats sailed through the town. When the water subsided, the promising town of Lafayette was gone. The only thing left standing was the public well. Many of the former residents of Lafayette moved uphill and relocated to Runnells.

Rutland (Humboldt)

(1985), (2007)

Rutland was platted in 1869 and named for Rutland, Vermont.

Ryan (Delaware)

(1998),

Ryan was plated in 1888 and incorporated in 1901.

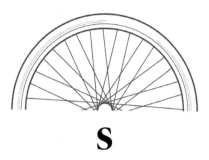

S

Sabula (Jackson)
(1998)
Sabula is Iowa's only island city. It was established in 1835 when, according to legend, Isaac Dorman crossed the Mississippi River from the Illinois on a log and decided to settle on the present site of Sabula. The name is French, meaning "sand," which refers to the sandy soil of the area.

Item of interest

In the late 19th century, the principal industry of the community was a large pearl button factory. It produced buttons from clam shells harvested from large clam beds located in the river adjacent to the shoreline.

SAC CITY (Sac) (County Seat)
(1975), (1995), (2012)
Sac City was platted in 1855 and incorporated in 1874. It was named for the Sac and Fox Indians who were in possession of the land at the time of the Louisiana Purchase. The meaning of Sac is "yellow earth people."

Items of interest

Sac City is home of the World's Largest Popcorn Ball, a title the town lost for a time. The town got the title back with they built a new, super-sticky popcorn boulder. The previous world's largest popcorn ball weighs 3,100 pounds. The new popcorn ball created in 2009, weighs 5,060 pounds. It took 253 volunteers, 12 hours and 40 minutes to make this ball. It took 900 pounds of popcorn, 2700 pounds of sugar, and 1400 pounds of syrup to form the new World's Largest Popcorn Ball.

The Allen Institute was established in 1893 and was a hospital for the cure of those addicted to liquor, tobacco and opium. Dr. J. I. Allen and Frank C, Hoagland were the originators and held similar remedies as were then popularly known as "Keeley Cures." They held the exclusive rights in Iowa for their remedy. The Keeley Cure was a remedy packaged in triangular bottles that contained a trace amounts of gold and marketed as therapies for drunkenness, opium habit and neurasthenia. The Keeley Cure was used from 1879 to 1965.

Salem (Henry)
(1975), (1992), (2003), (2019)

Salem was originally settled by Quakers with the intent to be a community of Friends. In 1835, Aaron Street, on his way westward came upon an uninhabited spot and declared "Now have mine eyes beheld a country teeming with every good thing...Hither will I come with my flocks and my herds, with my children and my children's children, and our city shall be called Salem, for thus was the city of our fathers, even near unto the seacoast." From the early years, members of other Christian denominations settled in Salem, so it was never an exclusively Quaker community.

Item of interest

Being only twenty miles from the Missouri border, Salem became an important spot on the Underground Railroad. Henderson Lewelling was a prominent abolitionists. His house is on West Main Street and is listed on the National Register of Historic Places as an Underground Railroad station.

Once known as the main ticket office of the Underground Railroad, the Lewelling Quaker House contains grim reminders of the anti-slavery movement. There were two trap doors: One in the kitchen and one in the small room off of the dining room. The original trap door in the kitchen leads to a crawl space under the kitchen, dining room and a small room off the dining room. The remains of the second trap door was found in this small room. A tour of the home reveals leg shackles on a chair by the fireplace. Several slaves would have been linked together with similar shackles and forced to walk with them on. Some of the Friends, had a dispute over the issue of abolition. They agreed in their opposition to slavery, but disagreed on actively helping slaves escape. In 1846, 50 members of the community, including Lewelling, were asked to leave the fellowship for their participation in the Underground Railroad.

In 1847, the Lewelling family traveled by covered wagon along the Oregon Trail with a special covered wagon. The wagon had been designed to transport more than 700 young fruit and nut trees including apples, pears, peaches, cherries, quince (a hard acid pear-shaped fruit), walnut, and hickory. The surviving trees become the parent stock of all of the early orchards in the Pacific Northwest.

There are five Underground Railroad stops in Iowa that have been preserved. They all have cellars, but there's not much proof that freedom seekers were actually hidden in these cellars, except possibly at the Hitchock House in Lewis. Favorite hiding places seem to have been in the attics of houses, or in out buildings like the haylofts of barns. Sometimes freedom seekers were hidden outside in the woods along creeks or rivers, or even in tall prairie grass.

Sanborn (O'Brien)
(2005)
Sanborn started in 1871 with the building of the Chicago, Milwaukee & St. Paul Railroad through the territory. It was named for George W. Sanborn, the railroad president. Sanborn was incorporated in 1880.

Sandusky (Lee)
(1981), (1992)
The community was named for Sandusky, Ohio.

Sandyville (Warren)
(2009)
Sandyville was laid out in 1851 and named for its founder, J. Moorman Sandy.

Santiago (Polk)
(2000)
The town was named for the nearby Santiago river.

Saratoga (Howard)
(2005),
Saratoga was laid out in 1858 and named for Saratoga Springs, New York.

Schaller (Sac)
(1977), (1987), (1998), (2001), (2012)
Schaller was incorporated in 1882 and named for Phillip Schaller.
Item of interest
Schaller was known as the popcorn capital of the world with brands of Bango and Jolly Time popcorn. The companies moved in the 1980s. For more than 60 years, popcorn was the major industry in the area and still is a major crop.

Schleswig (Crawford)
(1981), (2004)
Schleswig was laid out in 1899 and incorporated in 1900. It was named for the Schleswig, an area in Germany and Denmark, from where the original settlers came.

Schley (Howard)
(1993), (1996)
Schley is an unincorporated community. It was named for Rear Admiral Winfield Scott Schley, who in 1898, was the hero of the Battle of Santiago de Cuba in the Spanish-American War.

Scotch Grove (Jones)
(1974), (1985), (1991), (1998), (2002)
In 1837, the first settlers arrived in Scotch Grove. Some were descendants of Scottish farmer tenants who had been evicted during the Scottish Highland Clearance (1750 to 1860) which resulted from agricultural improvements and driven by the need of landlords to increase their income.
Item of interest
Scotch Grove is associated with two mental institutions. "The poor farm," was described as a "comfortable retreat for the lazy, able bodied,

and willingly dependent applicants," housed the poor, incurably insane and disabled. Tenants were given food and shelter in exchange for their labor on the agriculture and livestock farm. It was in operation from 1850 to 1910, during which time there were over 80 documented deaths, some from unknown causes. Their graves can be found in the nearby cemetery where their restless spirits are said to wander about at night. The poor farm was closed and demolished in 1910.

Several state mental institutions in Iowa have closed over the years, each with its own chilling history. One of the most notorious of these was Edinburgh Manor in Scotch Grove. The Manor, as it was called, has a history of horror. It still stands today, though closed. It was built in 1910-1911 to house the incurably insane, the poor, and elderly. It was closed a hundred years later (2010) when the last patients and employees left the building, never to return.

Scranton (Greene)
(1976), (1989), (2008), (2018)

Scranton was platted in 1869, shortly after the Cedar Rapids & Missouri River Railroad was built through that territory. It was incorporated in 1880. The town was named for Joseph H. Scranton of Scranton, Pennsylvania.

<u>Item of interest</u>

The Scranton's water tower was built in 1897 and is the oldest working water tower in Iowa and 9th oldest in the United States. A fire occurred at the tower in 1907 that got out of hand. The fire was intentionally set to melt the ice that had caused the town to be without water. Three men were injured attempting to put the fire out. They had climbed to the top of the water tower with buckets of water to throw down toward the flame, but failed because of the subzero weather. The men fell onto the ice in the water tower and were too weak to get out using the ropes that were extended to them. Twenty-one-year-old Howard Butler became a hero when he lowered the men to the ground. The tower itself did not suffer major damage.

Searsboro (Poweshiek)
(1973), (1975), (2001), (2006)

Searsboro was platted in 1870 by R. Sears, for whom the town was named.

The city attempted to no longer be incorporate in 2011, but the move failed when Poweshiek County refused to take control of the city's infrastructure.

Seneca (Kossuth)
(1982)
Seneca is an unincorporated community first settled in 1865.

Sergeant Bluff (Woodbury)
(2006)
Sergeant Bluff was incorporated in 1904 and named for Sergeant Charles Floyd, the only member of the Lewis and Clark Expedition to die on the journey. Clark diagnosed Floyd's condition as bilious colic, though modern doctors and historians believe Floyd's death was most likely caused by a ruptured appendix.

The town has been known by several names: Floyd's Bluff and Woodbury. When the Iowa State Legislature, issued a decree stating that the town would be called Sergeant's Bluff, the residents were forced to accept that name.

Shady Grove (Buchanan)
(2010),
Shady Grove was founded in 1857 and named when the post office was established. It was previously called Spring Creek.

Shambaugh (Page)
(2003),
Shambaugh was laid out in 1881 as a depot on the Chicago, Burlington and Quincy Railroad and named for its founder, James Shambaugh.

Sheffield (Franklin)
(1993)
Sheffield was platted in 1874 and incorporated in 1876. It was named for a personal friend of the founder.

Shelby (Pottawattamie)
(1976), (2000), (2008), (2013)
Shelby started in the late 1860s with the building of the railroad through the territory. Shelby was platted in 1870 by Benjamin F. Allen and Thusie Allen, and incorporated in 1877. Shelby was named for The Revolutionary War General Isaac Shelby.
Item of interest
Shelby has become the Purple Martin Capital of Iowa in an effort to use ecologically sound ways to control mosquitoes. Purple Martins are known as America's most wanted bird. A Purple Martin can eat 2,000 mosquitoes a day and will eat nearly any type of flying insect. They are the largest of the swallow family and get their name from the male which is all black, but gleams iridescent purple in direct sunlight. Martins nest only in North America and depend almost on man-made housing. Over fifty Purple Martin houses are in the community which helped establish this title.

Sheldahl (Polk, Boone, and Story)
(1973), (1988) (2011)
The Sheldahl area was settled by 120 Norwegian immigrants in 1855 which included Osmond and Anna Sheldahl, for whom the town is named. The town was incorporated on January 18, 1882.

Sheldon (O'Bfrien)
(1993), (2005), (2014)
Sheldon started in 1873 with the building of the Sioux City & St. Paul Railroad through the territory. It was named for Israel Sheldon, a railroad promoter.
Items of interest
In 1961, the city made headlines when it was discovered that Burnice Geiger had embezzled more than two million dollars over the course of many years from the Sheldon National Bank, which was operated by her father. Geiger worked as a cashier and was the bank's largest stockholder.
Her embezzlement was discovered when the federal bank examiners arrived unexpectedly. Geiger was reportedly exhausted by the time she was arrested because she had never taken a vacation. This turned out to

be a key component in her crime. The reason she never took a vacation was that she kept two sets of books and couldn't risk another employee discovering her embezzlement.

Bernice was said to be very generous, giving lots of the money away. Upon her arrest, the bank went under. She was sent to prison for 15-years but was paroled five years later. Upon her release, she moved back with her parents, who apparently forgave her. It was because of this discovery, that banking regulations were changed to require bank employees to take a vacation.

In 1924, Sheldon was the site of the first all-state meeting of the Ku Klux Klan with an estimated 25,000 members in attendance. This gathering included an induction ceremony for new members and the burning of a 40-foot wooden cross. A year later the Klan disbanded in Sheldon when the promoter disappeared with about $15,000 of the Klan's funds.

After the Civil War, the Klan was formed with the goal of protecting themselves and to terrorize the black slaves who were given their freedom following the Civil War. During World War I, the Klan was reorganized to appeal to whites who thought they were superior to immigrants, Catholics, Jews, and Blacks.

Shell Rock (Butler)
(1982), (1985)
Shell Rock was platted in 1853 and named for the Shell Rock River. The river was named for the fossil shells found along its banks.

Shellsburg (Benton)
(2012) (2015)
Shellsburg was founded in 1854 and incorporated in 1870. There are two theories has to how the town was named. One is that it was named for Schellsburg, Pennsylvania by Jacob Cantonwine who had come from Pennsylvania. The other is that it was first called Sellsburg for John Sells,

a pioneer of the township, but the people of the town preferred another name so it was changed to Shellsburg.

Shenandoah (Freemont and Page)
(1976), (1984) (1989), (1992), (2003), (2016)
Shenandoah was platted in 1870 shortly after the arrival of the Chicago, Burlington and Quincy Railroad. It was originally known as Fair Oaks, but the name was changed by early settlers in remembrance of the Shenandoah Valley in Virginia.
Items of interest
Shenandoah was once known as the "seed and nursery center of the world." It is home to the Earl May Seed Company which was founded in 1919. Earl May was a "natural born" salesman and quickly attracted a number of capable individuals to work with him in building a successful mail-order and retail seed and nursery business.

Radio station KMA has given many performers their start, including The Everly Brothers and Charlie Haden.

The Woman's Christian Temperance Union Public Fountain is located at Clarinda and Sheridan Streets. It was built in 1912 by the Woman's Christian Temperance Union to provide water as an alternative to alcohol consumption. The fountain was added to the National Register of Historic Places in 1984.

Shenandoah's downtown streetscape includes the "Walk of Fame," which has 125 Iowa-shaped sidewalk plaques along Sheridan Avenue which pays tribute to famous Iowans. They include a former President of the United States, scientists, famous artists, and musicians. Some of the names on the Walk of Fame are the Blackwood Brothers, the Everly Brothers, Henry Field, Dr. W. Eugene Lloyd, Earl May, Jesse Field Shambaugh and Charlie Hayden.

Shueyville (Johnson)
(1991)
Shueyville was founded in 1855 by Jacob Shuey and name for him.

SIBLEY ((Osceola) (County Seat)
(1979), (1985), (1996)
Sibley started in the 1872 with the building of the Sioux City & St. Paul Railroad through that territory. Sibley is named for Henry Hastings Sibley, a prominent General during the Dakota War of 1862, who later became the first governor of Minnesota.

Item of interest
In 2018, the city of Sibley lost a lawsuit brought against it by the American Civil Liberties Union (ACLU). Local resident Josh Harms had criticized local officials for failing to stop the "rancid dog food" smell coming from a local pork blood processing plant, which he believed would prevent people from moving into the town. The city of Sibley threatened to sue him and instructed him not to speak to the media about the issue. The ACLU successfully argued that this violated Harms' First Amendment rights of free speech. An injunction was granted, preventing Sibley's officials from "directing Harms not to speak with reporters."

SIDNEY (Fremont) (County Seat)
(1976), (1984), (1992)
Sidney was laid out in 1851 and originally named Dayton. The surveyors who were laying out the town, were boarding with the Milton Richards family. Richard's wife suggested they rename the city for her hometown of Sidney, Ohio.

Item of interest
The American Legion Post No. 128 has held the Sidney Iowa Championship Rodeo since 1924 and claims to be the world's largest continuously operated outdoor rodeo. The event is held in late July or early August. with approximately 38,000 visitors attending each year.

SIGOURNEY (Keokuk) (County Seat)
(1975), (1979), (1988), (1995), (2016), (2018)

Sigourney (pronounced "SIGG-ur-nee") started when Keokuk County was opened for white settlement in 1843, and in 1844 S.A. James built the first cabin. It was named in honor of the popular poet Lydia Sigourney, an American poet during the early and mid 19th century. She was commonly known as the "Sweet Singer of Hartford."

Items of interest

Until the year 1837, the Native Americans held undisputed possession of the territory in Keokuk County. It was not until October 1837 that the Native Americans first parted with their title to certain lands, now within the limits of Keokuk County, and the white man gained the right to a permanent settlement. The larger part of the County still remained in the hands of the Native Americans. It was not until October 1842 that the original possessors of this land gave up with their right to occupy the land and unwilling left to the far off and unknown regions west of the Missouri River. On May 1, 1843, Keokuk County was entirely open to white settlement.

The Dumont Museum_is located south of Sigourney. It is a 30,000-square foot museum featuring a large variety of collectibles which include:

- over 100 restored tractors
- gigantic Lionel Train layout
- buggies & horse drawn equipment
- hundreds of pedal tractors & cars
- toys, dolls, & collectibles
- Roy Rogers memorabilia collection

The museum represents a lifetime of collecting by Lyle & Helen Dumont.

Silver City (Mills)
(1980), (2003) (2011)

Silver City started in 1879 with the building of the Wabash, St. Louis and Pacific Railroad through that territory. The town was name for Silver Creek, which runs parallel to the eastern city limits.

Sioux Center (Sioux)
(2002), (2012)

Sioux Center was platted in 1881 and incorporated in 1891. It was named because it is located in the center of Sioux County. The county is named in honor of the Sioux Indian tribe, which was once prosperous in the area. Sioux means 'Snakes' or 'Little Snakes'.

Item of interest

Sioux Center is a Dutch community and home to Dordt College, a private liberal arts school associated with the Christian Reformed Church. Dordt was founded in 1955 and welcomes all students who are interested in a biblical, Christ-centered education. Dordt takes its name from the historic Synod of Dordrecht, held in the Netherlands from 1618-1619. The Canons of Dort, one of the three major confessional statements of Reformed Churches, came from that synod. The Canons of Dort were a response to statements made by the followers of Jacob Arminius and emphasized the sovereignty of God through his grace.

SIOUX CITY (Woodbury and Plymouth) (County Seat for Woodbury)

(1973), (1978), (1988), (1990), (1993), (1996), (2001), (2010), (2015)

Sioux City was laid out in the winter of 1854-55 and became a major entry point to the western plains, including Mormons heading to Salt Lake City and speculators heading to the Wyoming gold fields. Sioux got it name for the Dakotas Sioux Indians that lived in the area.

Items of interest

Sioux City is where RAGBRAI (Register's Annual Great Bike Ride Across Iowa) began in 1973 with Des Moines Register's columnist Donald Kaul and copy editor John Karras.

The first documented US citizens to record their travels through this area were Meriwether Lewis and William Clark during the summer of 1804. Sergeant Charles Floyd, a member of the Lewis and Clark Expedition, died here on August 20, 1804, the only death during the two and a half-year expedition. The Sergeant Floyd Monument is located at the burial site of U.S. Army Sergeant Charles Floyd. (See Sergeant Bluff)

The city gained the nickname of "Little Chicago" during prohibition due to its reputation for being a supplier of alcoholic beverages.

On December 14, 1949, the clocks in the Swift meat packing company building froze at 11:33 a.m., marking the moment a mighty explosion ripped through the structure. Twenty-one people died and more than 90 people were injured.

On July 19, 1989, United Airlines Flight 232 crash landed at Sioux Gateway Airport, killing 111 people.

In 1900, Sioux City residents and the rest of the country were the victims of a fraud perpetrated by a former Sioux City land speculator, developer, and later a notorious wheeler-dealer named John Peirce. Peirce was a colorful and flamboyant character, a decorated Union Army veteran who was wounded in the Civil War and a major promoter of Sioux City's during the 19th century boom years.

Sioux City historians and civic promoters held Peirce in high esteem for his years of dedication to the growth of Sioux City, especially of the North Side. More recent investigation has shown that Peirce was a very clever person who actually got away with his crime. Like most other businessman, Peirce had been badly hurt by the financial panic of 1893. Most of Sioux City's leading businessmen honorably spent years, working and rebuilding to pay back their debts. Peirce began scheming for a way to bilk the public out of the funds he needed to support his relocation to the west coast. In 1900, he initiated a nationwide lottery to dispose of his north side mansion (which later became the Sioux City Museum). About 40,000 tickets were sold at one dollar each.

The drawing took place at the Union passenger depot on Christmas Eve of 1900. It was first announced that the winner was a jeweler from Vinton, Iowa. A few days later, it came out that the "winning ticket" was actually held by a New York millionaire, William Barbour, to whom Peirce owed a large debt. The abstract for the Peirce Mansion reveals that a warranty deed transferred the title to Barbour nine days before the actual drawing and nineteen days before Barbour was publicly known to hold the title to the property. Barbour promptly sold the mansion to William Gordon, in exchange for bonds which were issued by the company operating the Combination Bridge. Peirce wrote an emotional goodbye to Sioux City in the newspaper before heading west. He collected his money and disappeared from Sioux City forever. (The combination bridge was completed in 1896 to carry rail, foot and horse traffic across the Missouri River.)

Slater (Story)
(1973), (1975), (1986), (1988), (1994), (2011)
There has been a post office in Slater since 1887. The city was named for Michael Slater, the original owner of the town site.
Item of interest
The High Trestle Trail Bridge is one of the largest pedestrian bridges in the world. The bridge is a half-mile long and 13 stories high and located just west of town. The bridge is part of a 25-mile trail that is part of the 670-mile trail system going through Des Moines and central Iowa.

Soldier (Monona)
(1981), (1983), (1987), (2018)
Soldier was incorporated in 1901. It was named for the Soldier River which runs beside the city. The Soldier River was named for a Civil War soldier, who was on his way home, when he died along the bank of the river.
Item of interest
Soldier was once known as Ole Town because there were so many men named Ole.

Solon (Johnson)
(1990), (1991), (2008), (2015)
Solon was platted in 1840 and named for the classical Athenian statesman, lawmaker, and lyric poet Solon. Solon (630- 560 BC) is credited with restructuring the social and political organization of Athens and thereby laying the foundations for Athenian democracy. Such were his accomplishments that, in later centuries, he became a sort of semi-

mythical founding father figure who had set Athens on the path to the
glory and prosperity the city enjoyed in the Classical period.

South Amana (Iowa)
(2008), (2011)
(See Amana)

South English (Keokuk)
(1986), (1995)
South English had its beginning in 1845 and named for the English
River in the area.

SPENCER (Clay) (County Seat)
(1979), (1990), (1999), (2007), (2017)
Spencer_was platted in 1871 and incorporated in 1880. It was named
for George Spencer who was an Alabama Congressman and a member of
the team which surveyed the town. Since Spencer was first established,
it has been inhabited by a class of people who were public spirited, high
minded and successful, and have made the name of Spencer synonymous
with "push, pluck and prosperity."
Items of interest
Spencer was the home of Dewey, a Small-Town Library Cat Who
Touched the World, a best-selling non-fiction book published in
September of 2008. It covers the life and times of Dewey Readmore Books,
the cat in residence at the Spencer Public Library.
The book discusses Dewey's life from his discovery in the library drop
bin on a cold winter's night, to his unlikely fame, and his death in 2006.
Dewey is portrayed as a loving cat who primarily lived in the library and
connected with patrons. The book also talks about the life of his caretaker,
Vicki Myron, including her early life and struggles with illness and single
motherhood.

On June 27, 1931, two small boys in the Otto Bjornstad
Drug Store, lit a sparkler and dropped it into a pile of sky
rockets, firecrackers, roman candles, cherry bombs, and
pin wheels. The resulting fire and blast moved from the

drug store to buildings to the north and within minutes the flames, pushed by strong winds, sent embers to the east side of Main Street wiping out many businesses. The can-do spirit of Spencer flourished following the disaster and within months the downtown area was rebuilt in an architectural style known as "Art Deco."

According to <u>Iowa Haunted Places</u>, a story is told that a very long time ago about a boy who was ice fishing on Moose Pond. It was getting late and the boy was packing up when the ice broke and he fell into the 40-foot deep pond and drowned. The tale is if you go down to the pond at 8:47 pm on December 23rd, you can hear the thumping on the ice and the screams of a young child.

In the Spring of 1881, the town of Spencer held its first city election. There were two parties at the time, one in favor of the saloon and one against it. Jacob Merrit was the candidate on the anti-saloon ticket, and W. C. Gilbreath was the candidate on the ticket in favor a saloon. Mr. Gilbreath was elected by a large majority. This indicated that the little town was in favor of the saloon. The first two years the saloon-favoring candidates were elected. The third year the saloon-favoring candidates were badly defeated and E. E. Snow was elected as mayor. The following year it was again reversed and those in favor of the saloon were again in power. But the next year their candidate was badly beaten and since then, Spencer did not have and saloons in the city. Spencer now has taverns.

Today the Clay County Fair is not only one of the largest county fairs in America, but has the added the honor of being considered one of the most rural-oriented fairs still in operation.

Spillville (Winneashiek)
(1977), (1996), (1999), (2005)
Spillville was founded in 1860 and mainly settled by Bohemian, German and Swiss immigrants. The town was named for its founder Joseph Spielman, but the spelling was change to Spillville.

Items of interest

The Czeck composer Antonín Dvořák spent the summer of 1893 in Spillville, where he composed the monumental Symphony No. 9 in E minor, "From the New World" as well as two of his most famous chamber works, the "String Quartet in F" ("The American") and the "String Quintet in E –Flat."

Dvorak made American composers think about their music differently. It was said that the history of 20th century American music changed because of his meeting with George Gershwin, Aaron Copeland and other composers, where he encouraged them to focus on American music instead on European style music. This meeting resulted in George Gershwin looking to jazz, and creating *Rhapsody in Blue* and the opera *Porgy and Bess* while Aaron Copland looking at American folk music in ballets like *Appalachian Spring* and *Rodeo.*

Thanks to Dvorak, American music, whether it is African-American, Native American, ragtime, or Louisiana bayou music, it has now become accepted as a rich part of the fabric of our musical life in America.

Spillville is home to the Bily Clocks Museum, a collection of intricately designed clocks created by two local brothers. It is housed in the building where Dvořák lived during his stay in Spillville. The hand carved clocks, by Joseph and Frank Bily, each depict a moment in history, religion, or culture. To pass the time during the slow winter months, these farmers took up clock making as a hobby, fashioning elaborate wooden facades and carving finely detailed statues for time pieces that grew ever larger and more complex.
They went on to make over 20 clocks during the next three decades. Their creations featured fully automated displays with multiple figurines and internal music boxes. Their largest clock, *The Apostles' Parade*, stands 9 feet 10 inches

tall and features miniatures of all twelve disciples of Jesus. Their masterpiece, *American Pioneer History*, took them four years to complete and Henry Ford offered to buy the clock for a million dollars in 1928, but they turned him down. Another notable clock in the collection was made in 1928 to commemorate Charles Lindbergh's historic Transatlantic flight.

They never sold a single clock, and rejected offers for commissioned projects. In 1946, they bequeathed their collection to the town of Spillville on the conditions that the clocks would be neither sold nor moved.

SPIRIT LAKE (Dickinson) (County Seat)
(2014)
Spirit Lake was incorporated in 1879. The Dakota Sioux originated the name of "Spirit Lake" referring to it as "The Lake of The Spirit." In 1856, three brothers-in-law created the town of Spirit Lake. In 1856 five cabins near Okoboji Lakes and Spirit Lake had been built and occupied by white settlers. These settlers did not get along peacefully with the natives. On March 13, 1857, Chief Inkpaduta, of the Sioux, led a revolt against the non-native settlers. After a severe winter, the Sioux attacked, killing 32 men, women, and children and abducted four women, of which two were subsequently killed, one released voluntarily, and one ransomed. A relief expedition sent from Ft. Dodge arrived only in time to bury the dead. Another was sent from Ft. Ridgely in Minnesota to pursue Inkpaduta, who fled westward, but failed to overtake him.

This was the last attack of Native Americans against settlers in Iowa. Historians have considered it a foreshadowing of the Sioux uprising in Minnesota in 1862. The events worsened relations between the Sioux and settlers in the territory, with mistrust and fear growing higher on both sides. Whites reacted by attacking some innocent Sioux who were hunting near their settlements. Because of competition over the lands, white settlers feared that the remaining free Indians would attack them, so they called for their removal by the United States Government. The Sioux resented the failure of the government to fulfill their treaty obligations. They were starving because of inadequate rations. By 1862, seeing thousands of children and elders die from starvation while whites broke the laws by seizing prime Sioux lands, the Sioux rebelled in what historians called the Sioux "Uprising."

Spragueville (Jackson)
(2004)

Spragueville is named for an early settler, Sprague, who arrived there in 1841.

Springbrook (Jackson)
(1989), (1991), (1998), (2002)

Springbrook was incorporated in 1897. It is believed to be named after the many springs and brooks located in the area.

Springbrook State Park (Jackson)
(2013)

Springbrook State Park has deer, red and gray fox, coyote, raccoon, beaver, muskrat and wild turkey. Almost every kind of bird that visits Iowa can be found there. The park is 920 acres and has a 17-acre spring fed lake.

Springdale (Cedar)
(1976), (1995), (2001), (2006), (2011)

Springdale was settled predominantly by Quakers around 1844. It was a way-station on the Underground Railroad. Its most famous resident was the militant abolitionist John Brown who resided at a house near Springdale while making preparations for the raid on the Federal Armory in Harpers Ferry, West Virginia.

Spring Hill (Warren)
(2019)

Spring Hill was laid out in 1872. It was named after the large spring that supplied the town with water.

Springville (Linn)
(1978), (1991), (2012), (2015)
Springville was laid out in 1856 and named for the large springs in the area.
Item of interest
Springville is located on land surrendered to the United States government by the Sac and Fox Indian tribes. In 1837, they turned over an elongated arrowhead-shaped stretch of land known as the Second Black Hawk Purchase to the United States Government.

Stacyville (Mitchell)
(2005)
Stacyville was platted in 1856 and named for its founder, Homer I. Stacy.

Stanley (Buchanan and Fayette)
(2002)
Stanley was named for Captain G. M. Stanley a relative of the Soule family who was one of the first settlers in the area.

Stanton (Montgomery)
(1984), (1984), (1989), (2009)
Stanton was laid out in 1870. Stanton was first settled by Swedish immigrants and first called Holmstad, after Malcolm Holm an early settler. Because the name was too hard to say, the railroad changed the name to Stanton for Edwin Stanton, who was Secretary of War under President Abraham Lincoln.
Item of Interest
Stanton is best known for its two water towers, which are painted and shaped like a giant coffee pot and coffee cup and billed as "the largest Swedish coffee pot in the world." The Swedish-style pot, painted with decorative hearts and flowers, holds 50,000 gallons of water (or 800,000 cups of coffee). Stanton was the home town of actress Virginia Christine, who was best known to television viewers as "Mrs. Olsen" in classic commercials for Folgers coffee.

St. Ansgar (Mitchell)
(1987), (1996), (2005)
St. Ansgar started in the mid 1800s and was named for the patron saint of Scandinavia, a French monk Ansgar who Christianized much of Denmark, Sweden, and northern Germany between 830 and 865 A.D.

St. Anthony (Marshall)
(1986), (1998), (2012)
St. Anthony was incorporated in 1897 and named by combining the names of two of its founders, John Q. Saint and Anthony R. Pierce.

St. Benedict (Kossuth)
(1990)
St. Benedict was platted in 1899 and named for St. Benedict, who was born in Rome in 480. He went to the town of Subiaco and sat on a mountain forty miles from Rome where he lived in a cave on the side of a cliff for three years. Sometimes a raven brought him food. When people heard about this holy man, more than 140 monks were living with him in a monastery at Subiaco. Benedict urged the monks to live a balanced life of prayer, work, and recreation and was guided by his desire to cherish Christ above all.

St. Charles (Madison)
(1991), (2009)
St. Charles was platted in 1852 and incorporated in 1876. It was named for St. Charles, Missouri

St. Lucas (Fayette)
(1987), (1996), (1999), (2005)
St. Lucas was incorporated in 1900 and named for Luke, who wrote both the Gospel of Luke and the Acts of the Apostles. This means that Luke contributed over a quarter of the text in the New Testament.

St. Marys (Warren)
(1991), (1992), (2009)
St. Marys (originally spelled St. Mary's with the apostrophe) was laid out about 1870 and named for Mary, the mother of Jesus.

St. Olaf (Clayton)
(2005)
St. Olaf was founded in 1872 and incorporated in 1900. It was named for Olaf II Haraldsson (995-1030), later known as St. Olaf (and traditionally as St. Olave), who was the King of Norway from 1015 to 1028 and posthumously given the title "Perpetual King of Norway" and canonized one year after his death. His sainthood resulted from encouraging the widespread adoption of the Christian religion among the Vikings.

St. Paul (Lee)
(1997)
St. Paul was laid out in 1866 and named for Paul, commonly known as Saint Paul as well as by his Jewish name Saul of Tarsus. Paul is generally considered one of the most important figures of Christianity.

State Center (Marshall)
(1974), (1976), (1994), (2008), (2018)
State Center began in 1864 with the building of the railroad through the territory. The town was first called Centre Station, but changed its name to State Center for its location near the geographical center of the state.
Item of interest
State Center is the "Rose Capital of Iowa." The annual Rose Festival is held the third weekend of June.

Steamboat Rock (Hardin)
(1978), (1983), (1989), (1995), (1998), (2004), (2015)
Steamboat Rock was platted in 1855 and gets its name from a large rock on the river bluff which is said to resemble a steamboat from a distance.

Stillson (Hancock)
(1985)
Stillson was platted in 1893. It was named for O. H. Stillson.

Stockport (Van Buren)
(1988), (1997), (2019)
The Stockport name is locally descriptive because the railroad station was used for loading live stock. It was incorporated in 1903.

Stockton (Muscatine)
(2011)
Stockton was laid out in 1855 when the railroad was built through the area. It was first called Farnham or Fulton. There was already a town called Fulton, so finally the name was changed to Stockport. The name came from being a large shipping point for the cattle and hogs raised in the area. It was incorporated in 1902.

Stone City (Jones)
(1982), (1991), (1994)
Stone City was founded in 1850 along the banks of the Wapsipinicon River where early settlers discovered dolomite and limestone. In its earliest history, Stone City was known as the Anamosa Quarries, then Stone City Quarries, and finally Stone City.

<u>Item of interest</u>
Stone City was once the location of an art colony. In 1932, Grant Wood, Edward Rowan, and Adrian Dornbush established the Stone City Art Colony. In a 1930 painting by Grand Wood called "Stone City," he depicts the landscape of the Stone City area. This was Wood's first major landscape painting. The Stone City painting was made the same year that Wood painted American Gothic. (See Anamosa)

STORM LAKE (Buena Vista) (County Seat)
(1973), (1978), (1987), (2001), (2010), (2015)
Storm Lake was incorporated in 1873. There are several stories about how Storm Lake got its name:
- A Trapper experienced a severe storm.
- A Sioux maiden was forbidden by her chief to marry a suitor from another tribe. The two tried to elope and started across the lake in a canoe when a storm upset the canoe drowning the two.

The saddened Chief cursed the waters and in his grief named the waters "Storm Lake."

- A tribe of Native Americans while traveling, pitched their wigwams on the bank of the lake. They found several poorly constructed canoes which a number of young braves took the canoes to go fishing. A sudden storm came up, capsized the canoes and the braves drowned. When the remaining tribe members left, they named the lake "Storm Lake."

Item of interest

Storm Lake is home of Buena Vista College which was founded by the Presbyterian Church (USA) in 1891. It became Buena Vista University in 1995.

STORY CITY (Story)

(1979), (1983), (1989), (1998), (2012)

Story City was laid in 1878 and incorporated in 1881. In Story City's early history, it was known as Fairview, but in 1881 when it was noted that there was already a Fairview, the name was changed to Story City, in honor of Supreme Court Justice Joseph Story.

Item of interest

Story City has a restored antique carousel, Iowa's only operating antique carousel. One of a vanishing species, this fun machine was built in 1913 by the Herschell-Spillman Co. of New York. The splendid wooden figures are hand-carved from poplar which include 20 horses, two chickens, two pigs, two dogs, two chariots, and a whirling tub. The calliope tunes are generated by a 1936 Wurlitzer Military Band organ housed in the center of the carousel. The carousel is located at North Park, 102 Park Avenue.

Stout (Grundy)

(2007), (2010)

Stout was incorporated in 1909 and named for A. V. Stout, the original owner of the town site.

Stratford (Hamilton and Webster)

(1973), (1980), (2012)

Stratford was platted in 1880 and named after Stratford-upon-Avon, the birthplace and gravesite of playwright and poet William Shakespeare.

Item of interest

One unusual person in Stratford's history has to be John Jonas Johnson, who took a trip to California and back, walking and pushing a wheelbarrow loaded with his possessions. He left for the gold fields with only 85 cents, but returned with enough money to start hardware stores in Mineral Ridge, Hook's Point, and Stratford.

Strawberry Point (Clayton)

(2014)

Strawberry Point was laid out in 1853 and incorporated in 1887. When the army moved 2,900 Winnebago Indians from Wisconsin to their new home in Winneshiek county, they made camp near a spring a mile west of Strawberry Point. The spring was located in an area that was abundant with wild strawberries. This is how the town got its name.

Items of interest

A Neutral Ground was established in 1830 as a means of protecting the Winnebago Indians from the hostile Sac and Fox tribes; therefore, Fort Atkinson was established to protect Indians from Indians.

Strawberry Point is home to the world's largest strawberry.
It is a 15-foot strawberry made of fiberglass.

Strawberry Point was once known as the "Cream City." In 1887, the town processed 10,731,428 gallons of whole milk, making Strawberry Point one of the top locations for processing whole milk in the entire state.

Stuart (Adair)

(1984), (1991), (2000), (2019)

Around the 1850s, Stuart began as a small Quaker community. The location was chosen for its high point where the prairie and timberlands met. In the late 1860s, the Chicago, Rock Island and Pacific Railroad built through Stuart. It was named for Charles Stuart, who was instrumental in bringing the railroad to the city.

Item of interest

On April 16, 1934, the First National Bank was robbed by the infamous crime couple of Bonnie Parker and Clyde Barrow. This location was the last bank robbery by the famous couple.

Sully (Jasper)
(1973), (1975), (2006), (2018)
Sully was platted in 1882 and incorporated in 1901. The town was named for railroad man Alfred Sully.

Sumner (Bremer)
(1980), (1999), (2002), (2014)
Sumner was established in 1870, and incorporated in 1894. The town was named for American political leader Charles Sumner, a lawyer and a powerful orator. Sumner was the leader of the anti-slavery forces in Massachusetts and a leader of the Radical Republicans in the U.S. Senate during the Civil War. The village of Cassville moved their buildings to Sumner so they would be near the railroad.
Item of interest
Sumner has had a bicycling club dating back to the 1890's.

Sutherland (O'Brien)
(2017)
Sutherland was laid out in 1882 and named for the Duke of Sutherland. The Dukes of Sutherland was one of the richest land owning families in the United Kingdom.

Sutliff Cider (Linn)
(2015)
Sutliff Cider Company makes their own hard cider. They have live music every Sunday during spring, summer and fall. Historically, Americans used to drink more hard cider than any other alcohol, and Iowa grows exceptionally flavorful apples. Sutliff Cider Company is located at 382 Sutliff Road, Lisbon.

Swaledale (Cerro Gordo)
(1999), (2010), (2017)
Swaledale was platted in 1887 and incorporated in 1892. The name Swaledale come from the dales (valleys) in the Yorkshire Dales National Park in northern England. The dale of the River Swale on the east side of the Pennines in North Yorkshire, resulted in the name Swaledale.
Item of interest
In 1954, a Braniff DC-3 crashed during a thunder storm 3.5 miles outside of Swaledale, killing eleven and injuring eight.

Swisher (Johnson)
(1991),
Swisher was incorporated in 1933. The community was named for Benjamin Swisher, the landowner.

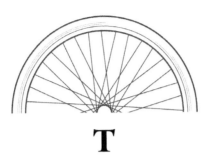

T

Tabor (Fremont and Mills)
(1989), (2016)
Tabor was founded by several Christian clergymen who were active abolitionists. The founders were impressed with the high location and mutually selected the name "Tabor" after the Biblical Mount Tabor, a mountain near Nazareth and the town of Jesus' childhood. Tabor was incorporated in 1868.

Items of interest
The founders of the town started a Christian college which became Tabor College. It was in operation from 1853 to 1927 before closing its doors for financial reasons. The buildings housed German P.O.W.s during World War II.

Tabor played a significant role in the 1850s as a center of the western antislavery movement. In the 1850s, the abolitionist, John Brown, kept a store of weapons in Tabor and met with other supporters to plan his raids in Kansas and Virginia, including the raid on Harpers Ferry.

The Pulitzer Prize Winning novel Gilead is a fictional town based on the real town of Tabor. The character of the narrator's grandfather is loosely based on the real-life story of the Rev. John Todd, a Congregationalist minister from Tabor who was a conductor on the Underground Railroad. He stored weapons, supplies and ammunition used by abolitionist John Brown in his 1857 invasion of Missouri to free a group of slaves.

Talleyrand (Keokuk)
(1975), (1986), (2000)
The town was named for Charles-Maurice de Talleyrand (1754-1838), a French gentleman and scholar who was also a diplomatic genius. He

was the foreign minister under Louis XVI as well as *five other regimes.* He managed to stay in a position of power throughout the French Revolution.

Tama (Tama)
(1979), (1994), (1995), (2008)
Tama started in 1862 with the building of the Cedar Rapids and Missouri River Railroad through the territory. Tama is named for Taimah, a 19th century Meskwaki leader.
Item of interest
Tama is located a few miles from the Meskwaki Settlement, Iowa's only significant Native American community.

Templeton (Carroll)
(2011), (2018)
Templeton was platted in 1882 and incorporated in 1883. It is thought that the city was named for a railroad worker.
Item of interest
The city is perhaps best known as the home of Templeton Rye, a brand of rye whiskey manufactured during prohibition that was very popular in Chicago, Omaha, and Kansas City. Many enterprising Carroll County farmers found this to be a viable way to supplement income during the Great Depression. The 18th Amendment to the U. S. Constitution was enacted to forbid the manufacture and sale of whiskey and other alcoholic beverages. At the height of the bootlegging era during the Great Depression, Templeton with a population of less than 500 people, was using 3 railroad cars of sugar a month.

Tennant ((Shelby)
1976), (2000), (2008), (2013)
Tennant was incorporated in 1915 and started with the building of the Chicago & Great Western Railroad through that territory.

Tenville (Montgomery)
(1984), (1997)
Tenville was started in 1852. It was named because it was at the intersection of highways 34 and 71 and was 10 (Ten) miles from some unidentified place.

Terril (Dickinson)
(1985), (2014)
Terril (formerly spelled Terrill) was platted in 1895 and first called Trilby, but because there was another town with that name, it was changed to Terrill after an early settler.

Thompson (Winnebago)
(1996), (2005)
Thompson was platted in 1892 and incorporated in 1894. It was named for J. F. Thompson, Vice President of the Chicago and Iowa Western Land and Town Lot Company.

Thor (Humboldt)
(1978), (1987), (2007)
The town was mainly settled by Scandinavian immigrants and started in 1869 with the filing of a claim by Ole Willicksen, a native of Stavanger, Norway. Thor was platted in 1882 and named for the mythical deity Thor, a hammer-wielding god associated with thunder, lightning, storms, oak trees, strength and the protector of mankind and fertility in old Norse mythology.

Thornburg (Keokuk)
(1975), (1979), (1988)
Thornburg was incorporated in 1883. The town was founded by the railroad and named in memory of Major Thomas T. Thornburgh, who died in the Meeker Massacre.

The Meeker Massacre, the White River War, Ute War, or the Ute Campaign, were conflicts that began when the Utes attacked an Indian agency on September 29, 1879. They killed the Indian agent, Nathan Meeker, 10 male employees, and took women and children as hostages which resulted in a further conflict. Following the massacre of Meeker, The United States Army sent troops from Fort Steele in Wyoming which followed with an attack at Milk Creek by the Indians on the troops led by Major Thomas T. Thornburgh. The major and 13 troops were killed within minutes.

Thornton (Cerro Gordo)
(2017)
Thornton was founded in 1885 and incorporated in 1892. It was named for J. Thornton Knapp.
<u>Item of interest</u>
In 1908, Thornton was almost wiped from the map by fire. Seven business blocks, almost the entire business section of the city, was destroyed. The property loss was about $70,000 with only $12,000 covered by insurance. The fire originated in a bowling alley and was first noticed about 2 am. The alarm was given promptly. Thornton had no fire-fighting apparatus and the flames were soon beyond control. The structures were all of frame construction and the flames spread rapidly from one building to another. The buildings were so quickly consumed that it was impossible to remove the stocks of goods which were almost entirely consumed by the fire.

Thurman (Freemont)
(1984), (1992),
Thurman was established in 1856 and incorporated in 1879. Thurman is a town of many names. It was first called Studyville, then Fremont City, and Plum Hollow which lasted until 1885, when during the first administration of Grover Cleveland, it was changed to Thurman in honor of Vice President Allen G. Thurman.

Tingley (Ringgold)
(1981)
Tingley was founded and incorporated in 1883. The name Silver Street was submitted to the U.S. Post Office Department, but was rejected because there was another post office by the same name in Iowa. It was suggested that William Tingley Cornwall send in his own name, which he did. It was approved and Tingley Cornwell was appointed as the first post master.

TIPTON (Cedar) (County Seat)
(1982), (2008)
Tipton was platted in 1840 and incorporated in 1857. It was named for General John Tipton, a personal friend of the founder, Henry W. Higgins.

Titonka (Kossuth)
(1977), (1982), (1999), (2002), (2005), (2014)
Titonka started in 1898 with the building of the Burlington, Cedar Rapids and Northern Railroad through that territory. Titonka was incorporated in 1898. Titonka is a Sioux Indian word meaning "Big Black," the name given by the Indians to the buffalo. Originally known as Ripley, but the name was changed when it was discovered that another town had a similar name.

TOLEDO (Tama) (County Seat)
(1979), (1994), (1995), (2008)
Toledo was founded in 1853 and incorporated in 1866. It was named for Toledo, Ohio.
Item of interest
Toledo is the former home of The Iowa Juvenile Home and Girls State Training School, a correctional facility for juveniles. It held girls who were judged as delinquents and youth of both genders who were judged as needing assistance. Because of a number of issues about the treatment of those detained, it was closed in 2013.

Trenton (Henry)
(1975), (1990), (1992)
Trenton was first settled in 1836. It was originally called Lancaster but renamed Trenton after Trenton, New Jersey. Trenton is an unincorporated community.

Tripoli (Bremer)
(1980), (1999), (2002), (2014)
Tripoli was settled around 1873 and incorporated in the 1880's. The town was first called Martinsburg after its founder Asa Martin, but was renamed Tripoli because there was already another town named Martinsburg. One source said that Martin chose Tripoli because of his birthplace in Tripoli, New York.

Troy (Davis)
(1981), (2003), (2019)

Troy is an unincorporated community. It was named for Troy, Ohio, the former home of J. I. Earhart, an early settler.

Troy Mills (Linn)
(1983), (2002)
Troy Mills was laid out in 1870 and first called Hoosier Mills. In 1853, three men attempted to build a dam for a fish trap when they got excited because they had found the perfect place to build a mill where they could harness the water of the Wapsipinicon River. Two years later they build a saw mill and later a flour mill. Today the dam is still there.

Truro (Madison)
(2009)
Truro was platted in 1881 and named for Truro in Cornwall, United Kingdom. The name was suggested by the local train conductor, whose hometown was Truro, Cape Cod, Massachusetts.

Turin (Monona)
(1977), (1983), (1987), (1995), (2004), (2018)
Turin was platted in 1887 and named for Turin, Italy.

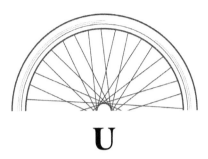

U

Underwood (Pottawattamie)
(1974), (1991), (1994), (1997), (2000), (2008), (2013), (2019)
Early settlers arrived in the Underwood area from 1845 to 1850. The name Underwood came from the first Milwaukee Railroad engineer to pass through the area on the new train tracks. Two farmers had cut corn stalks to clear a path to the tracks so the depot could be built. This path later became Main Street. The town was incorporated in 1902.

Union (Hardin)
(1986), (2004)
Union was laid out in 1868 and incorporated in 1874. It is thought that the name is the result of residents feeling patriotic after the Civil War.

Unionville (Appanoose)
(1981), (1997), (2003), (2009), (2016)
Unionville was founded in 1849 and incorporated in 1922. The city's name most likely was in support of the Union in response to the Civil War.

Unique (Humboldt)
(1978)
The town post office opened in 1878. A rusted metal sign is all that remains of Unique. It formerly said "Unique, Iowa," but is now illegible.

University Heights (Johnson)
(1973), (1976)
At the turn of the 20th century, the area of present-day University Heights was known as West Lucas Township and consisted of several small farms and properties. At that time, the University of Iowa and Iowa City had not expanded westward past the Iowa River.

In the early 1920s, brothers Lee and George Koser began purchasing and developing the land that became the city of University Heights, because they anticipated the westward expansion of the University and the city. With the construction of the University's General Hospital in 1928 and Kinnick Stadium in 1929, those predictions came true. By 1933, Iowa City began annexing land on the west side of the river and in 1935, the city of University Heights was incorporated. By the 1960s, most of the remaining lots were developed and the land surrounding University Heights had been annexed by Iowa City, limiting the future growth of University Heights.

Urbana (Benton)
(1974), (1978), (1983), (1985)
Urbana was laid out in 1847 and was previously known as Hoosier Point and Marysville. In 1857, the government changed the name of Maryville to Urbanna because there were other towns with that name. The spelling of Urbanna was used until 1880 when one "n" was dropped.
Item of interest
During the late 1850s, bands of Native Americans still roamed the countryside. They had a favorite camping site along the Cedar River near Thomas Way's cabin. The place was perhaps chosen because Mr. Way, known as "Uncle Tom," always has a good supply of fire water. They came every year and spent several days to celebrate some of their mystic rites and religious dances. On one occasion, James Rice gave them a fine puppy which they sacrificed to the Great Spirit with much ceremony and holding a war dance as part of the exercises. The Native Americans were often accused of committing crimes for which they were not guilty and were convenient scapegoats for horse thieves. Thomas Way's son Berry, would during the night, often run off the Indians' ponies during their annual encampment. Berry would always be home the next morning when the Indians came by to complain. He would always be on hand to assist in finding the horse, but would send them on the wrong trail, a wild goose chase.

Ute (Monona)
(1981), (1987), (2018)

Ute was platted and incorporated in 1887 and named by Isaac Cummins for the Ute tribe that rescued him and his family in Utah while heading west during the California Gold Rush. The Ute tribe is a branch of the Shoshone tribe of Indians.

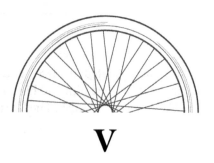

V

Vail (Crawford)
(1994)

Vail was laid out in 1871, and incorporated in 1875. The city was named for C. E. Vail, a relative of railroad magnate John Insley Blair.

Item of interest

From 1875 to 1878 there was a severe invasion of grasshoppers around Vail. One of the methods used by farmers to control the grasshoppers was to fill a trough with kerosene and attach it behind a drag. When the drag came through the field, the grasshoppers would jump up and many would land in the kerosene and be killed.

Van Horne (Benton)
(1994), (2004)

Van Horne was incorporated in 1883. It was named for Sir William Cornelius Van Horne (1843-1915), a Chicago-Milwaukee Railroad Superintendent.

Van Meter (Dallas)
(2013)

Van Meter was laid out in 1869 and incorporated in 1877. The city was named for Jacob Rhodes Van Meter and his family. They were Dutch settlers from Meteren, in the Netherlands.

Item of interest

In reality, there are two fields of dreams in Iowa. The first one was developed in the mid 1930s near Van Meter, on a farm owned by Bill Feller, the father of Bob Feller.

Van Meter is the birthplace of baseball Hall of Famer Bob Feller and home to The Bob Feller Museum built to honor him. Feller, who died in 2010 at the age of 92, spent 18 seasons with the Cleveland Indians after signing with them at the age of 17. He won 266 games, had a lifetime ERA of 3.25, threw three no-hitters and had 44 career shutouts.

The young Bob Feller developed his tremendous fastball in a little patch of grass on the west side of the barn. In his prime, he was believed to be the fastest pitcher in major league history.

Varina (Pocahontas)
(1973), (1978), (1987), (2010)
Varina started in 1899 with the building of the Chicago, Milwaukee and St. Paul Railroad through the territory. It was named for Varina Farms, a plantation established by John Rolfe in Jamestown, Virginia. (See Pocahontas and Rolfe)

Ventura (Cerro Gordo)
(1977), (1985), (1999), (2014), (2017)
The town was first known as Thayer's Siding. Mr. Thayer was the first to sell baled hay from the railroad siding he built. When the railroads came to an area, they would often pass through towns that were named for the settlers who living on the land. This was probably the case for the Thayer's Siding name. The story of how the town changed its name to Ventura is that when asked what they wished to call Thayer's Siding, the Skene Brothers, who sold marsh hay, replied that being in the area was quite a venture. In the process of naming the landing for the railroad, the name was changed from Venture to Ventura.

Item of interest
Ventura was a battle ground for various Native American tribes. There were deer and buffalo on the prairie nearby, so it was the hunting ground for many tribes. The Sioux held the region of Northern Iowa. Their bands included the Oto, Omaha and Santee. Trouble constantly occurred between the Sioux and the Native Americans south of them. This compelled the government to interfere. At the 1825 council of Indians at Prairie du Chien, a boundary was fixed. The Sioux were to stay north and the Sacs and Fox were to stay south of this line. Regardless, war parties kept fighting until the United States secured ground that was forty miles wide from the Mississippi to Des Moines River and named this area Neutral Ground.

Ventura was within this strip of land where Native Americans of any tribe could hunt and fish without a charge of trespassing. In 1833, the Winnebago from Wisconsin were moved into the Neutral Ground by the government. The Winnebago claimed to be ancestors of other Iowa Indians. At first, they resented living between other tribes; however, after they were removed to Minnesota in 1846, they would persist in migrating back to the Iowa area that they had learned to love. There are several accounts of the Native Americans camping and trading with the people of Ventura on their journeys.

The Mesquakies live on their settlement in Tama County and are of the Fox Native American tribe. They are now the only Native Americans in Iowa. Their settlement is different from a reservation in that they purchased the land from private parties and the land is not owned by the government. Mesquakies camped east of the Ventura's City limits on a hill north of the lake. This was a favorite spot, especially in the summer because the lake breezes kept the bugs away. The last conflict with the Sioux occurred in 1852. The scene was on the west bank of the east branch of the Des Moines River, about six miles north of Algona. A band of Mesquakies had gone from Tama County to the Clear Lake and Ventura area. Chief Ko-ko-wa and his band heard that a party of Sioux was encamped on the Des Moines River. The temptation was too great for the Mesquakies who put on their war paint, and headed out through the Ventura area to fight their last battle with the Sioux.

Vernon (Van Buren)
(1981), (1997), (2003)
Vernon was founded in 1837 and first called South Bentonsport. The town is believed to be named for Admiral Edward Vernon (1684-1746) of the British Navy. General George Washington's home of Mount Vernon was also named in honor of Admiral Vernon. George Washington's older brother, Lawrence Washington, had served under Admiral Vernon.

Victor (Poweshiek)
(1976), (1991), (1995), (2006), (2011)
Victor was laid out in the 1860s. The town was originally called Wilson, for George W. Wilson, who owned the town site, but changed the name to Victor for Victor, New York.

Item of Interest
In 1872, the Moravian Church organized a mission in Victor for German-speaking settlers, The Victor congregation was associated with the larger Harmony Moravian Church only 8 miles away. In 1883, Moravian activity here ceased and the little chapel (former schoolhouse) was sold for 200 dollars.

Village Creek (Allamakee)
(1977)
The town was formed in 1857 and named for the creek called Village Creek.

Villisca (Montgomery)
(1992), (2009), (2016)
Villisca began as a small settlement called The Forks. The name "The Fork" was derived from the merging of the Middle Nodaway and West Nodaway Rivers. The first plat was laid out in 1858 by D. N. Smith of the Chicago, Burlington, and Quincy (C.B.&Q.) Railroad. The town's name was changed to Villisca, which in the Native American language means "pretty place" or "pleasant view." Villisca, was incorporated in 1868.
Item of interest
Villisca is well known in the area for the mystery of the axe murders. On the night of June 9, 1912, the Moore family and two guests were brutally murdered with an axe. It wasn't until the morning of June 10, 1912 that they were found in their home by neighbor Ross Moore, the brother of Josiah Moore.
Josiah B. Moore and Sarah Montgomery were married on December 6, 1899. They had four children: Herman, Katherine, Boyd, and Paul. Joe was a prominent and well-liked businessman. By 1912, the Moore Implement Company was a competitor with other Villisca and area hardware stores, including the Jones Store which was owned by his former employer, F.F. Jones. Sarah was active in the Presbyterian Church and assisted with children's day exercises. On the morning of June 10, 1912, Joe (43) and Sara (39), their four children, and two visiting children (Lena and Ina Stillinger), were found to be beaten to death with Moore's own axe. Their unsolved murders began a chain of events that split Villisca

and forever changed the course of the town's history and the lives of its inhabitants.

Vining (Tama)
(1986), (1994), (1995), (2008)
Vining was incorporated in 1913.

VINTON (Benton) (County Seat)
(1978), (2012), (2015)
Vinton was founded in 1849 and incorporated in 1869. It was named for Hon. Plynn Vinton, a state legislator.
Items of interest
Vinton is home to the Iowa Braille School. It's best known student was probably Mary Ingalls. Laura Ingalls frequently mentioned this school in her Little House books and referred to some of the skills that Mary learned at the school such as piano, beadwork, and using a writing guide so she could write letters home to her family.

Mary was born in Pepin County, Wisconsin on January 10, 1865. Her father, Charles Ingalls was a pioneer farmer who later homesteaded near De Smet, South Dakota. Mary became totally blind at the age of fourteen from what was then called brain fever. Some speculate that it was actually scarlet fever that caused her blindness. On November 23, 1881, at the age of sixteen, she was enrolled at the Iowa College for the Blind.

In June of 1889, at the age of twenty-four, Mary graduated from the school and spent most of her remaining life living with her family near De Smet. Mary and her mother were very active in their church and Mary taught Sunday School classes. After her father's death, she made fly nets which helped with the family income. When her mother died in 1924, she went to live with her sister Grace and then her sister Carrie. On October 20, 1928, at the age of sixty-three, Mary died of pneumonia and was buried in the family plot near De Smet. She did not live long enough to know that her sister, Laura Ingalls Wilder, would immortalize the family through her writing of the Little House books.

Vinton is the hometown of Seaman A. Knapp whose farming experiments led to the formation of the U. S. Department of Agriculture's Cooperative Extension System.

Myrtle Cook's last words probably got her killed. Cook was sitting near the window of her home across the street from the busy Vinton train depot, rewriting and rehearsing her speech for the upcoming Women's Christian Temperance Union (WCTU) meeting.

As President of the Benton County WCTU, Cook did more than give speeches. She had recently published the names of people she suspected of bootlegging. These claims could, and did, lead to legal problems and jail time for those on her lists. She was also bad for the bootlegging business.

When it came to the subject of prohibition, she was not at all diplomatic. One newspaper, after her death, said she caused some people to "emphatically detest her." Her house had been egged the previous July 4 and believed the youths who threw the eggs had been hired by bootleggers to intimidate her. She told a friend that she worried that "this work may be the end of me yet." Cook's mother-in-law was upstairs the night of September 7, 1925, listening to her recite her speech over the noise of a thunderstorm and the rumbling from the railroad tracks.

The mother-in-law heard what she thought was thunder, and then silence. She headed downstairs where she saw Cook on the floor, gasping and bleeding from her chest. A bullet had come through the window and entered Cook's heart. She was dead within an hour.

In 1923, Vinton was one of the confirmed stops for Bobbie the Wonder Dog. After being separated from his family while on a trip to Indiana, Bobbie was able to find his way back home to Oregon, a journey of almost 3,000 miles. The story of Bobbie the Wonder Dog made national news and appeared in Ripley's Believe It or Not book and the film *The Call of the West*. The family received hundreds of letters from all over the world about their heroic dog.

The story told about a stranger accompanied by a woman who appeared in Vinton in 1849. He gave his name as Ketchum and soon after his arrival was engaged in the saloon business. Then another woman came to town and gave her name as Mrs. Ketchum, the lawfully wedded wife of the saloon keeper. She did not tolerate Ketchum's weakness for getting married while she was still able to get around. She was an energetic woman who had a warrant for her husband's arrest and placed it in the hands of Deputy Marcus Webb within two hours of her arrival. Webb made the arrest and took his prisoner before Justice Brubacher; however, having other business to attend to, Brubacher left him in the custody of Constables Stanbury and Quail. Doctor Buffum was engaged by the prisoner to defend him and had gone with him to Justice Brubacker's office. Pending the appearance of witnesses, a jug of whiskey was sent to the Justice and the attorney for the defense, who sat down to play a friendly game of "seven-up." Quail, having been out late the night before, went into an adjoining room and laid down and went to sleep. About the time Brubacher was two points ahead in his second game with Buffum when Ketchum asked permission to leave the room for a few minutes. Brubacher granted his request. That was the last ever seen of Ketchum in Benton County. A diligent search was made, but he was beyond the reach of the officers. Brubacher was indicted at the next term of the District Court for keeping a gambling house and both he and Buffum were indicted for gambling. Because of problems with the paperwork, both were discharged.

Viola (Linn)
(1978), (1991), (1994), (2004), (2012)

Viola was laid out in 1861. It was named for Miss Viola Leonard, daughter of a landowner. Viola was first called "Crow Creek Station" from the creek that ran through the town.

Item of interest

The story is that if at night you go North of Viola to the Matsell Bridge and park your car near the middle of the bridge and turn off the motor, you will be pushed across the bridge. You will see and hear things outside your car. If you have your windows down you will hear a lot of noises and voices in the woods. After you leave and get to a light, you will see handprints on your car. Be careful, if you go there too many times you will be recognized and they will get mad and try to push you off the bridge or break your windows.

Viola Center (Audubon)
(1980)
A post office was established in Viola Center in 1881. The town was named for Viola Emma Sanborn, the first person born in the town.

Volga (Clayton)
(1980), (1996)
Volga (formerly Volga City) was laid out in 1852. It was named for the nearby Volga River, which was named for the Volga River in Russia.

Voorhies (Black Hawk)
(1983)
Voorhies was platted in 1900, shortly after the Chicago and Northwestern Railroad reached the town. Voorhies is an unincorporated community.

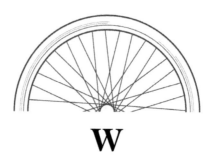

W

Wadena (Fayette)
(1993), (1996), (1999)

Wadena was established in 1857 and incorporated in 1895. The name Wadena came from an Indian chief who was a close friend of Major Herriman, one of the founders and an Indian agent.

Item of interest

Wadena is remembered in Iowa for the Woodstock-like rock festival held on a nearby farm on August 1–3, 1970. A second rock-fest was held in late July 1995.

Walcott (Muscatine and Scott)
(1973), (1982), (2011), (2015)

Walcott was platted in 1854. The first passenger train route west of the Mississippi River was in 1855 and helped Walcott grow. William Walcott, who was a director of Chicago and Rock Island Railroad, donated $500 in 1855 for the construction of a school building, with the stipulation that the town along the railroad tracks near Davenport be named for him.

Items of interest

In 1911, Dunn & Co., as published by the Bankers' Journal of New York, declared Walcott as the richest town in the United States determined by bank deposits for its population of 300.

Walcott is the home of the world's largest truck stop. The Iowa 80 Truck stop began serving truckers out of a small white building in 1964, before Interstate 80 was completely built. Bill Moon, Iowa 80 founder, located the spot at what is now Exit 284, for Standard Oil. They built and opened the truck stop with Bill taking over management a year later. After Interstate 80 was complete, thousands of truckers and travelers have stopped by to fuel, grab a bite to eat and head on down the road. In 1984, Standard Oil (now Amoco) decided to sell the facility. Bill Moon, who had been managing the place for nearly 20 years, jumped at the chance to buy it. He and his wife Carolyn leveraged everything they had, including borrowing money from friends, to purchase the Iowa 80 truck stop.

Today after 28 expansions and several remodels, the truck stop is now run by the second generation of the Moon Family. The truck stop includes the Iowa 80 Kitchen, a 300-seat restaurant, gift store, the Super Truck Showroom, a dentist office, a barber shop, a chiropractor's office, a workout room, laundry facilities, a 60-seat movie theatre, a trucker's TV lounge, 24 private showers, a food court (featuring Wendy's, Dairy Queen, Orange Julius, Taco Bell, Pizza Hut and Caribou Coffee), a convenience store, a custom embroidery and vinyl shop, 42 gas islands, 16 diesel lanes, a fuel center, a 7-bay truck service center, a 3-bay Truckomat truck wash, a CAT Scale, a Dogomat Pet Wash, and the Iowa 80 Trucking Museum.

Iowa 80 Truck Stop currently serves 5,000 customers per day and has parking spaces for 900 tractor-trailers, 250 cars and 20 buses. Each year in July, the Iowa 80 hosts the Walcott Truckers Jamboree, a 3-day event dedicated to celebrating America's truckers.

Wales (Montgomery)
(1997)
Wales was settled around 1910 and named for Wales on the British Isle of England.

Walker (Linn)
(1982), (1990)
Walker began as an outgrowth of the Burlington, Cedar Rapids and Northern Railroad and was laid out in 1873. It was named in honor of W. W. Walker, chief engineer of the railroad.

Wallingford (Emmet)

(1996), (2005)

Wallingford was platted in 1882 and incorporated in 1913. No one knows how the town got its name. Some believe it is where there was a crossing (ford) of the river near the town and others believe it was name for an early settler from England, but that may not be correct because most of the settlers were Norwegian.

Wall Lake (Sac)

(1981), (1988), (1995), (2004)

Wall Lake was platted in 1877 and named for nearby Wall Lake. Wall Lake (originally on the early maps called "Walled Lake") got its name from a pile of prairie boulders which have been heaved up by the frosts of many winters. These boulders form a wall around the lake.

Items of interest

Wall Lake is the birthplace of Howard Andrew "Andy" Williams (December 3, 1927 – September 25, 2012) who was an American singer that recorded 43 albums in his career, of which 15 have been gold-certified and three platinum-certified. He sold more than 100 million records worldwide.

Walnut (Pottawattamie)

(1976), (2001), (2016), (2019)

The town was platted in 1869 and incorporated in 1877. The town was first known as Walnut Creek, but later shortened to Walnut. Walnut Creek was named for the black walnut trees which lined the creek before early settlers cut them down.

Item of interest

In 1987, the Governor designated Walnut as Iowa's Antique Capital.

Walnut City (Appanoose)

(1981), (2019)

Walnut City was laid out in 1858 and incorporated in 1877. Walnut was originally name "Walnut Creek" because of a lone Walnut tree that stood beside Walnut Creek. The town changed Creek to City in its name. The town quickly became a trade center for the Rock Island Railroad. The

Walnut Flour Mill used the railroad to ship its product, much of which eventually went to Europe.

WAPELLO (Louisa) (County Seat)
(1979)
Wapello was platted in the late 1830s and named for the Meskwaki Indian Chief Wapello, a powerful ruler. Wapello means "the prince."

Washburn (Black Hawk)
(1985), (2010)
Washburn was platted in 1880 and named for Levi Washburn, an area farmer.

WASHINGTON (Washington) (County Seat)
(1975), (1986), (1990), (2000), (2016)
Washington was founded in 1839 and first named Slaughter, for William B. Slaughter, Secretary of the Wisconsin Territory. The town's name was later changed to Washington for the nation's first president.
Item of interest
Washington has twice been voted among the best 100 small towns in America.

Washta (Cherokee)
(1973), (1978), (2001), (2010), (2015)
Washta's name dates back to 1868 when a local man named Whisman turned his farm into a trading post and mail stop. When asked what the name of his town would be, he recalled an interesting encounter with two Native Americans the previous year. While Whisman was out hunting, the two Native Americans came upon him and removed his gun, they looked at it and handed it back while saying, "Wash-tay, Wash-tay," meaning good. Changing the pronunciation slightly, Whisman decided he would call the town Washta.
Item of interest
On January 12, 1912, the town had the distinction of being "The Coldest Spot in Iowa" with a recorded temperature of 47 degrees below zero, not including the wind chill.

WATERLOO (Black Hawk) (County Seat)
(1974), (1985), (1989), (2010)
Waterloo was originally known as Prairie Rapids Crossing and was first settled in 1845. Tradition has it that as the future postmaster flipped through a list of other post offices in the United States and came upon the name Waterloo. The name struck his fancy and on December 29, 1851, a post office was established under that name.

Items of interest

Waterloo is home of the John Deere Tractor & Engine Museum. John Deere entered into the engine and tractor business in 1918 with the purchased of the Waterloo Gasoline Engine Company for $2.5 million. At the museum visitors can witness the evolution of farming from horse drawn to horsepower, and discover how innovations of the past help to shape our future. The museum has tractors dating from the Waterloo Boy, the company's first tractor, to current day tractors. They can trace the history of John Deere from a simple steel plow to today's modern working machines. They can grip the handles of a steel plow and test their strength against real horsepower and explore the history of John Deere in their interactive exhibits.

Among the most interesting stories from Waterloo's history is that of The Sullivan brothers. They enlisted in the U. S. Navy on January 3, 1942, with the stipulation that brothers would serve together. The Navy had a policy, though not strictly enforced, of separating siblings. George and Frank had served in the Navy before, but their brothers had not.

All five were assigned to the light cruiser USS Juneau. Beginning in August of 1942, the Juneau participated in a number of naval engagements during the months-long Guadalcanal Campaign. Early on the morning of November 13, 1942, during the Naval Battle of Guadalcanal, the ship was struck by a Japanese torpedo and forced to withdraw. Later that day, as it was leaving the Solomon Islands' area for the Allied base at Espiritu Santo with other surviving US warships from battle, the Juneau was again struck, this time by a torpedo from the Japanese submarine I-26. The torpedo likely hit the thinly armored light cruiser at or near the ammunition magazines. The ship exploded and quickly sank.

Eight days after the Juneau went down, ten survivors were found by a search aircraft and then retrieved from the water. The survivors reported that Frank, Joe and Matt died instantly, Al drowned the next day, and George survived for four or five days, suffering from delirium as a result of hypernatremia, though some sources say he was "driven insane with grief" over the loss of his brothers. George went over the side of the raft he occupied and was never seen or heard from again.

As a direct result of the Sullivan's' deaths and the deaths of four of the Borgstrom brothers within a few months of each other, two years later the U.S. War Department adopted the Sole Survivor Policy. This Policy describes a set of regulations that are designed to protect members of a family from the draft or combat duty if they have already lost a family member while in military service. It also placed restrictions on family members serving together.

In 1910, a significant number of black railroad workers were brought into Waterloo as strikebreakers. Again in 1940, black strikebreakers were brought in this time to work in the Rath meat plant. In 1948, a black strikebreaker accidentally killed a white union member as he tried to escape the striker's ire. Instead of a race riot, a strike broke out against the Rath Company. The National Guard was called in to end the 73-day strike.

Waterville (Allamakee)
(2017)
Waterville was first settled in 1850 and incorporated in 1912. It received its name from the availability of water to operate mills.

Waucoma (Fayette)
(1987), (1999), (2005)
The town was incorporated in 1883. It was named for Waucoma, an Indian maiden who became the wife of Chief Decorah.

Waukee (Dallas)
(2006)
Waukee was laid out in 1869 and incorporated in 1878. It is thought to be named for Milwaukee, Wisconsin.

WAUKON (Allamakee) (County Seat)
(1977), (2017)
The first white settler arrived in 1849 and the town was incorporated in 1883. Waukon is often said to be named for Waukon Decorah, a Ho Chunk (Winnebago) leader who was a United States ally during the 1832 Black Hawk War. Other sources say that it was named for his son, Chief John Waukon.
Item of interest
The Allamakee County towns of Lansing and Waukon had a long and bitter fight over who would have the county seat. Originally, the Iowa legislature selected Jefferson Township as the county seat. In the 1851 election, the voters rejected Jefferson Township and selected Columbus as the county seat. In 1853, the legislature granted a petition to seek a county seat closer to the center of the county. Waukon was approved in a two-thirds vote. The battle continued into 1859, when Lansing offered to build an $8,000 courthouse if the county seat was moved to Lansing.

In 1861, the Waukon courthouse was completed at a cost of $13,635. In that same year, Columbus and Lansing teamed up to fight for the county seat and beat out Waukon by 22 votes in the election. Waukon was unsuccessful in getting the county seat back in the 1864 election. In June of 1866, the county sheriff, a Waukon resident, led a posse to the courthouse in Lansing and removed the county records. On their way back to Waukon, the Lansing horsemen intercepted the posse and returned the records to Lansing. The Iowa Supreme Court intervened in 1867 and ruled that Waukon was indeed the county seat, a ruling which still stands today.

WAVERLY (Bremer) (County Seat)
(1980), (1999), (2014)
In 1852, the first settler arrived in what is now Waverly. The town was incorporated in 1859. The story of how the town got its name is that the speaker at the naming ceremony was a fan of Sir Walter Scott's series of

novels called Waverly. When it came time to name the town, which settlers wanted it to be call Harmonville or Harmon, he inadvertently called it Waverly. The myth goes that Jennie Harmon Case later wrote that it was her father who was the speaker and that he made the decision to name the town after his favorite book, instead of the proposed "Harmonville."

Item of interest

Waverly is home to Wartburg College, a four-year liberal arts college associated with the Evangelical Lutheran Church in America. The college is named for Wartburg Castle in Eisenach, Germany, where Martin Luther was protected during the stormy days of the Reformation.

Wayland (Henry)
(1975), (1990), (1992), (2000)
Wayland was surveyed around 1837 and originally known as Crooked Creek. From 1851 to 1880 it was known as Marshall until the name was changed to Wayland because of confusion with Marshalltown.

Webb (Clay)
(1979), (2002), (2007)
Webb was founded in 1900 and originally known as Glenora. The name was changed to Webb by F. D. White in honor of his mother's maiden name.

Webster (Keokuk)
(1995)
Webster was platted in 1854 and incorporated in 1909.

WEBSTER CITY (Hamilton) (County Seat)
(1980), (1995), (2012), (2015)
Webster City was originally called Newcastle by settlers. In early June of 1835, three companies of United States Dragoons were the first white men to see the area now occupied by Webster City. (The word dragoon originally meant mounted infantry who were trained in horse riding as well as infantry fighting skills.) Commanded by Col. Stephen W. Kearney, the mounted soldiers first reached the Boone River and named it in honor of a Dragoon officer, Captain Nathan Boone, son of Daniel Boone.

There is a long history of how Webster City got its name. Newcastle, the original town's name was in Webster County. There was no Hamilton County until January 1, 1857, when Webster County was divided into two counties. State representative Willson, aided by William Hamilton, got the new county established and the towns name of Newcastle was changed to Webster City.

There are three theories as to why the name of the town was changed to Webster City.

- The first theory is that the town was named for a popular stagecoach driver that often visited Willson's hotel.
- The second theory is that the town was named for Daniel Webster for whom the original county was named.
- The last theory is that the town was named Webster City because it was custom to name the town after the county it resided in, which was originally Webster County.

Items of interest

In September, the town annually hosts a celebration of the Doodle Bug motor scooter, a motor scooter built from 1946 to 1948 by the Beam Manufacturing Company of Webster City. It was sold through the Gambles store chain to compete with Cushman scooters. It was also sold under the Allstate brand by Sears. Gambles sold the Doodle Bug, which was powered by 1½ horse power Briggs & Stratton or Clinton engine, under the "Hiawatha" name.

On June 24, 1888, the Ringling Brothers Circus was performing in Webster City. That evening, their strong man, James Richardson (AKA Monsieur Dialo) tried to break up a fight and was shot and killed. Ringling Brothers vowed never to return to Webster City. Each Memorial Day, flowers mysteriously appear on Richardson's grave.

Wellman (Washington)
(2018)

Wellman was founded in 1878 and incorporated in 1885. It was named for Joseph Edward Wellman, who in 1879, provided 40 acres of his farmland for railroad construction, including lots for development near the depot.

Items of interest

Wellman was the "turkey capital of the world" through the 1950's.

Wellsburg (Grundy)
(1989), (1998)
Wellsburg was named for George Wells, an early settler in the region who, in 1880, gave one square mile of his land to establish a town.

Welton (Clinton)
(1985)
Welton started in 1871 with the building of the Davenport and St. Paul Railroad. It was incorporated in 1908.

Wesley (Kossuth)
(2010), (2017)
Wesley was incorporated in 1892. There are two theories of how the town got its name. One is that Wesley was the son of a railroad worker and another is that it was named for John Wesley, a railroad foreman who help build the depot.

West Amana (Iowa)
(1976), (1991), (2008), (2011)
(See Amana)

West Bend (Kossuth and Palo Alto)
(1977), (1985), (1990), (1993), (1999), (2010), (2017)
West Bend started in the early 1880s with the building of the Burlington, Cedar Rapids and Northern Railroad through that territory. It was originally called Ives after the president of the railroad, but the townspeople had it changed to West Bend, for the sharp bend in the Des Moines River. It was established in 1856 and incorporated in 1884.

Item of interest

West Bend is the site of the Grotto of the Redemption, a series of nine contiguous grottos occupying a full city block, constructed of minerals, rocks, and semiprecious gems. It was the inspiration and life work of Fr. Paul Dobberstein (1872-1954), a Catholic priest who settled in West Bend around 1902. For a decade, he gathered rocks and semi-precious stones from around the world. Construction began in 1912. For the next 42 years, Fr. Dobberstein created hundreds of intricate rock settings that form the Grotto's walls and ceilings, evoking a spiritual experience. Matt Szerensce, a parishioner and Fr. Louis Greving, the next Catholic pastor in West Bend, worked side-by-side with Fr. Dobberstein and furthered his work after his death in 1954. Although the Grotto was technically finished in the late 1980s, it is an ongoing work with restorations and repairs made yearly.

The Grotto of the Redemption is the largest man-made grotto in the world. The nine separate grottoes each depict a scene in the life of Jesus of Nazareth or of the testament of God. The theme of redemption gives unity to this sacred space. Although the Grotto was built by a Catholic priest, he wanted it to be appreciated and enjoyed by all religions. His hope was to have the Grotto speak to all through the natural beauty of the stones and their arrangements. The Grotto has been considered the "Eighth Wonder of the World" and The Iowan magazine described it as a "Miracle in Stone."

West Branch (Cedar and Johnson)
(1973), (1976), (1995), (2001), (2006), (2011)
West Branch was laid out in 1869 by Joseph Steer and incorporated in 1875. The city was first settled by Quakers from Ohio. Its name is derived from the Quaker meeting place on the west branch of the Wapsinonoc Creek.

Items of interest
Before the Civil War, the areas in and around West Branch were stops on the Underground Railroad. John Brown, the famous abolitionist, traveled with a son, riding a mule and leading a horse from Kansas to the Quaker settlement of Cedar County. Among the Quaker Friends he found kind treatment. In December of 1856 he stopped at the Traveler's Rest at West Branch and dismounting. He surprised the landlord by asking: "Have you ever heard of John Brown?" Without replying, Mr. Townsend took a piece of chalk from his breast pocket then removed Brown's hat and marked it with a large "X" and then replaced the hat. He then marked Brown's back with a "XX," followed by placing a broad "X" on the back of

the mule then said, "Just put the animal into the stable and walk right into the house; thou art surely welcome."

> In 1874, President Herbert Hoover was born to a Quaker blacksmith and his wife in West Branch. In 1962, The Herbert Hoover Presidential Library-Museum was dedicated in West Branch by Hoover and his close friend, President Harry Truman. This historical site is an extraordinary lesson in how an orphan boy became a multi-millionaire then president of the United States. Hoover had his reputation damaged by his oversight during the Great Depression but then restored it with his humanitarian work later in life. The site includes the Library-Museum, the Hoover Birthplace Cottage and the gravesites of President and Lou Henry Hoover.

West Burlington (Des Moines)
(2009), (2019)
West Burlington was first known as Leffler's Station, which was a stop on the railroad for mail and passengers. Around 1883, when the shops moved to north of the tracks, West Burlington was born.

West Chester (Washington)
(2016)
West Chester was laid out in 1872 and first called Chester for C. F. Chester, an early settler. Later it was found that there was another Chester, Iowa, so in 1873 the name was changed to West Chester.

Westgate (Fayette)
(1990), (2014)
Westgate celebrated its 125th anniversary on July 16, 2011. The town was named for the Sylvester S. Westgate family who gave land west of the railroad tracks for the town. It was incorporated in 1896.

West Grove (Davis)
(2019)
West Grove was laid in 1853 and was first known as Weeping Willow, but in 1856 its name was changed to West Grove for West Grove Township. The township was first known as Deadman's Grove because it was where the remains of a murdered man had been found, but later changed its name to West Grove Township.

West Le Mars (Plymouth)
(1982)
(See Le Mars)

West Liberty (Muscatine)
(1976), (1995), (2001), (2006), (2015), (2018)
West Liberty was incorporated in 1867. Prior to incorporation, the town stood about half a mile north of where it is currently located. It was relocated in order to be closer to the railroad. The settlement was originally known as Wapsinonoc Township, which means smooth surfaced, meandering creek or stream. The town changed its name to Liberty for Liberty, Ohio, the former home of many of the new settlers. Its name is attributed to the wife of the township's first postmaster, Simeon A. Bagley. It is believed that the town came to be known as West Liberty after it was relocated, possibly influenced by the town being west of Liberty, Ohio.

<u>Items of interest</u>

In the winter of 1837-8, a party of Native Americans were encamped near Moscow. One evening, three or four of the Native Americans were at a West Liberty drinking house or grocery kept by a man named Ross. In company of some half dozen other white men, Ross got the Native Americans to perform a war dance. In order to make the dancing livelier, both the Native Americans and the white men freely drank from a barrel that stood in one corner of the filthy shanty marked OLD WHISKY. They kept up the dancing and drinking until they all became decidedly drunk. The Native Americans, as is usual under these circumstances, demanded more from the barrel, which in their own language was called, Scutah Oppo signified FIRE WATER. This finally resulted in a war of words.

It happened that Powsheik, who was chief of that particular band of Native Americans, had a brother who was one of the party in this quarrel. Ross and his friends wanting to get the Native Americans out of the shanty and started to force them to leave. In the scuffle which started, Ross struck the chief's brother with a heavy stick of wood and knocked him senselessly to the ground. The rest of the Native Americans became frightened and ran away. Ross then dragged the fallen brave outdoors and deliberately beat him to death with a heavy rail.

The Native Americans were angered at this outrage and were determined on getting revenge. They were often seen with their faces painted as a demonstration of their displeasure, but were kept quiet by the assurance that Ross would be punished by the laws of the white man. Ross was indicted for murder, but owing to some trifling defect in the indictment, was set free.

The Native Americans could not understand why a man who everyone acknowledged was guilty of a brutal murder, should be permitted to escape punishment for his crime, just because of the omission of a word or two in the manuscript which they could neither read or understand. The Native Americans therefore determined to seek justice in their own way. With the utmost contempt for the inefficient laws of the white man, they set out to find Ross. Ross knew that if he did not flee the country, his fate was sealed. Therefore, he left as quietly as possible. The Native Americans, being unable in their attempts to find Ross, quietly waited for an opportunity to avenge their wrong upon one of the same hated race. It so happened that their victim was a Methodist minister, whose name was Oliver Atwood.

One bitter cold winter day, the congregation gathered to attend a church service in a school house which was conducted by a minister. No fire had been started so the room was very uncomfortable. Many were inclined to forego the service, but the preacher had come to preach the Gospel and they had come to hear it. When the service started, the preacher used a desk near the back of the room as his pulpit, but the stove was near the front of the room. He did not remove his overcoat or his cap because of the cold. After the preliminaries of the service, the preacher

arose to address the congregation. One of his first acts was
to reach in his pocket and take out a plug of tobacco from
which he took a liberal chew. As he warmed up with his
subject, his jaws worked faster and the saliva accumulated
till it threatened to interfere with his sermon. He would start
for the stove and continued talking, then open the stove
door and unload his burdened mouth, then returned to the
pulpit without missing a word. Many did not remember the
text or the point of the sermon, but do vividly remember
the man and the earnestness of his faith. Many look back
to his ministry as the beginning of a better life, and it was
easier to forget his uncouthness than his love for his fellow
man.

Weston (Pottawattamie)
(1994), (2000), (2013)

West Point (Lee)
(1988), (1997), (2013), (2019)
West Point was incorporated in 1858. The name of West Point was
chosen by officers of the garrison at Fort Des Moines and likely named for
the Military Academy at West Point, New York.
Item of interest
West Point is home to Iowa's Largest Sweet Corn Festival. The four-
day event in August has historically resulted in an estimated 25,000 visitors
and over 17 tons of sweet corn being consumed.

Westphalia (Shelby)
(1983)
Westphalia was founded in 1874 by a colony of German Catholics
and named for the region of Westphalia, Germany.

WEST UNION (Fayette) (County Seat)
(1987), (1993), (1999), (2005)
West Union was originally called Knob Prairie which was founded
by William Wells who named the town for his hometown of West Union,
Ohio.

What Cheer (Keokuk)
(1988)
What Cheer was founded in 1865 as Petersburg, named for Peter Britton, its founder but the name was rejected by the post office. Joseph Andrews, a major and veteran of the Civil War, suggested the name What Cheer, and was officially renamed in 1879.

Sources differ as to why the name What Cheer was chosen. The phrase "what cheer with you" is an ancient English greeting dating back at least to the 15th century.

- One theory is that a Scottish miner exclaimed "What Cheer!" on discovering a coal seam near town.
- A more elaborate theory suggests that Joseph Andrews chose the name because of a myth at his native town of Providence, Rhode Island. According to the story, in 1636 when Roger Williams arrived at the site that would become Providence, he was greeted by Narragansett Native Americans with "What Cheer, Netop." Netop was the Narragansett word for friend. The Narragansetts had picked up the What Cheer greeting from English settlers.

White Oak (Polk)
(2011)
White Oak was named for the grove of white oak trees in the area.

Whittemore (Kossuth)
(1977), (1990), (1999), (2005), (2010), (2017)
Whittlemore was platted in 1878 and named for a Milwaukee Railroad engineer, Don Whittemore.

Whitten (Hardin)
(1986)
In 1880, the Northwestern Railroad System platted the town. The town was named for C. C. Whitten, an official of the railroad. Whitten was incorporated in 1882.

Whittier (Linn)

(1978), (1994), (2004), (2015)

Whittier was founded as a Quaker community, and named for the Quaker poet and abolitionist John Greenleaf Whittier.

Wichita (Guthrie)
(1986), (1989), (2006)

Wichita is an unincorporated community.

Wildcat Den State Park (Muscatine)
(2018)

Wildcat Den State Park is located on the Mississippi River. The park features 75-foot cliffs, rock formations, and several historic structures. The 1848 Pine Creek Gristmill and Pine Mill Bridge are both on the National Register of Historic Places.

Willey (Carroll)
(1980), (2011)

The town was likely named for Josiah Richard Willey, an early settler. It was incorporated in 1911.

Williams (Hamilton)
(2015)

Williams was platted in 1869 and named for Major William Williams.
Items of interest

In 1911, the wooden water tower collapsed, sending a rush of water across the street to the home of 90-year-old Thomas Duffy. The flood water broke through the windows and sent Mr. Duffy across the room where he suffered a broken collarbone from this incident.

In 1930, Williams was chosen by Bell Telephone as the first rural community west of the Mississippi River to have dial telephones.

The Hemken Collection, located downtown Williams, is a collection of vintage cars featuring American convertibles: Chevys, Lincolns, Hudsons and Packards from 1947 and 1948. The cars comprise the collection of Daryl Hemken.

Williamsburg (Iowa)
(1973), (1995), (2001), (2006)
Williamsburg was laid out in 1856 and first named Stellapol, but was renamed for its founder, Richard Williams. It was incorporated in 1885.

Wilton (Cedar and Muscatine)
(1973), (1982), (2011), (2015), (2018)
The first settler to Wilton arrived in 1846. The town was platted in 1854 and incorporated in 1908. The town was first called Glendale but renamed for Wilton, Maine, the home town of an early settler.

Items of interest
The Candy Kitchen is the oldest ongoing Ice Cream Parlor and Soda Fountain in the world and has been serving ice cream, lunches, and candy for over 160 years. Since 1860, the ownership of the store has been in the Nopoulos family and run by George and Thelma Nopoulos.

Since her husband's death, Thelma Nopoulos had been looking for someone who could continue the legacy of the Candy Kitchen. In 2014, the Ochiltrees were interested in purchasing it and came to Thelma with an offer which she accepted. Lynn Ochiltree and his wife Brenda had operated a funeral home in Winterset for a number of years. They sold the Winterset business to return to Lynn's hometown of Wilton.

When speaking of The Candy Kitchen, Lynn Ochiltree said it had its beginning when a young immigrant named Gus Nopoulos came to town and rented the building to make chocolates and sell soda and ice cream. The Nopouluses were legendary. Gus came here when he was 17 years old as a Greek immigrant, said Ochiltree. When he was 19, he saw a sign in the window of the store. It was a confectionery soda fountain that was closed. He reopened the store in 1910, and his son George took ownership along with his wife, Thelma.

An event on June 20, 1874 will always be remembered with special interest. It was the discovery of the fossil remains of the Wilton Mastodon, which was discovered and dug up a short distance south of the city limits. The Mastodon has been extinct for 10,000 to 20,000 years. The bones were the largest ever found. The length of the scapula (shoulder blade) is three feet and five inches long, and two feet and five inches wide in the widest place, and weighs fifty and one-half pounds. Some of the vertebrae measured eight and one-half inches in diameter. Only parts of the bones were recovered.

Windham (Johnson)
(2006)
Windham was platted in 1854. There is no record of how the town got its name but some believed it possible that a person named Windham was an early settler.

Winfield (Henry)
(2000)
Winfield was laid out in 1852 and named for General Winfield Scott.
No one person had more influence on the United States Army during its first 100 years of existence than General Winfield Scott. He was known as Old Fuss and Feathers because of his attention to detail and a liking for gaudy uniforms. Winfield Scott fought in the War of 1812, the Blackhawk War, the Seminole Wars, the Mexican-American War, and the Civil War.

Winnebago Heights (Cerro Gordo)
(1982)
Winnebago was named for the Winnebago Indians.

WINTERSET (Madison) (County Seat)
(1991), (1997), (2019)
Winterset was platted during a cool spell in the summer of 1849. The town was originally to be called "Summerset," but the unseasonable coldness made the commissioners revise it to "Winterset."
Items of interest
Winterset is the birth place of Marion Mitchell Morrison (May 26, 1907 – June 11, 1979), known professionally as John Wayne and nicknamed "Duke." He was an American actor and filmmaker, an Academy Award-

winner (for True Grit) and among the top box office draws over three decades. Although he was born in Winterset, he grew up in Southern California.

The modest 4-room home where John Wayne was born is open to tourist along with the John Wayne Birthplace Museum. The museum features the largest diversified exhibit of John Wayne artifacts in existence including original movie posters, film wardrobe, scripts, letters, artwork and sculpture, and even one of his customized automobiles. The museum has a small theater which had a documentary on John Wayne's life, with a special welcome by his daughter Aissa. The museum is located at 205 South John Wayne Drive.

The Bridges of Madison County by Robert Waller is a 1995 American romantic novel and drama film that takes place near Winterset.

George W. Carver arrived in Winterset in 1888 after being turned away from college in Kansas. Although discouraged about his educational possibilities, he became an active member of the Winterset community, working in a hotel kitchen, taking in laundry in his home, roaming the hills studying nature, and participating in the First Baptist Church choir. At the church, he was noticed by Mrs. Helen Milholland who invited him into the Milholland home to enjoy their mutual interests of plants, art, and music. The family encouraged him in 1890 to enroll in Simpson College located in Indianola. This set him on a course to Iowa State College (now Iowa State University), the Tuskegee Institute, and his scientific contributions to the world. (See Ames and Indianola for more information)

Madison County is home to the oldest tree in Iowa which has been determined to have germinated around 1634, not long after the Pilgrims arrived at Plymouth Rock in 1620.

Winthrop (Buchanan)
(1989), (1990), (2002), (2007), (2010), (2014)
Winthrop was platted in 1857. The towns name was suggested by E. S. Norris for a friend of the man who platted the town.

Wiota (Cass)
(1991), (2001), (2019)
Wiota started in 1972. Legend has it that an Indian boy named Iota fell into the creek. The Indians thought it was so funny that they called that place Wiota.

Woden (Hancock)
(1977),)1982), (1999), (2002), (2005)
Woden was platted in 1898 and incorporated in 1904. Woden was first called Bingham and then Ripley. The post office turned down both names for their similarity to other towns. The name Woden was said to have been chosen because there was so much noise caused by the dynamiting by the railroad that it sounded like war. Woden is the Norse god of war.

Wooden Wheel Vineyards (Washington)
(2016)
Isabella, the great, great grandmother of Mike Vincent, was the original owner of the Wagon Wheel Vineyards which is now owned by Mike Vincent. Isabella's father, a veteran of the War of 1812, died when she was 2 years old. As an orphan and minor child of a veteran, she became eligible for an 80-acre land grant. Her brother, who was traveling in Iowa, learned of the program and returned on horseback to Ohio to have Isabella complete the paper work. She turned in her claim two weeks before her eighteenth birthday, after which she would have no longer qualified for this program as a minor child. The vineyard was passed down to Mike's father and in 1978, Mike and Connie Vincent purchased it. The farm crisis of the 1980's sent them away, but they always hoped to return. In 2010, they sold their insurance company and returned to plant their first vines and began construction of the winery and events center.

Woodland (Decatur)
(1988), (1992)
Woodland started in 1856 and named for the valuable and heavy growth of timber which once grew there.

Woodward (Dallas)
(1983), (1986), (1994), (2001)
Woodward started when the Chicago, Milwaukee and St. Paul Railway Company constructed its lines through the community. The original name for the town was Xenia, but the town moved to accommodate the railroad and was renamed Colton for one of the landowners. It was found that another town had already adopted that name so the name was changed to Woodward. There are two stories about how the town was named Woodard:

- The town was named for a beautiful garden in California.
- A former State Senator liked the railroad ticket taker Frank Wordwork and named it for him. Because of a handwriting error, on August 1883, the town was incorporated as Woodward.

Woolstock (Wright)
(2004),
Woolstock was platted in 1881 and incorporated in 1895. Many early residents in the area raised large flocks of sheep. They would travel to the southwestern part of the township to the little village called "Wool Stock" where they met with traders who would buy their wool. Unfortunately, the wool trade was a failure. Harsh winters and lack of prepared shelter for the sheep caused many to die or be eaten by wolves. The rest were destroyed or sold at a reduced price.

Items of interest
No other place in the United States or the English-speaking world goes by the name of Woolstock.

Woolstock is the birth place of George Reeves, television's first 1950's Superman. George Reeves was born George Keefer Brewer in Woolstock on January 5, 1914. In 1935, he joined the Pasadena Community Playhouse. His first film role was a minor part in "*Gone With The Wind.*" Reeves acted in movies and army training films and in 1951, he took the title role on the popular television series "*The Adventures of Superman.*" His mysterious 1959 death was considered a suicide, but some speculate it was murder. After Reeves death, one of his replacements as Superman was Brandon Routh who grew up in Norwalk, Iowa.

Worthington (Dubuque)
(1989), (1999), (2007)
Worthington was platted 1858 and incorporated in 1893. The town got its name from an early settler named Amos Worthington.

Wyoming (Jones)
(1978), (1985)
Wyoming was incorporated in 1873 and named for Wyoming County, New York.

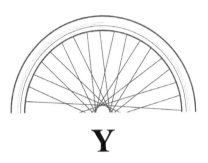

Y

Yale (Guthrie)
(1983), (2001), (2013)
Yale was platted in 1882 and named for its founder, Milo Yale.

Yarmouth (Des Moines)
(1990), (2000)
Yarmouth started with the building of the Burlington and Northwestern Railroad through the territory and named for Yarmouth, which is on the east coast of England.

Yellow River State Forest (Allamakee)
(2017)
The Yellow River State Forest was established in 1933 by the Civilian Conservation Corps with the purchase of 1500 acres of land at the mouth of the Yellow River. The forest is located in the "Driftless Area" of Iowa, a region that did not have glaciers passing through it during the last ice age.

Yetter (Calhoun)
(1981)
Yetter was platted in 1899 and incorporated in 1903. It was named for its founder, L. M. Yetter.

Yorktown (Page)
(1989),
Yorktown was platted in 1882 by C. E. Perkins and incorporated in 1898. The early citizens of Yorktown had a disagreement about what the town should be called. The Government named the post office York and the town Yorktown, but the people wanted the town to be named Loy in honor of the first postmaster, Jacob Loy. The town held the name of Loy for only a few months. As a publicity stunt, a local correspondent for the

Shenandoah Post started a contest to rename the town Yorktown, which emphasized the famous surrender of Cornwallis at Yorktown, Virginia. The stunt was successful and the town was renamed Yorktown.

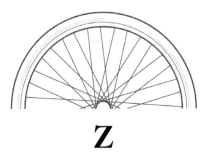

Z

Zaneta (Grundy)
(1978)
Zaneta was founded in the 1800s and named after Zanesville, Ohio. The "ta" was added to Zane because some thought it sounded better.

Zearing (Story)
(1979), (1986), (1998), (2012)
Zearing was founded in 1881 and incorporated in 1883. It was named for William Mitchell Zearing, a judge from Chicago who donated a bell to the first church in the community.

Zwingle (Dubuque)
(1999)
Zwingle was first settled in 1845 and named for the Swiss religious reformer, Ulrich Zwingle.

Full list of Iowa Bike Towns
1973-2020

Overnight towns are in all caps.

I, August 26-31, 1973 (six days)

SIOUX CITY, Kingsley, Washta, Quimby, STORM LAKE, Varina, Pioneer, Clare, FORT DODGE, Coalville, Lehigh, Stratford, Boone, Luther, AMES, Slater, Sheldahl, Kelley, Polk City, Ankeny, DES MOINES, Altoona, Mitchellville, Colfax, Prairie City, Reasnor, Sully, Lynnville, Searsboro, Montezuma, Deep River, Millersburg, WILLIAMSBURG, University Heights, Iowa City, West Branch, Rochester, Moscow, Wilton, Durant, Walcott, DAVENPORT

II (SAGBRAI), August 4-10, 1974

COUNCIL BLUFFS, McClelland, Underwood, Bentley, Hancock, ATLANTIC, Elk Horn, Kimballton, Hamlin, GUTHRIE CENTER, Panora, Minburn, Granger, CAMP DODGE, Ankeny, Bondurant, Maxwell, Colo, State Center, MARSHALLTOWN, Green Mountain, Gladbrook, Morrison, Hudson, WATERLOO, Evansdale, Elk Run Heights, Gilbertville, Brandon, Urbana, Center Point, Central City, Prairieburg, MONTICELLO, Scotch Grove, Center Junction, Onslow, Cascade, Farley, Epworth, Centralia, DUBUQUE

III, August 3-9, 1975

HAWARDEN, Orange City, Alton, Granville, Marcus, CHEROKEE, Nemaha, Sac City, LAKE VIEW, Carnavon, Auburn, Lake City, Lanesboro, Churdan, Paton, Boxholm, Pilot Mound, BOONE, Luther, Slater, Farrar, Mitchellville, Colfax, Lambs Grove, NEWTON, Reasnor, Sully, Lynnville, Searsboro, Montezuma, Deep River, Thornburg, Keswick, SIGOURNEY, Talleyrand, Washington, Wayland, Trenton, MOUNT PLEASANT, Oakland Mills, Salem, Houghton, Denmark, FORT MADISON

IV, August 1-7, 1976
SIDNEY, Farragut, Shenandoah, Essex, RED OAK, Walnut, Avoca, Shelby, Tennant, HARLAN, Kimballton, Hamlin, Coon Rapids, Scranton, JEFFERSON, Grand Junction, Dana, Ogden, Boone, Gilbert, Ames, NEVADA, Colo, State Center, Melbourne, Kellogg, GRINNELL, Brooklyn, Carnforth, Victor, Ladora, Marengo, West Amana, High Amana, Middle Amana, Amana, Homestead, Oxford, University Heights, IOWA CITY, West Branch, Springdale, West Liberty, Atalissa, MUSCATINE

V, July 31-August 6, 1977
ONAWA, Turin, Castana, Mapleton, Danbury, Battle Creek, IDA GROVE, Galva, Schaller, Nemaha, Newell, Albert City, LAURENS, Mallard, West Bend, Whittemore, ALGONA, Titonka, Woden, Crystal Lake, Hayfield, Miller, Ventura, CLEAR LAKE, Burchinal, Rockford, Charles City, Ionia, NEW HAMPTON, Protivin, Spillville, Ridgeway, DECORAH, Freeport, Waukon, Elon, Dalby, Village Creek, LANSING

VI, July 30-August 5, 1978
SIOUX CITY, Pierson, Washta, Quimby, STORM LAKE, Varina, Pioneer, Unique, HUMBOLDT, Dakota City, Thor, Eagle Grove, Dows, Popejoy, IOWA FALLS, Cleves, Steamboat Rock, Holland, Zaneta, Hudson, Eagle Center, Dysart, Garrison, VINTON, Urbana, Center Point, Alice, Alburnett, Whittier, Springville, Paralta, MOUNT VERNON, Paralta (again), Springville (again), Viola, Fairview, Anamosa, Wyoming, Monmouth, Baldwin, MAQUOKETA, Goose Lake, Elvira, CLINTON

VII, July 29-August 4, 1979
ROCK RAPIDS, Sibley, May City, Hartley, SPENCER, Dickens, Gillett Grove, Webb, Marathon, Albert City, Fonda, Jolley, ROCKWELL CITY, Lohrville, Churdan, Paton, Boxholm, Pilot Mound, STORY CITY, Roland, McCallsburg, Zearing, Bangor, Liscomb, Green Mountain, Le Grand, Montour, TAMA-TOLEDO, Haven, Brooklyn, Deep River, Thornburg, Keswick, Sigourney, Ollie, Packwood, FAIRFIELD, Lockridge, Rome, Mount Pleasant, Mount Union, Morning Sun, WAPELLO, Oakville, Kingston, BURLINGTON.

VIII, July 27-August 2, 1980
GLENWOOD, Silver City, Henderson, ATLANTIC, Elk Horn, Kimballton, Audubon, Viola Center, Dedham, Willey, CARROLL, Willey (again), Dedham (again), Coon Rapids, Cooper, Rippey, PERRY, Rippey (again), Pilot Mound, Ridgeport, Stratford, WEBSTER CITY, Clarion, Belmond, Alexander, Aredale, Bristow, Allison, Clarksville, WAVERLY, Bremer Station, Tripoli, Sumner, Fayette, Volga, ELKADER, Elkport, Garber, GUTTENBERG

IX, July 26-August 1, 1981
MISSOURI VALLEY, Magnolia, Pisgah, Moorhead, Solider, Ute, MAPLETON, Schleswig, Boyer, Wall Lake, Lake View, Yetter, LAKE CITY, Glidden, Coon Rapids, Casey, GREENFIELD, Orient, Creston, Diagonal, Tingley, Ellston, (just missed Beaconsfield), Kellerton, Lamoni, Davis City, LEON, Garden Grove, Humeston, Cambria, Millerton, Bethlehem, Confidence, Walnut City, Mystic, CENTERVILLE, Rathbun, Moravia, Unionville, Paris, Drakesville, Bloomfield, Troy, Lebanon, Pittsburg, KEOSAUQUA, Vernon, Bentonsport, Bonaparte, Farmington, Donnellson, Argyle, Montrose, Galland, Sandusky, KEOKUK

X, July 25-31, 1982
AKRON, Ruble, West Le Mars, Le Mars, CHEROKEE, Peterson, Everly, Milford, ESTHERVILLE, Ringsted, Seneca, Bancroft, Titonka, Woden, Crystal Lake, FOREST CITY, Winnebago Heights, Mason City (east edge), Portland, Rockford, CHARLES CITY, Nashua, Bradford (by the Little Brown Church), Horton, Shell Rock, Finchford, Dunkerton, Littleton, Otterville, INDEPENDENCE, Quasqueton, Walker, Central City, Stone City, Anamosa, Morley, Mechanicsville, TIPTON, Moscow, Wilton, Durant, Walcott, DAVENPORT

XI, July 24-30, 1983
ONAWA, Turin, Soldier, Dunlap, Earling, Panama, Westphalia, HARLAN, Jacksonville, Kimballton, Hamlin, Gardner, GUTHRIE CENTER, Yale, Perry, Bouton, Woodward, Luther, AMES, Roland, Story City, Ellsworth, Jewell, Kamrar, CLARION, Dows, Bradford, Faulkner, Ackley, Cleves, Steamboat Rock, Holland, GRUNDY CENTER, Morrison,

Reinbeck, Voorhies, Eagle Center, La Porte City, Brandon, Urbana, Center Point, Troy Mills, Robinson, MANCHESTER, Earlville, Dyersville, Bankston, Asbury, DUBUQUE

XII, July 22-28, 1984
GLENWOOD, Bartlett, Thurman, Sidney, SHENANDOAH, Essex, Stanton, Tenville, Dickieville, Corning, Prescott, CRESTON, Orient, Greenfield, Stuart, Redfield, ADEL, Dallas Center, Granger, Polk City, Crocker, Ankeny, Enterprise, Bondurant, Mitchellville, Colfax, Lambs Grove, Newton, Reasnor, Galesburg, PELLA, Flagler, Bussey, Hamilton, Lovilia, Albia, Munterville, Bidwell, OTTUMWA, Dahlonega, Farson, Packwood, Brookville, Fairfield, Lockridge, Rome, MOUNT PLEASANT, Prairie Grove, BURLINGTON

XIII, July 21-27, 1985
HAWARDEN, Rock Valley, Doon, George, SIBLEY, May City, Milford, Terril, Graettinger, EMMETSBURG, West Bend, Ottosen, Rutland, HUMBOLDT, Dakota City, Livermore, Lu Verne, Corwith, Stillson, Hutchins, Britt, Garner, Ventura, Clear Lake, Burchinal, MASON CITY, Dougherty, Greene, Clarksville, Shell Rock, Finchford, Cedar Falls, WATERLOO, Washburn, Gilbertville, Brandon, Urbana, Center Point, Alice, Central City, Prairieburg, MONTICELLO, Scotch Grove, Center Junction, Onslow, Wyoming, Oxford Junction, Lost Nation, Welton, Elvira, CLINTON

XIV, July 20-26, 1986
COUNCIL BLUFFS, Mineola, Emerson, RED OAK, Marne, Elk Horn, Kimballton, AUDUBON, Wichita, Guthrie Center, Panora, PERRY, Bouton, Woodward, Madrid, Slater, Maxwell, Iowa Center, Fernald, McCallsburg, Zearing, Clemons, St. Anthony, New Providence, Gifford, ELDORA, Gifford (again), Union, Whitten, Conrad, Beaman, Green Mountain, Garwin, Clutier, Vining, Chelsea, BELLE PLAINE, Luzerne, Blairstown, Marengo, Ladora, Millersburg, North English, South English, Harper, Keota, Talleyrand, WASHINGTON, Riverside, Lone Tree, Nichols, MUSCATINE

XV, July 19-25, 1987

ONAWA, Turin, Soldier, Ute, Charter Oak, DENISON, Deloit, Kiron, Arthur, Galva, Schaller, STORM LAKE, Varina, Palmer, Plover, Pioneer, Clare, FORT DODGE, Badger, Thor, Hardy, Renwick, Kanawha, Denhart (century loop), Corwith (century loop), Britt, Crystal Lake, FOREST CITY, Joice, Kensett, Bolan, St. Ansgar, OSAGE, New Haven, Elma, Alta Vista, Jerico, Jackson Junction, Waucoma, St. Lucas, WEST UNION, Elgin, Gunder, Elkader, Communia, Elkport, Garber, GUTTENBERG

XVI, July 24-30, 1988

SIOUX CITY, Bronson, Anthon, Battle Creek, IDA GROVE, Arthur, Odebolt, Wall Lake, Breda, Mount Carmel, CARROLL, Lidderdale, Lanesboro, Adaza, Churdan, Farlin (century loop), Dana, BOONE, Luther, Slater, Sheldahl, Polk City, Johnston, DES MOINES, Pleasant Hill, Rising Sun, Woodland, Adelphi, Runnells, Pleasantville, Knoxville, Harvey, OSKALOOSA, What Cheer, Thornburg, Keswick, Sigourney, Ollie, Packwood, FAIRFIELD, Stockport, West Point, FORT MADISON

XVII, July 23-29, 1989

GLENWOOD, Bartlett, Tabor, Randolph, Shenandoah, Yorktown, CLARINDA, Stanton, Griswold, Lewis, ATLANTIC, Exira, Wichita, Bayard, Scranton, JEFFERSON, Paton, Boxholm, Pilot Mound, STORY CITY, Randall, Jewell, Ellsworth, Steamboat Rock, Wellsburg, Holland (century loop), Dike, CEDAR FALLS, Waterloo, Dunkerton, Jesup, Independence, Winthrop,Masonville, Manchester, Delaware, Earlville, DYERSVILLE, Worthington, Cascade, Andrew, Springbrook, BELLEVUE

XVIII, July 22-28, 1990

SIOUX CENTER, Newkirk, Hospers, Primghar, Royal, SPENCER, Dickens, Ayrshire, Curlew, Mallard, West Bend, Whittemore, ALGONA, St. Benedict, Corwith, Kanawha, Goodell, Meservey, Alexander, HAMPTON, Aredale, Bristow, Allison, Clarksville, Westgate, OELWEIN, Hazleton, Aurora, Winthrop, Quasqueton, Walker, Alburnett, Robins (not on map), CEDAR RAPIDS, Ely, Solon, Iowa City, Hills, Riverside, WASHINGTON, Wayland, Trenton, Mount Union, Yarmouth, BURLINGTON

XIX, July 21-27, 1991

MISSOURI VALLEY, Beebeetown, Underwood, Bentley, Hancock, ATLANTIC, Wiota, Anita, Adair, Casey, Menlo, Stuart, Dexter, Earlham, WINTERSET, Hanley, St. Charles, St. Marys, New Virginia, Medora, Lacona, Bauer, Melcher-Dallas (maybe), KNOXVILLE, Pella, Galesburg, Kilduff, Oakland Acres, GRINNELL, Brooklyn, Carnforth, Victor, Ladora, Marengo, West Amana, High Amana, Middle Amana, AMANA, East Amana, Swisher, Shueyville, Solon, Lisbon, Mount Vernon, Paralta, Springville, Viola, Stone City, ANAMOSA, Amber, Scotch Grove, Canton, Emeline, Iron Hill, Andrew, Springbrook, BELLEVUE

XX, July 19-25, 1992

GLENWOOD, Bartlett, Thurman, Knox, Sidney, SHENANDOAH, Essex, Coburg, Villisca, Nodaway, Dickieville, Corning, Gravity, BEDFORD, Redding (century loop), Blockton (century loop), Benton, Mount Ayr, Kellerton, Decatur City, Leon, OSCEOLA, Liberty, Medora, New Virginia, St. Marys, Martensdale, Prole, Norwalk, DES MOINES, Pleasant Hill, Woodland, Adelphi, Monroe, Knoxville, OSKALOOSA, Rose Hill (maybe), Delta, Hayesville, Richland, Brighton, Coppock, Wayland, Trenton, MOUNT PLEASANT, Oakland Mills, Denova, Salem, Houghton, Mount Hamill, Farmington, Donnellson, Argyle, Montrose, Sandusky, KEOKUK

XXI, July 25-31, 1993

SIOUX CITY, Ellendale, Merrill, Le Mars, Oyens, Carnes, Orange City, Alton, Granville, SHELDON, Archer, Primghar, Royal, Gillett Grove, Ayrshire, EMMETSBURG, Mallard, West Bend, Ottosen, Bode, Livermore, Renwick, CLARION, Belmond, Sheffield, Dougherty, Rockford, Rudd, OSAGE, Riceville, Schley, Cresco, DECORAH, Ossian, West Union, Elgin, Wadena, Arlington, Lamont, MANCHESTER, Delaware, Earlville, Dyersville, Farley, Epworth, Centralia, Asbury, DUBUQUE

XXII, July 24-30, 1994

COUNCIL BLUFFS, Weston, Underwood, Beebeetown, Persia, Portsmouth, HARLAN, Irwin, Manilla, Vail, Breda, Mount Carmel, CARROLL, Lidderdale, Lanesboro, Churdan, Jefferson, Grand Junction,

Rippey, Angus, PERRY, Bouton, Woodward, Madrid, Slater, Huxley, Cambridge, Nevada, Colo, State Center, Lamoille, MARSHALLTOWN, Le Grand, Montour, Tama, Toledo, Vining, Elberon, Van Horne, Newhall, Atkins, Palo, Hiawatha, Cedar Rapids, MARION, Whittier, Viola, Stone City, Anamosa, Morley, Olin, Hale Village, Oxford Junction, Lost Nation, Elwood, MAQUOKETA, Elwood (again), Grand Mound, DeWitt, Elvira, CLINTON

XXIII, July 23-29, 1995
ONAWA, Turin, Castana, Mapleton, Danbury, Wall Lake, LAKE VIEW, Sac City, Jolley, Knieirm, Barnum, FORT DODGE, Coalville, Kalo, Lehigh, Homer, Webster City, Blairsburg, Alden, IOWA FALLS, Ackley, Cleves, Steamboat Rock, Holland, Grundy Center, Beaman, Conrad (century spur), Gladbrook, Le Grand, Montour, TAMA-TOLEDO, Vining, Chelsea, Belle Plaine, Victor, Keswick, SIGOURNEY, Webster, South English, North English, Parnell, Williamsburg, Iowa City, CORALVILLE, Iowa City (again), West Branch, Springdale, West Liberty, MUSCATINE

XXIV, July 21-27, 1996
SIOUX CENTER, Orange City, Alton, Granville, Paullina, Archer, SIBLEY, Ocheyedan, May City, Milford, ESTHERVILLE, Wallingford, Ringsted, Bancroft, Thompson, LAKE MILLS, Northwood, Carpenter, Grafton (century loop), Bolan (century loop), Kensett (sesquicentennial loop), Joice (sesquicentennial loop), St. Ansgar, Osage, CHARLES CITY, Colwell, Deerfield, Alta Vista, Elma, Schley, CRESCO, Protivin, Spillville, Fort Atkinson, St. Lucas, Hawkeye, Randalia, FAYETTE, Wadena, Volga, Elkader, Clayton Center, Garnavillo, GUTTENBERG

XXV, July 20-26, 1997
MISSOURI VALLEY, Beebeetown, Underwood, Bentley, Hancock, Oakland, Carson, Wales, RED OAK, Tenville, Corning, Prescott, CRESTON, Lorimor, Winterset, Cumming, Norwalk, DES MOINES, Indianola, Milo, Lacona, Oakley, CHARITON, Millerton, Bethlehem, Confidence, Iconium, Moravia, Unionville, Paris, Drakesville, BLOOMFIELD, Pulaski, Milton, Lebanon, Pittsburg, Keosauqua, Vernon,

Bentonsport, Bonaparte, Stockport, FAIRFIELD, Stockport (again), Houghton, St. Paul, Pilot Grove, West Point, FORT MADISON

XXVI, July 19-25, 1998
HAWARDEN, Ireton, Craig, Brunsville, Le Mars, Remsen, CHEROKEE, Quimby, Galva, Schaller, Nemaha, Jolley, ROCKWELL CITY, Rinard, Farnhamville, Gowrie, Paton, Boxholm, Pilot Mound, BOONE, Story City, Roland, McCallsburg, Zearing, Bangor (century loop), Clemons (century loop), St. Anthony (century loop), New Providence, ELDORA, Steamboat Rock, Wellsburg, Dike, CEDAR FALLS, Dunkerton, Jesup, Rowley, Quasqueton, Monti, Ryan, Buck Creek, MONTICELLO, Scotch Grove, Canton, Andrew, Springbrook, SABULA

XXVII, July 25-31, 1999
ROCK RAPIDS, George, Ashton, Melvin, Hartley, Moneta, SPENCER, Dickens, Ayrshire, Curlew, Mallard, West Bend, Whittemore, ALGONA, Oak Lake, Titonka, Woden, Crystal Lake, Hayfield, Miller, Ventura, CLEAR LAKE, Swaledale, Rockwell, Dougherty, Bristow (century loop), Aredale (century loop), Greene, Packard, Clarksville, WAVERLY, Bremer Station, Tripoli, Sumner, Alpha, Waucoma, St. Lucas, Fort Atkinson, Spillville, Ridgeway, DECORAH, Ossian, West Union, Elgin, Wadena, Arlington, Lamont, Dundee, MANCHESTER, Delaware, Earlville, Worthington, Cascade, Hugo, Garryowen, Bernard, Zwingle, La Motte, Cottonville, BELLEVUE

XXVIII, July 23-29, 2000
COUNCIL BLUFFS, Weston, Underwood, Neola, Minden, Shelby, Tennant, HARLAN, Elk Horn, Exira, Anita, Canby, Fontanelle, GREENFIELD, Orient (century loop), Arbor Hill, Stuart, Redfield, Adel, Dallas Center, Granger, Andrews, Polk City, Crocker, ANKENY, Enterprise, Bondurant, Santiago, Mitchellville, Colfax, Lambs Grove, Newton, Reasnor, Galesburg, Pella, KNOXVILLE, Bussey, Hamilton, Lovilia, Albia, Blakesburg, OTTUMWA, Farson, Packwood, Richland, Talleyrand, Dublin, WASHINGTON, Wayland, Olds, Winfield, Mount Union, Yarmouth, Mediapolis, Kossuth, Kingston, BURLINGTON

XXIX, July 22-28, 2001
SIOUX CITY, Kingsley, Washta, Quimby, STORM LAKE, Schaller, Galva, Ida Grove, Arthur, Kiron, Deloit, DENISON, Manilla, Irwin, Walnut, ATLANTIC, Wiota, Anita, Adair, Casey, Guthrie Center, Yale, PERRY, Bouton, Woodward, Madrid, Huxley, Cambridge, Maxwell, Mingo, Ira, Baxter, GRINNELL, Searsboro, Montezuma, Deep River, Millersburg, Parnell, Williamsburg, CORALVILLE, Iowa City, West Branch, Springdale, West Liberty, Atalissa, Moscow, MUSCATINE

XXX, July 21-27, 2002
SIOUX CENTER, Orange City, Alton, Granville, Marcus, CHEROKEE, Rembrandt, Marathon, Webb, Ayrshire, EMMETSBURG, Fenton, Lone Rock, Titonka, Woden, Crystal Lake, FOREST CITY, Plymouth, Rock Falls, Nora Springs, Rudd, CHARLES CITY, Nashua, Bradford, Bremer Station, Tripoli, Sumner, OELWEIN, Stanley, Aurora, Winthrop, Quasqueton, Troy Mills, Central City, ANAMOSA, Amber, Scotch Grove, Canton, Andrew, Springbrook, BELLEVUE

XXXI, July 20-26, 2003
GLENWOOD, Silver City, Henderson, Emerson, Essex, SHENANDOAH, Coin, College Springs, Shambaugh, Clarinda, New Market, BEDFORD, Benton, Mount Ayr, Kellerton, Decatur City, Leon, OSCEOLA, New Virginia, Medora, Lacona, Melcher-Dallas, Attica, Bussey, Beacon, OSKALOOSA, Cedar, Kirkville, Chillicothe, Blakesburg, Unionville, Paris, Drakesville, BLOOMFIELD, Troy, Lebanon, Pittsburg, Keosauqua, Vernon, Bentonsport, Bonaparte, Hillsboro, Salem, Oakland Mills, MOUNT PLEASANT, New London, Lowell, Denmark, FORT MADISON

XXXII, July 25-31, 2004
ONAWA, Turin, Castana, Mapleton, Schleswig, Kiron, Wall Lake, LAKE VIEW, Rockwell City, Knierim, Barnum, FORT DODGE, Badger, Eagle Grove, Woolstock (century loop), Dows, Popejoy, IOWA FALLS, Ackley, Cleves, Steamboat Rock, Eldora, Gifford, Union, Bangor, MARSHALLTOWN, Garwin, Clutier, Elberon, Keystone, Van Horne, Newhall, Atkins, Palo, HIAWATHA, Whittier, Viola, Fairview, Anamosa,

Morley, Olin, Hale, Oxford Junction, Lost Nation, Elwood, MAQUOKETA, Spragueville, Preston, Goose Lake, Charlotte, Elvira, CLINTON

XXXIII, July 24-30, 2005
LE MARS, Oyens, Granville, Alton, Orange City, Newkirk, SHELDON, Archer, Primghar, Sanborn, Melvin, May City, Milford, ESTHERVILLE, Wallingford, Ringsted, Fenton, Whittemore, ALGONA, Oak Lake, Titonka, Woden, Crystal Lake, Thompson, Lake Mills, NORTHWOOD, Carpenter, St. Ansgar, Stacyville, Riceville, Saratoga, Lime Springs, CRESCO, Protivin, Spillville, Fort Atkinson, Jackson Junction, Waucoma, St. Lucas, Douglas, WEST UNION, Elgin, Gunder, St. Olaf, Clayton Center, Garnavillo, GUTTENBERG

XXXIV, July 23-29, 2006
SERGEANT BLUFF, Bronson, Anthon, Battle Creek, IDA GROVE, Boyer, Arcadia, Manning, AUDUBON, Wichita, Guthrie Center, Montieth, Redfield, Adel, WAUKEE, Granger, Polk City, Elkhart, Bondurant, Mitchellville, Colfax, Lambs Grove, NEWTON, Reasnor, Sully, Lynnville, Searsboro, Montezuma, Brooklyn, Carnforth, Victor, Ladora, MARENGO, Williamsburg, Holbrook, Windham, Cosgrove, CORALVILLE, Iowa City, West Branch, Springdale, West Liberty, Atalissa, Moscow, MUSCATINE

XXXV, July 22-28, 2007
ROCK RAPIDS, George, Ashton, Melvin, Hartley, Moneta, SPENCER, Dickens, Gillett Grove, Webb, Marathon, Albert City (century loop), Laurens, Havelock, Rolfe, Bradgate, Rutland, HUMBOLDT, Dakota City, Thor, Eagle Grove, Clarion, Cornelia, Alexander, HAMPTON, Aredale, Dumont, Kesley, Aplington, Stout, CEDAR FALLS, Denver, Klinger, Dunkerton, Fairbank, INDEPENDENCE, Winthrop, Lamont, Dundee, Manchester, Earlville, DYERSVILLE, Worthington, Cascade, Garryowen, Bernard, La Motte, BELLEVUE

XXXVI, July 20-26, 2008
MISSOURI VALLEY, Beebeetown, Underwood, Neola, Minden, Shelby, Tennant, HARLAN, Kimballton, Elk Horn, Exira, Coon Rapids, Scranton, JEFFERSON, Grand Junction, Dana, Ogden, Boone, AMES,

Nevada, Colo, State Center, Albion, Green Mountain, Le Grand, Montour, TAMA-TOLEDO, Vining, Chelsea, Belle Plaine, Luzerne, Blairstown, West Amana, South Amana, Homestead, NORTH LIBERTY, Solon, Lisbon, Mount Vernon, Martelle, Morley, Mechanicsville, TIPTON, Bennett, New Liberty, Maysville, Eldridge, Argo, LE CLAIRE

XXXVII, July 19-25, 2009
COUNCIL BLUFFS, Mineola, Henderson, Emerson, RED OAK, Stanton, Villisca, Nodaway, Corning, Prescott, Fontanelle, GREENFIELD, Orient, Macksburg, East Peru, Truro, St. Charles, St. Marys, Martensdale, Prole, INDIANOLA, Ackworth, Sandyville, Milo, Lacona, Oakley, CHARITON, Millerton, Bethlehem, Confidence, Iconium, Moravia, Unionville, Blakesburg, OTTUMWA, Hedrick, Martinsburg, Pekin, Packwood, Pleasant Plain, Brighton, Germanville, Lockridge, Rome, MOUNT PLEASANT, New London, Lowell, Middletown, West Burlington, BURLINGTON

XXXVIII, July 25-31, 2010
SIOUX CITY, Kingsley, Washta, Quimby, STORM LAKE, Varina, Pocahontas, Plover, Rolfe (century loop), West Bend, Whittemore, ALGONA, Wesley, Hutchins, Britt, Garner, CLEAR LAKE, Swaledale, Rockwell, Cartersville, Rockford, CHARLES CITY, Clarksville, Parkersburg, Stout, Dike, Hudson (not on original map)*, WATERLOO, Washburn, Gilbertville, Jubilee, Shady Grove, Rowley, Quasqueton, Winthrop, MANCHESTER, Delaware, Earlville, Dyersville, Bankston, Graf, DUBUQUE

XXXIX, July 24-30, 2011
GLENWOOD, Silver City, Carson, Griswold, Lewis, ATLANTIC, Elk Horn, Kimballton, Manning, Templeton, Dedham, Willey, CARROLL, Lidderdale, Lanesboro, Churdan, Paton, Dana (century loop), Pilot Mound, BOONE, Luther, Kelley, Slater, Shehldal, Alleman, White Oak, Elkhart, Bondurant, ALTOONA, Mitchellville, Colfax, Baxter, GRINNELL, Brooklyn, Carnforth, Victor, Ladora, Marengo, West Amana, South Amana, Homestead, Oxford, CORALVILLE, Iowa City,

West Branch, Springdale, Moscow, Wilton, Durant, Stockton (?) (not on map), Walcott, DAVENPORT

XL, July 22-28, 2012
SIOUX CENTER, Orange City, Alton, Granville, Marcus, CHEROKEE, Aurelia, Hanover, Schaller, Nemaha, Sac City, LAKE VIEW, Auburn, Lake City, Lohrville, Farnhamville, Gowrie, Harcourt, Dayton, Stratford (century loop), Lehigh, WEBSTER CITY, Kamrar, Jewell, Ellsworth, Story City, Roland, McCallsburg, Zearing, St. Anthony, Clemons, MARSHALLTOWN, Garwin, Clutier, Garrison, Vinton, Shellsburg, Palo, Covington, CEDAR RAPIDS, Mount Vernon, Springville, Viola, Fairview, ANAMOSA, Hale, Oxford Junction, Lost Nation, Elwood, Delmar, Charlotte, Goose Lake, CLINTON

XLI, July 21-27, 2013
COUNCIL BLUFFS, Underwood, Neola, Minden, Shelby, Tennant, HARLAN, Kimballton, Elk Horn (century loop), Hamlin, Guthrie Center, Springbrook State Park, Yale, PERRY, Minburn, Dallas Center, Van Meter, West Des Moines, DES MOINES, Pleasant Hill, Adelphi, Runnells, Monroe, KNOXVILLE, Pella, Bussey, Beacon, OSKALOOSA, Cedar, Fremont, Hedrick, Martinsburg, Packwood, FAIRFIELD, Birmingham, Keosauqua, Bentonsport, Bonaparte, West Point, FORT MADISON

XLII, July 20-26, 2014
ROCK VALLEY, Hull, Boyden, Sheldon, Melvin, May City, Milford, West Okoboji, Arnolds Park, OKOBOJI/SPIRIT LAKE/MILFORD (officially listed as "Okoboji"), Terril, Graettinger, EMMETSBURG, Ringsted, Bancroft, Burt (century loop), Lone Rock (century loop), Titonka, Gruis Recreation Center (not Woden), Crystal Lake, FOREST CITY, Ventura, Clear Lake, MASON CITY, Nora Springs, Rockford, Marble Rock, Greene, Packard, Clarksville, WAVERLY, Bremer, Tripoli, Sumner, Westgate, Oelwein, Otterville, INDEPENDENCE, Winthrop, Lamont, Strawberry Point, Edgewood, Elkport (not on original map), Garber, GUTTENBERG

XLIII, July 19-25, 2015

SIOUX CITY, Kingsley, Washta, Quimby, Hanover, STORM LAKE, Lakeside (not on map), Newell, Fonda, Pomeroy (gravel loop), Manson, Clare, FORT DODGE, Duncombe, Webster City, Blairsburg, Boondocks station, Williams, Alden, Buckeye, Radcliffe (century loop), ELDORA, Steamboat Rock, Cleves, Ackley, Austinville, Aplington, Parkersburg, New Hartford, CEDAR FALLS, Hudson, Eagle Center (not on map), La Porte City, Mount Auburn, Vinton, Shellsburg, Palo, HIAWATHA, Robins (not on map), Whittier, Springville, Mount Vernon, Lisbon, Sutliff Cider, Solon, CORALVILLE [Iowa River Landing], University Heights, Iowa City, West Liberty, Atalissa, Moscow, Wilton, Durant, not Stockton, Walcott, DAVENPORT

XLIV, July 24-30, 2016

GLENWOOD, Malvern, Tabor, Randolph, Imogene (gravel loop), SHENANDOAH, Essex, Bethesda, Villisca, Nodaway, Corning, Prescott, CRESTON, Diagonal, Mount Ayr, Kellerton, Decatur City, LEON, Garden Grove, Humeston, Cambria, Millerton, New York, Bethlehem, Confidence, Iconium (century loop), Honey Creek State Park (century loop), Mystic, CENTERVILLE, Rathbun, Moravia, Unionville, Blakesburg, OTTUMWA, Hedrick, Hayesville, Sigourney, Wooden Wheel Vineyards, West Chester, WASHINGTON, Columbus Junction, Fredonia, Letts, Ardon Creek Vineyard, MUSCATINE

XLV, July 23-29, 2017

ORANGE CITY, Alton, Granville, Paullina, Primghar, Sutherland (gravel loop), Hartley, SPENCER, Dickens, Gillett Grove, Ayrshire, Curlew, Mallard, Plover (century loop), West Bend, Whittemore, ALGONA, Wesley, Hutchins, Britt, Garner, Ventura, CLEAR LAKE, Thornton, Swaledale, Rockwell, Cartersville, Rockford, CHARLES CITY, Ionia, New Hampton, Lawler, Protivin, CRESCO, Decorah, Ossian, Castalia, Postville, WAUKON, Waterville, Harpers Ferry, LANSING

XLVI, July 22-28, 2018

ONAWA, Turin, Soldier, Moorhead (gravel loop), Ute, Charter Oak, DENISON, Aspinwall, Manning, Templeton, Dedham, Coon Rapids,

Scranton, JEFFERSON, Grand Junction, Dana, Ogden, Boone, ~~Ledges State Park~~ (eliminated late due to flooding), Luther, Napier, AMES, Nevada, Colo, State Center, Melbourne, Baxter, Lambs Grove (not on map), NEWTON, Reasnor, Sully, Lynnville, New Sharon (century loop), Peoria (century loop), Montezuma, Deep River, Keswick, SIGOURNEY, Harper, Keota, Wellman, Kalona, Riverside, Hills, IOWA CITY, West Liberty, Atalissa, Moscow, Wilton, Wildcat Den State Park, Montpelier, Blue Grass, DAVENPORT

XLVII, July 21-27, 2019
COUNCIL BLUFFS, McClelland (gravel loop), Underwood, Neola, Minden, Avoca, Walnut, Marne, ATLANTIC, Wiota, Anita, Adair, Casey, Menlo, Stuart, Dexter, Earlham, WINTERSET, Howell's Greenhouse ("Iowa Ag Oasis"), Cumming, Norwalk, Spring Hill (not on map), INDIANOLA, Lake Ahquabi State Park, Liberty Center, Lacona, Chariton, Millerton, Bethlehem, Confidence, Iconium (century loop, not on map), Honey Creek Resort (century loop), Walnut City, Mystic, CENTERVILLE, West Grove, Bloomfield, Troy, Lebanon, Leando, Douds, Libertyville, FAIRFIELD, Stockport, Salem, Houghton, Geode State Park, Middletown, West Burlington, BURLINGTON, West Burlington (again), Middletown (again), Geode State Park (again), Denmark, West Point, Franklin, Donnellson, Montrose, KEOKUK

List created by Jeff Morrison

2020
The 2020 ride was cancelled because of the coronavirus for the safety of the riders and communities on the route.

Iowa Bike Counties

Adams
Corning
Dickieville
Nodaway
Prescott

Adair
Adair (also Guthrie)
Arbor Hill
Canby
Casey (Also Guthrie)
Fontanelle
Greenfield
Orient
Stuart

Allamakee
Dalby
Elon
Hanover
Harper's Ferry
Lansing
Postville
Village Creek
Waterville
Waukon
Yellow River State
Forest

Appanoose
Centerville
Honey Creek Resort
Iconium

Moravia
Mystic
Rathbun
Unionville
Walnut City

Audubon
Audubon
Exira
Gardner (Also
Guthrie)
Hamlin
Kimballton
Viola Center

Benton
Atkins
Belle Plaine
Blairstown
Garrison
Keystone
Luzerne
Mount Auburn
Newhall
Shellsburg
Urbana
Van Horne
Vinton

Black Hawk
Cedar Falls
Dunkerton
Eagle Center

Elk Run Heights
Evansdale
Finchford
Gilbertville
Hudson
Jesup (Also
Buchanan)
Jubilee
La Porte City
Voorhies
Washburn
Waterloo

Boone
Angus
Boone
Boxholm
Ledges State Park
Luther
Madrid
Napier
Ogden
Pilot Mound
Ridgeport
Sheldahl (Also Polk
and Story)

Bremer
Bremer
Bremer Station
Denver
Horton
Klinger

Sumner
Tripoli
Waverly

Buchanan
Aurora
Brandon
Fairbank (Also
Fayette)
Hazleton
Independence
Jesup (Also Black
Hawk)
Lamont
Littleton
Monti
Otterville
Quasqueton
Rowley
Shady Grove
Stanley (Also Fayette)
Winthrop

Buena Vista
Albert City
Marathon
Newell
Rembrandt
Storm Lake

Butler
Allison
Aplington
Aredale
Austinville
Bristow

Clarksville
Dumont
Greene
Kesley
New Hartford
Packlard
Parkersburg
Shell Rock

Calhoun
Farnhamville (Also
Webster)
Jolley
Knierim
Lake City
Lohrville
Manson
Pomeroy
Rinard
Rockwell City
Yetter

Carroll
Arcadia
Breda
Carroll
Coon Rapids (Also
Guthrie)
Dedham
Glidden
Lanesboro
Liddendale
Manning
Mount Carmel
Templeton
Willey

Cass
Anita
Atlantic
Griswold
Lewis
Marne
Wiota

Cedar
Bennett
Durant (Also
Muscatine and Scott)
Mechanicsville
Rochester
Springdale
Tipton
West Branch (Also
Johnson)
Wilton (Also
Muscatine)

Cerro Gordo
Burchinal
Carterville
Clear Lake
Dougherty
Mason City
Meservey
Nora Springs
Plymouth
Portland
Rock Falls
Rockwell
Swaledale
Thornton
Ventura

Winnebago Heights

Cherokee
Aurelia
Cherokee
Marcus
Quimby
Washta

Chickasaw
Alta Vista
Bradford
Deerfield
Ionia
Jerico
Lawler
Nashua
New Hampton
Protivin

Clarke
Knox
Liberty
Osceola

Clay
Dickens
Everly
Gillett Grove
Peterson
Royal
Spencer
Webb

Clayton
Buck Creek

Clayton Center
Communia
Edgewood (Also
Delaware)
Elkader
Elkport
Garber
Garnavillo
Gunder
Guttenberg
St. Olaf
Strawberry Point
Volga

Clinton
Charlotte
Clinton
Delmar
Dewitt
Elvira
Elwood
Goose Lake
Grand Mound
Lost Nation
Welton

Crawford
Aspinwall
Boyer
Charter Oaks
Deloit
Denison
Dunlap (Also
Harrison)
Kiron
Manilla

Schleswig
Vail

Dallas
Adel
Bouton
Dallas Center
Dexter
Granger (also Polk)
Minburn
Perry
Redfield
Van Meter
Waukee
Woodward

Davis
Bloomfield
Drakesville
Pulaski
Troy
West Grove

Decatur
Davis City
Decatur City
Garden Grove
Lamoni
Leon
Woodland

Delaware
Delaware
Dundee
Dyersville
Earlville

Edgewood (Also
Clayton)
Manchester
Masonville
Robinson
Ryan

Des Moines
Burlington
Geode State Park
(Also Henry)
Kingston
Kossuth
Mediapolis
Middletown
Prairie Grove
West Burlington
Yarmouth

Dickinson
Arnolds Park
Milford
Okoboji
Spirit Lake
Terril

Dubuque
Asbury
Bankston
Bernard
Cascade (Also Jones)
Centralia
Dubuque
Epworth
Farley
Gaf

Hugo (Also Jackson)
Worthington
Zwingle

Emmert
Estherville
Ringsted
Wallingford

Fayette
Alpha
Arlington
Douglas
Elgin
Fairbank (Also
Buchanan)
Fayette
Hawkeye
Oelwein
Randalia
Stanley (Also
Buchanan)
St. Lucas
Wadena
Waucoma
Westgate
West Union

Floyd
Charles City
Colwell
Marble Rock
Rockford
Rudd

Franklin
Ackley (Also Hardin)
Alexander
Dows (Also Wright)
Faulkner
Hampton
Popejoy
Sheffield

Freemont
Bartlett
Farragut
Imogene
Randolph
Shenandoah (Also
Page)
Sidney
Tabor (Also Mills)
Thurman

Greene
Adaza
Churdan
Cooper
Dana
Farlin
Grand Junction
Jefferson
Paton
Rippey
Scranton

Grundy
Beaman
Conrad

Coon Rapids (Also
Carroll)
Dike
Holland
Morrison
Stout
Zaneta

Guthrie
Adair (Also Adair)
Bayard
Casey (Also Adair)
Coon Rapids (Also
Carroll)
Gardner (Also
Audubon)
Guthrie Center
Menlo
Montieth
Panora
Reinbeck
Wellsburg
Wichita
Yale

Hamilton
Blairsburg
Boondocks Station
Ellsworth
Homer
Jewell
Kamrar
Randall
Stratford (Also
Webster)
Webster City

Williams

Hancock
Britt
Corwith
Crystal Lake
Denhart
Forest City
Garner
Goodell
Hayfield
Hutchins
Kanawha
Miller
Stillson
Woden

Hardin
Ackley (Also
Franklin)
Alden
Buckeye
Cleves
Eldora
Gifford
Iowa Falls
New Providence
Radcliffe
Steamboat Rock
Union
Whitten

Harrison
Beebeetown
Dunlap (also
Crawford)

Magnolia
Missouri Valley
Persia
Pisgah

Henry
Coppock (Also
Jefferson and
Washington)
Denova
Geode State Park
(Also Des Moines)
Hillsboro
Lowell
Mount Pleasant
Mount Union
New London
Oakland Mills
Olds
Rome
Salem
Trenton
Wayland
Winfield

Howard
Cresco
Elma
Lime Springs
Riceville (Also
Mitchell)
Saratoga
Schley

Humboldt
Bode

Bradgate
Dakota City
Hardy
Humboldt
Livermore
Lu Verne (Also
Kossuth)
Ottosen
Pioneer
Renwick
Rutland
Thor
Unique

Ida
Arthur
Battle Creek
Galva
Ida Grove

Iowa
Amana Colonies
East Amana
High Amana
Holbrook
Homestead
Ladora
Marengo
Middle Amana
Millersburg
North English (Also
Keokuk)
Parnell
South Amana
West Amana
Williamsburg

Jackson
Andrew
Baldwin
Bellevue
Canton (Also Jones)
Cottonville
Emeline
Garryowen
Hugo (Also
Dubuque)
Iron Hill
La Motte
Maquoketa
Monmouth
Preston
Sabula
Spragueville
Springbrook
Springbrook State
Park

Jasper
Baxter
Colfax
Galesburg
Ira
Kellogg
Kilduff
Lambs Grove
Lynnville
Mingo
Monroe
Newton
Oakland Acres
Prairie City
Reasnor

Rock Creek State
Park
Sully

Jefferson
Brookville
Coppock (Also
Henry and
Washington)
Fairfield
Libertyville
Lockridge
Packwood
Pekin
Pleasant Plain

Johnson
Camp Dodge
Coralville
Cosgrove
Hills
Iowa City
Lone Tree
North Liberty
Oxford
Shueyville
Solon
Swisher
University Heights
West Branch (Also
Cedar)
Windham

Jones
Amber
Anamosa

Canton (also
Jackson)
Cascade (Also
Dubuque)
Center Junction
Fairview
Hale
Hale Village
Martella
Monticello
Morley
Olin
Ollie
Onslow
Oxford Junction
Scotch Grove
Stone City
Wyoming

Keokuk
Delta
Harper
Hayesville
Hedrick
Keswick
Martinsburg
North English (also
Iowa)
Richland
Sigourney
South English
Talleyrand
Thornburg
Webster
What Cheer

Kossuth
Algona
Bancroft
Burt
Fenton
Lone Rock
Lu Verne (also
Humboldt)
Oak Lake
Seneca
ST. Benedict
Titonka
Wesley
West Bend (Also
Palo Alto)
Whittemore

Lee
Argyle
Denmark
Donnellson
Fort Madison
Franklin
Galland
Houghton
Keokuk
Montrose
Mount Hamill
Pilot Grove
Sandusky
St. Paul
West Point

Linn
Alburnett
Alice

Cedar Rapids
Center Point
Center City

Covington
Ely
Hiawatha
Lisbon
Marion
Mount Vernon
Palo
Paralta
Paris
Prairieburg
Robins
Springville
Sutliff Cider
Troy Mills
Viola
Walker
Whittier

Louisa
Ardon Creek
Vineyard
Columbus Junction
Fredonia
Letts
Morning Sun
Oakville
Wapello

Lucus
Chariton
Oakley

Lyon
Doon
George
Rock Rapids

Madison
Earlham
East Peru
Hanley
Macksburg
St. Charles
Truro
Winterset

Mahaska
Beacon
Cedar
Freemont
New Sharon
Oskaloosa
Peoria
Rose Hill

Marion
Attica
Bauer
Bussey
Flagler
Hamilton
Harvey
Knoxville
Melcher-Dallas
Pella
Pleasantville

Marshall

Albion
Bangor
Clemons
Green Mountain
Le Moille
Le Grand (also
Tama)
Liscomb
Marshalltown
Melbourne
St. Anthony
State Center

Mills
Emerson
Glenwood
Henderson
Malvern
Mineola
Silver City
Tabor (Also
Fremont)

Mitchell
Carpenter
New Haven
Osage
Riceville (Also
Howard)
Stacyville
St. Ansgar

Monona
Castana
Mapleton
Moorhead

Onawa
Soldier
Turin
Ute

Monroe
Albia
Lovilia

Montgomey
Coburg
Red Oak
Stanton
Tenville
Villisca
Wales

Muscatine
Atalissa
Blue Grass (Also
Scott)
Durant (Also Cedar
and Scott)
Montpelier
Moscow
Muscatine
Nichols
Stockton
Walcott (Also Scott)
West Liberty
Wildcat Den State
Park
Wilton (Also Cedar)

O'Brian
Archer

Hartley
Moneta
Paullina
Primghar
Sanborn
Sheldon
Sutherland

Osceola
Ashton
May City
Melvin
Ocheyedan
Sibley

Page
Bethesda
Clarinda
Coin
College Springs
Essex
Shambaugh
Shenandoah (Also
Fremont)
Yorktown

Palo Alto
Ayshire
Curlew
Emmetsburg
Graettinger
Mallard
West Bend (Also
Kossuth)

Plymouth
Akron
Brunsville
Craig
Ellendale
Kingsley
Le Mars
Merrill
Oyens
Remsen
Ruble
Sioux City (Also
Woodbury)
West Le Mars

Pocahontas
Fonda
Havelock
Laurens
Palmer
Plover
Pocahontas
Rolfe
Varina

Polk
Adelphi
Alleman
Altoona
Ankeny
Bondurant
Crocker
Des Moines
Elkhart
Enterprise
Farrar

Granger (Also
Dallas)
Johnston
Mitchellville
Pleasant Hill
Polk City
Rising Sun
Runnells
Santiago
Sheldahl (Boone and
Story)
White Oak

Pottawattamie
Avoca
Bentley
Carson
Council Bluffs
Hancock
McClelland
Minden
Neola
Oakland
Shelby
Underwood
Walnut
Weston

Poweshiek
Brooklyn
Carnforth
Deep River
Grinnell
Montezuma
Searsboro
Victor

Ringgold
Benton
Diagonal
Ellston
Kellerton
Mount Ayr
Redding
Tingley

Sac
Auburn
Carnavon
Lake View
Nemaha
Odebolt
Sac City
Schaller
Wall Lake

Scott
Argo
Blue Grass (Also
Muscatine)
Davenport
Durant (Also Cedar
and Muscatine)
Eldridge
Le Claire
Maysville
New Liberty
Walcott (Also
Muscatine)

Shelby
Earling
Elk Horn

Harlan
Irwin
Jacksonville
Panama
Portsmouth
Tennant
Westphalia

Sioux
Alton
Boyden
Carnes
Germanville
Granville
Hawarden
Hospers
Hull
Ireton
Newkirk
Orange City
Rock Valley
Sioux Center

Story
Ames
Cambridge
Colo
Fernald
Gilbert
Huxley
Iowa Center
Kelley
Maxwell
McCallsburg
Nevada
Roland

Sheldahl (Polk and
Boone)
Slater
Story City
Zearing

Tama
Chelsea
Clutier
Dysart
Elberon
Garwin
Gladbrook
Haven
Le Grand (Also
Marshall)
Montour
Tama
Toledo
Vining

Taylor
Bedford
Blockton
Gravity
New Market

Union
Creston
Lorimor

Van Buren
Bentonsport
Birmingham
Bonaparte
Farmington

Keosauqua
Leando-Douds
Lebanon
Milton
Pittsburg
Stockport
Vernon

Wapello
Bidwell
Blakesburg
Chillicothe
Dahlonega
Farson
Kirkville
Munterville
Ottumwa

Warren
Ackworth
Cumming
Indianola
Lacona
Lake Ahquabi State
Park
Liberty Center
Martendale
Medora
Milo
New Virginia
Norwalk
Prole
Sandyville
Spring Hill
St. Marys

Washington
Brighton
Coppock (Also
Henry and Jefferson)
Dublin
Kalona
Keota
Riverside
Washington
Wellman
West Chester
Wooden Wheel
Vineyards

Wayne
Bethlehem
Cambria
Confidence
Humeston
Millerton
Milo
New York

Webster
Badger
Barnum
Clare
Coalville
Dayton
Duncombe
Farnhamville (Also
Calhoun)
Fort Dodge
Gowrie
Harcourt
Kalo

Lehigh
Stratford (Also
Hamilton)

Winnebago
Lake Mills
Thompson

Winneshiek
Castalia
Decorah
Fort Atkinson
Freeport
Jackson Junction
Ossian
Ridgeway
Spillville

Woodberry
Anthon
Bronson
Danbury
Leeds
Pierson
Sergeant Bluff
Sioux City (Also
Plymouth)

Worth
Bolan
Grafton
Joice
Kensett
Northwood

Wright
Belmond
Clarion
Cornelia
Dows (Also Franklin)
Eagle Grove
Woolstock